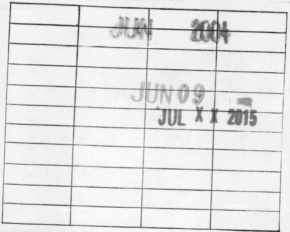

77–581

PN
1785
R4
v. 7

Renaissance Drama.

JUL 2000

Date Due

	JUN 2004	
	JUN 09	
	JUL X X 2015	

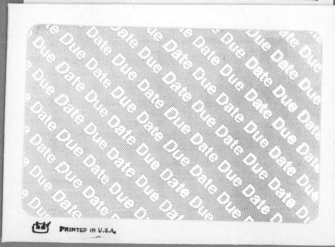

Date Due

PRINTED IN U.S.A.

RENAISSANCE DRAMA

New Series VII ❧ *1976*

Renaissance Drama

New Series VII

Drama and the Other Arts

Edited by Joel H. Kaplan

Northwestern University Press

EVANSTON 1976

Copyright © 1977 by Northwestern University Press
All rights reserved
Library of Congress Catalog Card Number 67-29872
ISBN 0-8101-0460-1
Printed in the United States of America

THE ILLUSTRATION on the front cover is Hans Holbein's *The Ambassadors* (1533). Reproduced by courtesy of the Trustees, The National Gallery, London.

THE ILLUSTRATION on the back cover is a detail from *The Destruction of Troy,* the Brussels Series. Reproduced by courtesy of the Abegg-Stiftung, Bern.

Publication of this volume was made possible by a grant from the College of Arts and Sciences, Northwestern University.

Editorial Note

RENAISSANCE DRAMA, an annual publication, provides a forum for scholars in various parts of the globe: wherever the drama of the Renaissance is studied. Coverage, so far as subject matter is concerned, is not restricted to any single national theater. The chronological limits of the Renaissance are interpreted liberally, and space is available for essays on precursors, as well as on the utilization of Renaissance themes by later writers. Editorial policy favors articles of some scope. Essays that are exploratory in nature, that are concerned with critical or scholarly methodology, that raise new questions or embody fresh approaches to perennial problems are particularly appropriate for a publication which originated from the proceedings of the Modern Language Association Conference on Research Opportunities in Renaissance Drama.

The Guest Editor of Volume VII would like to thank Robert Adams, O. B. Hardison, Jr., S. K. Heninger, Jr., R. W. Ingram, J. A. Lavin, and G. B. Shand for their assistance in assembling the present essays. Special thanks are due to Leonard Barkan without whose aid and encouragement Volume VII could not have appeared. Perhaps this is also the place to express appreciation for the patience of our long-suffering readers and contributors which helped to see this volume through two lengthy Canadian postal strikes.

Beginning with Volume VIII (New Series), the editor of *Renaissance Drama* will be Professor Leonard Barkan of Northwestern University. Volume VIII has as its topic "The Celebratory Mode," and it will include articles on such subjects as Elizabethan Country-House Revels, Jonson's masques and dramas, Milton's "Arcades," Richelieu's theater, and various theatrical forms of pageantry in the Renaissance.

Volume IX of *Renaissance Drama* is concerned with "Renaissance Drama in the Theater." The editor is interested in articles in such areas as theater history, modern theater practice, and analytic literary criticism with a theatrical bias. Manuscripts, for which the deadline is 31 January 1977, should be sent to Professor Leonard Barkan, Department of English, Northwestern University, Evanston, Illinois 60201. Prospective contributors are requested to follow the recommendations of the *MLA Style Sheet* (revised edition) in preparing manuscripts.

Contents

RENAISSANCE DRAMA

New Series VII ❧ *1976*

Volpone *and* Reynard the Fox

R. B. PARKER

SURPRISINGLY, the relation between *Volpone* and the beast epic of *Reynard the Fox* has never been investigated. Even the admirable Herford and Simpson concentrate almost exclusively on borrowings from the classics; and, apart from cursory statements about a general relationship to the bestiary and the beast-epic traditions, there was no specific parallel drawn before D. A. Scheve's short article "Jonson's *Volpone* and Traditional Fox Lore" in 1950.[1] Scheve argues that the central situation of *Volpone* is a traditional story of the fox who feigns death, which Jonson could have read in his copy of Gessner's *Historia animalium* (1557) and which Scheve traces back, through such intermediaries as Pierre Gilles, Bartholomaeus Anglicus, Albertus Magnus, Odo of Cheriton, Alexander of Neckham, Isidore of Seville, the Greek and Latin *Physiologus* (or "The Naturalist"), and Aelian, to Oppianus's *Halieutica* in the first century A.D. He also mentions its treatment in chapter 24 of Caxton's translation of *The History of Reynard the Fox*—which identifies the fox's victim as the crow's wife (i.e., Celia in the play)—and, very

1. *RES*, N.S. I (1950), 242–244.

briefly, its appearance in medieval iconography. In 1964, Scheve's lead was taken further by Robert E. Knoll,[2] who added the ideas of the fox as an allegory of the devil, of Reynard's habitual escape from well-earned punishment, and the effect on the play's tone of a "distancing" recognition of its relation to the beast fables—especially in qualifying our reaction to the morally repugnant behavior of Corbaccio and Corvino. Knoll's suggestions are illuminating, but his main attention was then directed to the bestiary background of the other animals in the play—the fly, the carrion birds, the peregrine hawk, and the parrot who turns into a tortoise—topics which subsequent studies have added to without exploring the relation to the Reynard epic further.[3]

Yet it is inconceivable that there was no more influence than this. Since Charles Baskervill's pioneering study *English Elements in Jonson's Early Comedy*,[4] critics have become increasingly aware of Jonson's knowledge of and debt to the medieval as well as the classical traditions—a debt which becomes self-conscious in the old-fashioned devices of the final plays and the learned notes to his masques. Jonson was not Camden's pupil for nothing. Moreover, the epic of Reynard the Fox was perhaps the most widely known story in medieval Europe, with a popular appeal that extended well beyond the Renaissance: "in various forms from the twelfth century to the eighteenth," says Thomas Wright, "[*Reynard the Fox*] has enjoyed a popularity which was granted probably to no other book."[5] And that Jonson did indeed know the epic is proved by a passage in *Epicoene* (1609), the play he wrote immediately after *Volpone*:

LA-F[OOLE]

I, and there's an excellent booke of morall philosophie, madame, of RAY-NARD the foxe, and all the beasts, call'd DONES philosophie.

2. *Ben Jonson's Plays: An Introduction* (Lincoln, Nebr., 1964), pp. 79–104.

3. E.g., Malcolm South, "Animal Imagery in *Volpone*," TSL, X (1965), 141–150; Lloyd L. Mills, "Barish's 'The Double Plot' Supplemented: The Tortoise Symbolism," *The Serif*, IV (Sept. 1967), 25–28; Ian Donaldson, "Jonson's Tortoise," RES, N.S. XIX (1968), 162–166; P.B.R. Doob and G. B. Shand, "Jonson's Tortoise and Avian," *Renaissance and Reformation*, X (1974), 43–44.

4. (Austin, Tex., 1911).

5. Thomas Wright, *The History of Caricature and Grotesque in Literature and Art* (London, 1864), p. 77; a similar comment is made by Lucien Foulet, *Le Roman de Renart* (Paris, 1914), p. 498.

GEN[TAUR]

There is, indeed, sir AMOROUS LA-FOOLE. . . .

LA-F[OOLE]

I have read it, my lady CENTAVRE, all over to my cousin here.

MRS. OT[TER]

I, and 'tis a very good booke as any is, of the modernes.[6]

(IV.iv.83–91)

Sir Amorous's foolish mistake suggests that Jonson was also aware of the complicated relation between the beast epic and popular animal fables. The Reynard story was of French clerical origin, and there were many manuscript and printed versions, adaptations, imitations, and translations of it; but it was also always part of the oral tradition, drawing on fables and bestiary lore that antedate the epic and, in its turn, contributing names and incidents to the folklore which followed it. "Certainly the oral tradition," says Léopold Sudre, "was one of the main factors in the formation of the cycle. The greater part of its content was committed to memory more often than to paper: it was transmitted as much by voice as by writings, and it must have happened that, in these incessant journeys from mouth to mouth, it was transformed and infinitely varied."[7]

We are dealing with a popular tradition, then, not just a particular single source. Animal symbolism was everywhere in the Renaissance, almost a habit of mind; so, for example, Queen Elizabeth gave her courtiers animal nicknames—Burleigh was the fox, the French ambassador the ape—and in her first Christmas revels there appeared the strange figures of cardinals, bishops, and abbots with the heads of crows, asses, and wolves.[8] The animal analogies and stories were so pervasive, in fact, so taken for granted, that their influence functions "at an almost

6. Ben Jonson, *Works,* ed. C. H. Herford and Percy and Evelyn Simpson, 11 vols. (Oxford, 1925–1952), V, 232; all references to Jonson's works will be to this edition. Sir Amorous has confused Reynard with Sir Thomas North's English translation (1570; repr. 1601) of the Italian translation of Doni's Latin translation of a Greek text of the animal *Fables of Bidpai,* which derive ultimately from India.

7. Léopold Sudre, *Les Sources du "Roman de Renart"* (Paris, 1893), p. 91.

8. See E. Greenlaw, *Studies in Spenser's Historical Allegory* (Baltimore, Md., 1932), pp. 112 ff., and M. C. Bradbrook, *The Rise of the Common Player* (London, 1962), p. 124.

subterranean level";[9] and this obliquity of influence is nowhere truer than in England, where, apart from references in Latin by two popular preachers and in Anglo-Norman by a third, the only literary texts extant about Reynard are one mid-thirteenth century poem *The Vox and the Wolf,* Chaucer's *Nonnes Preestes Tale* (ca. 1390), and Caxton's translation of *The History of Reynard the Fox* (1481). The iconographic evidence, however, in church carvings, stained glass, and manuscript illuminations, is overwhelming proof that, after Caxton's translation, the story of Reynard "became, if possible, more popular in England than elsewhere, and that popularity hardly diminished down to the commencement of the [19th] century."[10]

It is a premise of this paper, then, that the Reynard stories familiar to Renaissance England, as evidenced particularly by their iconography, were wider and more various than the rather selective translation by Caxton of his late Flemish source.[11] From this premise it will be argued that Jonson's original audience would have recognized four or five key incidents in the play as very familiar and "expected" scenes, with im-

9. Charles C. Mish, *"Reynard the Fox* in the 17th Century," *HLQ,* XVII (1953–1954), 328.

10. Wright, p. 84. For similar assessments of the epic's popularity in England, see also: F. Mossé, *"Le Roman de Renart* dans l'Angleterre du Moyen Age," *Les Langues Modernes,* XLV (1951), 70–84; R. M. Wilson, *The Lost Literature of Medieval England* (London, 1952), pp. 136, 243 ff.; John Flinn, *"Le Roman de Renart" dans la littérature française et dans les littératures étrangères au Moyen Age* (Paris and Toronto, 1963), pp. 672–691, and his *L'Iconographie du "Roman de Renart"* (unpublished MS), p. 65; and Kenneth Varty, *Reynard the Fox: A Study of the Fox in Medieval English Art* (Leicester and New York, 1967), *passim.* Varty's purpose is, in fact, "to prove, from iconographical evidence, that Reynard was much better known in England than extant literary evidence suggests," p. 24.

11. Caxton, for instance, plays down the fact that a central incident of the epic is Reynard's trial for rape of the she-wolf, Hersent, a situation with obvious parallels to Celia's accusation of Volpone. In Caxton this is merely hinted at in the wolf's complaint in chap. 2 and sandwiched in with many other crimes in Reynard's confessions in chaps. 4 and 12; it is not actually recounted till chap. 33, by which time its centrality has been lost and the relation to Jonson's play obscured. See *The History of Reynard the Fox, Translated and Printed by William Caxton in 1481,* ed. Donald B. Sands (Cambridge, Mass., 1960). Hereafter cited as "Caxton."

portant effects on their sense of the play's unity and tone and on our own understanding of its staging.

I. The Development of the Reynard Epic

Before looking at the play, however, it is necessary to sketch out the very complex development of the Reynard epic itself.[12] When the first of its many "branches" appeared about A.D. 1175, there was already a substantial body of animal lore and fable it could draw on. The animal lore derived from the quasi-scientific observations of Aristotle, Pliny, Oppianus, and Aelian, which passed into the collections of such Renaissance scholars as Pierre Gilles, Conrad Gessner, and Edward Topsell via the indiscriminate collations of medieval encyclopedists. Its most popular manifestations were the *Physiologus,* compiled in Alexandria about A.D. 4 and constantly translated and supplemented, and the familiar *Bestiaries,* in which, like the *Physiologus,* the beast lore was made a vehicle for moral instruction.[13] These combined very easily with the moralizing animal fables of Aesop, Phaedrus, and Avian, which were available directly, in the original and in translation, and also via the popular *Romulus* collections and their vernacular equivalents the *Isopets* (from "Aesop"). The two strands of influence met on the common

12. The most thorough and reliable discussions of this development are those in Foulet and Flinn. A short but useful summary of their arguments can be found in R. Bossuat, *Le Roman de Renard,* rev. ed. (Paris, 1967). For the text of the *Roman de Renart* I have consulted the edition by E. Martin, 3 vols. (Strasbourg, 1882–1887). A useful selection of some of the main incidents can be found in *Les Grands Auteurs français du programme, I, Moyen Age,* ed. André Lagarde and Laurent Michard (Paris, 1962); and Foulet has excellent summaries of the various branches' content. I should also like to acknowledge here the generous advice and guidance of John Flinn, my colleague at the University of Toronto.

13. Thus in *Physiologus* the story of the fox who feigned death is glossed: "So also is the Devil very crafty in his ways. He who would partake of his flesh dies. To this flesh belong adultery, covetousness, lust, and murder" (trans. James Carlill in W. Rose, ed. *The Epic of the Beasts* [London, 1924], p. 191). Similarly, in *The Book of Beasts, being A Translation from a Latin Bestiary of the Twelfth Century,* ed. T. H. White (New York, 1954), p. 54: "The Devil has the nature of this same. With all those who are living according to the flesh he feigns himself to be dead until he gets them in his gullet and punishes them."

medieval ground of moral allegory, and their familiarity in England is attested by the didactic use made of them by such popular preachers as the twelfth-century Cistercian Odo of Cheriton in his *Liber parabolarum*, abridged in the fourteenth century by Jean de Sheppey, Bishop of Oxford, and in the Anglo-Norman *Contes moralisés* of the Franciscan Nichole Bozon, also in the fourteenth century.[14]

Preachers in France used the stories in the same way, and it is only a step from this use of established animal lore and fables to the invention of new, more extended stories in the same vein. For our purposes the two most important of these inventions were the *Ecbasis captivi* of a tenth-century monk of Saint-Evre-de-Toul in Lorraine, which includes an expansion of Aesop's story of the sick lion and the fox pretending to be a doctor, and *Ysengrimus*, written by a Flemish monk Nivard of Ghent about 1150, which places the fox-as-fake-doctor story within a wider feud between the fox and the wolf, during which the fox disguises himself as a cleric on one occasion and rapes Hersent the she-wolf on another.[15] It is *Ysengrimus* which has the most influence on the first branches of the *Roman de Renart*.

The development of the *Roman* itself is very complex. It consists of some twenty-seven or twenty-eight "branches" written by different authors at different times, with a great deal of repetition and overlapping. The sequence worked out by Lucien Foulet sees Branches II and V^a, written by Pierre de Saint Cloud about 1175, as the original version, in which for the first time the cunning fox of the bestiaries and fables becomes the malicious villain-hero of mock epic.[16] In this first story, Hersent the she-wolf hypocritically denies adultery with Reynard when her cubs accuse her to their father, Isengrin. She and Isengrin chase Reynard to his burrow, but Hersent, who is ahead, sticks in the opening and Reynard vindictively violates her while Isengrin is still panting up. Isengrin and Hersent then charge Reynard with rape before the lion, King Noble; but

---

14. See also G. R. Owst, *Literature and Pulpit in Medieval England* (London, 1933), pp. 204–205.

15. See: *Ecbasis captivi* . . . , trans. with introduction and notes by Edward H. Zeydel (Chapel Hill, N.C., 1964); *Ysengrimus*, ed. E. Voight (Strasbourg, 1884); and *Isengrimus*, trans. into German by Albert Schönfelder (Cologne, 1955).

16. Foulet, p. 212. Please note that the spelling of the fox's name will be regularized to "Reynard" and the wolf's to "Isengrin," except in titles.

Noble, suspecting that Hersent has really been Reynard's mistress, dismisses the case on condition that Reynard swear innocence to the impartial mastiff, Roenel. Isengrin suborns Roenel to bite Reynard, but the fox, seeing the trap, escapes to his hole, followed by the rest in full cry. Subsequent branches elaborate these incidents of the feud, the rape, the trial, and Reynard's escape, adding further crimes and further tricks in an overlapping, discontinuous way that defies any ordering into a single sequence. The nihilistic gaiety of the early branches is replaced in the later branches by a distinctly more moralizing and satiric tone; and this didactic trend is taken further in such later imitations of the *Roman* as: Rutebeuf's *Renart le Bestourné* (1260–1270), which satirizes the mendicant orders of the church; the anonymous *Le Couronnement de Renart* (1263–1270), where injustice, pride, and envy run riot while Reynard is king; *Renart le Nouvel* (1288–1289) by Jacquemart Gelée of Lille, in which Noble leads an abortive war against Reynard; and *Renart le Contrefait,* a political and religious allegory written early in the fourteenth century by a defrocked cleric of Troyes.[17]

The original branches were also developed by translation into other languages; and, in fact, when the vogue of Reynard petered out in France, just at the time of the Renaissance, it was the foreign adaptations which kept the story prominent and popular. The first was a German version, *Reinhart Fuchs,* by an Alsatian called Heinrich der Glîchezâre (Henry the Sneak) about 1190, who was the first to try to arrange the various French "branches" into some kind of logical sequence. A Venetian version, *Rainardo e Lesengrino,* of which two manuscripts survive, one from the fourteenth century, the other from the fifteenth, is a very lively treatment of the fox's trial for offenses against the she-wolf and the cockerel, and may be based on a lost French Branch 27. And of particular importance are two Flemish versions: *Reinaert de Vos,* written by one "Willem" about 1250 and usually referred to as *Reinaert I;* and *Reinaerts historie,* written at the end of the fourteenth century and usually called *Reinaert II,* which incorporates Willem's story of the fox's trial as its Book I and adds three more books about his further adventures, written with a more heavily moralizing tone. It is *Reinaert II* which kept the beast epic so lively for the Renaissance; it was translated into many

17. For other, lesser imitations, see Flinn, *"Roman,"* pp. 672–691.

languages, and via an intermediary prose version provided the main source for Caxton. At the same time, Flemish artisans seem to have carried the iconography of Reynard into every corner of Europe. We know from Branch 13 of the *Roman* itself, from protests by Gautier de Coincy, prior of Vic-sur-Aisne, and from thirteenth-century Latin advice to painters,[18] that scenes from the Reynard epic were painted in private apartments and even in the churches themselves; and there is a double record, by Jean de Saint-Victor and by Geffroi de Paris, that in Philippe le Bel's 1313 celebrations in Paris the trade guilds actually represented on stage *Reynard as Doctor* and *The Funeral Procession of Reynard.*[19]

In England, besides the *Vox and Wolf* poem and Caxton and Chaucer texts, the references by popular preachers, and the pervasive iconography already mentioned, there were six reprintings of the Caxton translation between 1481 and 1550; and, though there is then a gap between 1550 and 1620, there were two transfers of copyright in 1560 and 1586, and it seems probable that there were also editions during that time which no longer survive.[20] Certainly, after 1620, there were again frequent reprintings and also two interesting original sequels: *A Continuation, or Second Part of Reynard the Fox* (1672), and *The Shifts of Reynardine, the Son of Reynard the Fox* (1684), the latter of which will be discussed later.

It is important to bear two probabilities in mind, therefore, as we turn to *Volpone:* that Caxton's version represents only a very limited selection of the Reynard stories which could have been known in England; and that Jonson's own knowledge of these stories was probably wider than the average Englishman's, not only because of his antiquarian interests but also because of his period in Flanders as a soldier. In fact, as one examines the texts and iconography of the many Reynard versions, it becomes clear that certain incidents were much more popular than others, both to writers and to visual artists; and it is precisely these most popular aspects which seem relevant to *Volpone:* the two trials of the fox, accused of attempted rape and of feigning death to catch predators; the venality of the court, the mock pathos of an apparent funeral procession, and the

18. Cf. Flinn, *L'Iconographie,* pp. 3–5.
19. Cf. Foulet, pp. 531–534; Flinn, *"Roman,"* pp. 148–149.
20. See Mish, *passim.*

birds' attempted punishment of the fox from which he escapes jeeringly at the last minute; the fox's liaison with imitative apes, who aid him while he is sick but turn later into rivals; the fox as false doctor and false preacher; and the fox as seducing musician.

II. The Two Trials of Reynard

It is the trial of the fox, rather than his feigning of death, which is the most basic and recurrent of the beast-epic incidents.[21] The episode begins in *Ysengrimus* and is first developed in Branches II and V^a of the *Roman de Renart,* in which Reynard escapes from his first trial for raping the she-wolf. Some five years later (i.e., 1179–1180) a sequel, known as Branch I, was written to finish the story by bringing Reynard to a second trial. Briefly, it tells of the following events: at Ascension all the animals are summoned to Noble's court, where Reynard's enemies take advantage of his absence to renew accusations against him, particularly the charge of raping Hersent. Noble's initial reluctance to pursue this matter is changed to rage at the news that Reynard has murdered one of Chantecler's hens. Two messengers sent to summon Reynard, a bear and a cat, return much the worse for wear; but a third messenger, Grimbert the badger, persuades the fox to come to court. Reynard pleads his age and innocence, but Noble, angry at the flouting of his authority, orders the fox to be hanged. Reynard, however, simulating repentance, asks to go on pilgrimage instead. This is granted; but as soon as he is out of the court's reach, he throws off his pilgrim's garb and jeers at his accusers. They chase him, but again he gets safely to his earth.

The trials of Branch II and Branch I were first brought together in the German *Reinhart Fuchs;* but the full pattern does not emerge until the second Flemish version, *Reinaert II.* Its first book (which was originally *Reinaert I*—Willem's *Reinaert de Vos*) covers the Branch I incidents: Noble's summoning of the animals, complaints against the absent Reynard headed by Isengrin's accusation of rape, the three messengers summoning Reynard to court, the death sentence commuted to a pilgrimage, and the fox's immediate backsliding and insolence. One

21. See Varty, chap. 3, "The Fox's Trial," pp. 43–50.

interesting elaboration is that Noble is persuaded to commute the death
sentence by Reynard's promise to show him hidden treasure. Books II
and III then present a second trial of Reynard, in which the chief accuser is no longer Isengrin but a crow who complains that Reynard
trapped his wife by feigning death. The fox is again persuaded to come
to court, and, with prosy help from his aunt Rukenauwe the ape, he
again evades punishment, partly by recalling an occasion when his
father cured the lion's father of sickness. Only the wolf now remains
antagonistic; and in Book IV, after describing yet another rape of
Hersent by the fox, Isengrin challenges Reynard to single combat. After
lengthy advice from Rukenauwe, the fox wins the fight unfairly and is
rewarded by the lion. Caxton's translation follows the same pattern, except that, in order to avoid *Reinaert II's* double violation of Hersent, he
plays down the early accusation of rape in a way that obscures its importance (see note 11 above).

This pattern of a second trial provoked by the fox's insolence has interesting resemblances to the two trials of Volpone. There is no equivalent to Noble in the play, of course—though the Venetian court might be
dominated by the Lion of St. Mark, as it was in a recent production at
Bristol—but in both cases the courts are partial and venal, swayed by the
prospect of personal gain (cf. also Branch I', in which Reynard's wife
buys him off punishment with gold). In several versions of the *Reynard,*
moreover, there are specific comments on the fox's corruption of lawyers.[22]
In both epic and play Reynard arrives late at the trial and is first defended
by others (the ape and the badger in the epic). When he does arrive, he
pleads age as an excuse for not coming sooner and as a reason why the
court should disbelieve the crimes of which he is accused; and in at
least one version—an untitled fourteenth-century Latin text, provisionally
known as *Reynard in the Chancery*—he also pleads sickness.[23]

These alibis are reflected in two groups of iconography: not only the
widespread images of the fox who feigns death (which will be discussed
later), but also a less common sequence in which a sick fox is tended by

22. E.g., Caxton, pp. 120–121. Cf. Flinn's comment, *"Roman,"* p. 444: "Depuis
longtemps nous sommes habitués à lire ces accusations de renardie addressées aux
avocats . . ."

23. See Flinn, *"Roman,"* pp. 542–548.

Illustration 1. Ape Tends Sick Fox. Misericord (U.S., S. 19. 1520). Beverley Minster, Yorkshire. (Photo: J. C. D. Smith)

an ape. Varty lists six of these in England, and Flinn refers to another in France. The most interesting is perhaps that on a misericord in the Cathedral of St. John in Beverley, Yorkshire, which shows the fox in bed attended by a monkey (Varty #8, plate 7; Flinn, *L'Iconographie,* p. 73.) [24] At Boston in Lincolnshire Reynard is accompanied by a monkey who is holding a urinal (Varty #28, plate 89; Flinn, *L'Iconographie,* p. 73); and there are similar carvings at Beverley St. Mary's (Varty #15,

24. See Illustrations 1 and 2.

Illustration 2. A Fox Consults an Ape. Misericord (N. 19. 1390). St. Botolph's,
Boston, Lincolnshire. (Photo: D. R. Maxted)

plate 90) and at the parish church of Knowle in Warwickshire (Varty
#108, plate 12). Another particularly interesting example, mentioned but
not illustrated by Varty (#194), is a misericord in St. George's Chapel
at Windsor which has one ape pouring liquid down a recumbent fox's
throat and another ape inspecting his urinal. These images of foxes
feigning or suffering sickness attended by ape doctors or accomplices
have an obvious resemblance to Volpone and Mosca at the beginning of
the play; and, considering that the helpers are apes, perhaps also to Lady
Pol's unsolicited and garbled medical advice in Act III, scene iv.[25] Also
of interest in this connection are two carvings of an ape apparently help-
ing the fox disguise himself: one on a bench-end at All-Saints, Branston,

25. Flinn mentions a further example in a thirteenth-century *Bréviaire à l'usage
de l'abbaye du Saint-Sépulchre de Cambrai;* and of the image's frequency in
England he twice speculates that there may have been a lost English branch where
the monkey was actually doctor to the fox: *L'Iconographie,* pp. 69, 73.

In Lincolnshire, which Varty (#32) mentions but does not illustrate, and a very interesting misericord from St. George's Chapel, Windsor, on the left supporter of which is carved an ape with a comb or razor standing before a seated fox who holds a basin (Varty, #191, plate 87).[26]

The chief accusation against Reynard is always the rape of the she-wolf, a sexual relationship which is partly a parody of Courtly Love pretensions [27]—like Volpone's attack on Celia when high-flown blandishments have failed. The lubricity of the fox is extended to the rape of the lioness, Dame Fière, in Branch XI and the *Reinaert I,* and in *Renart le Nouvel* he is given three mistresses, the she-wolf, the lioness, and a leopardess. The she-wolf's behavior is more ambiguous. Lewis and Short's *Latin Dictionary* records "prostitute" as a secondary meaning of *lupa;* and certainly in *Ysengrim,* in the early branches of the *Roman,* and in *Reinaert* Hersent is presented as the fox's willing mistress. This is one of Reynard's defenses against the charge of rape and one of the reasons why Noble is reluctant to punish him for it. It has its most obvious equivalent in *Volpone* in the charges of fornication brought against Celia, but it also seems related to the would-be profligacy of Lady Pol. Very interestingly, although Lady Pol is mainly seen as a noisy, imitative parrot, at one point Volpone actually calls her his "shee-wolfe" (V.ii.66), a contradiction of her parrot image which seems pointless except in relation to the beast epic.

In other versions the she-wolf's guilt is left more open, and her rape when she is stuck in Reynard's hole resembles the attack on Celia when she is trapped in Volpone's bedroom. Celia's position, however, is also related to the second major charge against the fox: his attack on the crow's wife while feigning death. As Scheve and Knoll have pointed out, this relates to a very ancient and popular tradition.[28] It is brought into the French *Roman* fairly late, in Branches XIII and (with variations) XVII, but becomes prominent in chapter I of Book II of *Reinaert II,* and is

---

26. See Illustration 3.

27. See Gustave Cohen, *La Vie littéraire en France au Moyen Age* (Paris, 1949), p. 131.

28. See above, pp. 3–4. Stith Thompson also includes it as item K827.4 in his *Motif-Index of Folk Literature* (Bloomington, Ind., 1958).

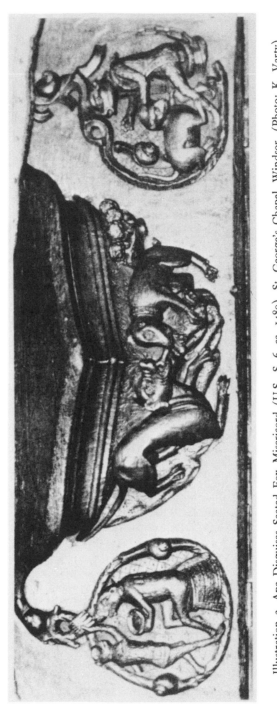

Illustration 3. Ape Disguises Seated Fox. Misericord (U.S., S. 6. ca. 1480), St. George's Chapel, Windsor. (Photo: K. Varty)

Illustration 4. Birds Peck Recumbent Fox, from the early 14th-century Queen Mary's Psalter of Sir George Warner (MS. Roy. 2. B.VII, p. 156). Reproduced by permission of the British Library Board.

taken over from there into chapter 24 of Caxton's translation: "How Corbant the Roke Complayned on the Foxe for the Death of His Wyf." [29] Curiously enough, it is based on fact: Varty prints some stills from a fascinating film made in 1961 by a Russian naturalist at the Moscow Pavlov Institute, which show a fox pretending to be dead and actually catching a crow. [30]

The large number of references to this trick in literature is matched by its frequency in iconography. One of the earliest examples in England is the famous Norman doorway at Alne in Yorkshire, which, under the inscription "Vulpis," shows a fox on its back with one bird on his body and another pecking at his jaws (see Varty #2, plate 157). The examples of this image are too numerous to list in full (Varty, for instance,

29. See Caxton, pp. 108–109.
30. See Varty, p. 91, and Plates 147, 148, 149, 150.

Illustration 5. Birds Peck Recumbent Fox, from 13th-century MS. (Douce 132, fol. 69 verso: Bodleian Library)

Illustration 6. Fox with Vulture. Late 12th-century MS. (Douce 218, fol. 38 verso: Bodleian Library)

records some twelve British manuscripts with illustrations of the fox feigning death, not to speak of the frequent representation of the scene in carvings); but some of particular interest are:[31] an illustration on page 156 of the early fourteenth-century manuscript of *Queen Mary's Psalter* (BL, MS. Roy. 2 B.VII) in which a fox feigning death is pecked by three birds while another looks on from a tree, then in the next drawing the fox springs to life and catches one of them; a thirteenth-century manuscript in Bodley (Douce 132, folio 69 verso); a twelfth-century manuscript, also in Bodley (Douce 218, folio 38 verso), which shows a recumbent fox attacked by what Varty (#282) identifies as a vulture; a twelfth-century bestiary in Cambridge University Library (MS. I. 1. 4. 26), reprinted by T. H. White (*Book of Beasts*, p. 53), which is interesting

31. See Illustrations 4, 5, 6, 7, and 8.

Illustration 7. Birds Peck "Dead" Fox in 12th-century Bestiary. (Cambridge University Library, MS I.1.4, 26)

because, besides the three birds pecking the fox, it shows three fox cubs peeping out to watch; and a misericord from Chester Cathedral, in the center of which a fox feigns death and three birds peck him while three others watch, and to the right of which the fox eats a bird he has caught (Varty #66, plate 155). Another fine misericord can be found in St. Mary's, Nantwich, Cheshire (Varty #133, plate 156); and there are many more on record, both in England and abroad.

One other aspect of the "trial" sequence may be pertinent here also. As will be discussed later, Reynard invariably escapes final punishment, no

Illustration 8. Birds Peck "Dead" Fox. Misericord (N. 14. 1390) from Chester Cathedral. (Photo: D. R. Maxted)

matter how near he comes to it; but his closest shave is perhaps in
Branch XVII where, after losing at chess to the wolf, Reynard is nailed
by his testicles to the chess board and apparently dies. There follow
funeral orations and an elaborate procession to the grave, at which point
Reynard revives and seizing the cock, Chantecler, makes his escape.
Chantecler then beats him in a duel, however, and Reynard, feigning
death again, is cast into a ditch, where he snaps off the leg of a scavenging
raven. Summoned to court to give an account of this behavior, he is
saved when his vixen persuades the court that the grave of a man called
Reynard is really her husband's. This branch gave rise to another subject
for iconography: the mock funeral procession of Reynard, and its variant,
the procession of Reynard to the scaffold. Perhaps the most famous of
these is the frieze sculpted on Strasbourg Cathedral in 1298, which was
destroyed in 1685 but recorded in detailed drawings.[32] Other examples
are at Tarragon Cathedral in Catalonia, on the "Porta della Pescheria"
of Modena Cathedral, and on an eleventh-century mosaic in the Cathedral
of Sainte-Marie-Majeure at Vercelli. But of particular interest for us is
an illustration on the manuscript "Smithfield Decretals" (BL, Roy.
10 E. IV, folio 49 recto), which shows the fox carried in funeral procession and tended by two weeping nuns (Varty, #227, plate 144).[33] It
seems possible that the elaborate entrance of the "dying" Volpone to his
first trial, at IV.vi.20 in the play, would be reminiscent of this at least as
a stage spectacle, with Lady Pol taking the role of the solicitous nuns.
The "Procession," it will be remembered, was one of the two Reynard
scenes represented on the stage at Paris in 1313.[34]

To summarize this section, then: I wish to suggest that behind the
main events of Jonson's play lie not only the tradition of the fox who
feigns death, but also the crafty "sick" and "old" fox attended by an ape,
the fox's double trial for rape and dissimulating death, at which his
victim's chastity is impugned by a biased and venal court, and possibly
also his "dying" procession which we know to be a trick: all of them
events treated frequently and freely in various versions of the beast epic,
and all of them to be found in popular iconography.

32. Reproduced by Wright, p. 81, Illustration 49.
33. See Illustration 9.
34. See p. 10 above.

Illustration 9. Fox Is Carried in Funeral Procession, from the "Smithfield Decretals" (MS. Roy. 10 E. IV., fol. 49 recto, ca. 1340). Reproduced by permission of the British Library Board.

III. Reynard the Doctor and Reynard the Preacher

The second scene represented at Paris in 1313 was "Reynard the Physician," another favorite subject for iconography, which, together with the sequence of "Reynard as False Preacher," I wish to relate to Volpone's disguise as the mountebank, Scoto of Mantua (II.ii).

The story of Reynard pretending to be a doctor is a very ancient one, deriving from Aesop's fable of "The Old Lion and the Fox."[35] It was this story which was incorporated into the tenth-century *Ecbasis;* it was combined with the fox's trial as early as *Ysengrimus;* and Léopold Sudre has argued that it was the nucleus of the *Roman de Renart* (p. 112). It does not appear in the *Roman* until Branch X, however, a "mediocre" (Foulet, p. 361) sequence composed about 1185 which tells the story of how Noble the Lion falls sick after Reynard has ignored his summons to court and maltreated two of his envoys (in this branch the mastiff and the stag). A third envoy (Grimbert the badger again), however, advises Reynard to take advantage of Noble's sickness to make his peace with the lion and at the same time injure his enemies at court. Accordingly, the fox gathers herbs and steals a famous ointment, "Aliboron," from a sleeping pilgrim. Arriving at court, he excuses his absence by lying that he has been to Rome, Montpellier, and Salerno to find a cure for Noble. He gravely acts the doctor, examining the lion's urine; then recommends that the lion be wrapped in the skin of the wolf, with the stag's "nerve" (thought to be in his antlers) for medicine. Isengrin is accordingly flayed and the stag polled; then Reynard cures the king with "Aliboron" and is given two castles as reward. A variant of the story in which the king's illness is caused by an ant in his ear turns up in Part III of *Reinhart Fuchs* (with Reynard poisoning the king after curing him); and in Book III of *Reinaert II* it becomes a reminiscence of how Reynard's father had cured the lion's father by getting him to eat a wolf's liver: it is this version which Caxton follows in chapter 32 of his translation. Other versions turn up in *Le Couronnement de Renart, Renart le Nouvel,* and *Renart le Contrefait;* and the popularity of the sequence is attested by the

---

35. *Fables of Aesop,* trans. S. A. Handford (London, 1954), p. 28. See also Varty, chap. 6, "The Fox Physician," pp. 68–75.

fact that in the thirteenth century English poem *The Vox and the Wolf* the main story of the fox and wolf in the well (Branch IV of the *Roman*) is preceded by an account of the fox pretending to be a doctor as an excuse for the bloodletting of hens.[36]

The fox as doctor also appears in iconography. Varty lists four English examples: a pillar carving in Salisbury Cathedral (Varty #156, plate 99); some fourteenth-century drawings in the All Saints' manuscript (MS. 6, folio 13 recto) of the Amesbury Psalter at Oxford (Varty, #262, plate 37), and two particularly interesting drawings from the "Smithfield Decretals" (BL, MS. Roy. 10 E. IV), folio 54 recto (Varty #231, plate 93) and folio 158 verso (Varty #246, plate 98).[37] Flinn adds two examples from the Continent: an illustration of the thirteenth-century *Douai Psaltery* (*L'Iconographie*, p. 80) and a frieze in the crypt of the Münsterkirche of Bâle (*L'Iconographie*, pp. 17–18). Another early iconographical sequence shows not Reynard but apes stealing medicaments from the sleeping pilgrim,[38] and this relates to a late version of the story which is of particular interest in connection with *Volpone*.

In chapters 11 through 15 of the second English continuation of Caxton, *The Shifts of Reynardine, the Son of Reynard the Fox* (London, 1684, pp. 45–62), Reynardine's young cousin, Zani the ape, advises the Fox to pretend to be a physician, helps him disguise himself, and provides him with instruments stolen from the pack of a sleeping peddler. Reynardine calls himself "Doctor Pedanto" and, attended by Zani, sets up in practice in the kingdom of Feraria as a rival to "Doctor Simpleton," the Ass, who tries to discredit him (cf. Scoto's feud with the "ground *ciarlitani*," II.ii.42 ff.). After describing the Fox's treatment for various disorders, the story goes on to tell how, pretending to cure his enemy old Firrapel the leopard, Reynardine kills him with a sleeping draught of opium (cf. Corbaccio's plan in *Volpone*, I.iv.12–18). He escapes suspicion for this, but he and Zani quarrel over the fee. Zani tries to set up as a rival physician, so Reynardine spreads rumors of his incompetence; and in revenge the ape discloses that "Doctor Pedanto" is really the fox.

36. See Brian Stone, trans., *Medieval English Verse* (London, 1964), p. 245.
37. See Illustration 10.
38. See Varty, #242, Plate 101; #196, Plate 105; #98, Plates 106, 107; #43, Plate 109; #7, Plate 110; also Francis Bond, *Wood Carvings in English Churches, I: Misericords* (Oxford, 1910), p. 75.

Illustration 10. Fox Examines Wolf's Urinal, from "Smithfield Decretals" (Fol. 158 verso: British Museum)

Suspicions immediately arising about Firrapel's death, Reynardine escapes, leaving the ape to be hanged. Reynardine then meets a mountebank "who pretended he could cut off diseased Arms, Legs, or particular Joynts affected, without Pain; and dexterously perform many other rare, strange, and unparallel'd Cures . . ." (p. 61). In return for testifying from the mountebank's stage that the operation was painless, Reynardine has his ears and tail cut off as disguise.

This is too late to be considered an "influence" on *Volpone,* of course; but because of the ape-robbing-the-peddler motif several scholars consider that it may draw on an older oral tradition.[39] In any case, it has several interesting analogies to the play. Reynardine is not himself a mountebank, but he becomes assistant to one; and his discussion of the necessary pretensions to be a doctor and subsequent advertisement as "Doctor Pedanto" are very close to Scoto's spiel in the play (II.ii.33 ff.):

I have read over *Gallens* Method of Physick, more than once; and am not a little Skilled in the use of Simples by him prescribed. Also I know how to prepare and administer *Emeticks, Catharticks, Diaphoreticks,* and *Diureticks.* What hard Names are these Cosin, said the Ape? These quoth the Fox, are only Terms of Art, used by Physicians, that their Patients may admire, what they cannot understand. A few Cramp words spoken by a Doctor, always creates Admiration in the Vulgar. . . . You say well Cosin, said the Ape; . . . but without some notable Disguise that cannot be done with Safety: Besides . . . it will also be necessary, that you present yourself as a great Travailler and Stranger, come from Forrain Parts; otherwise . . . you will hardly ever come to be Famous or Eminent. . . . Having thus agreed, the Ape in a few days had dyed the *Fox's* Coat, shaved his Tail, and made him a complete black Perriwig, that covered his Head and Ears; and then they sat together in consult how to manage their future Business to their best Advantage.

(pp. 46–47)

"Doctor Pedanto's" advertisement reads as follows:

Good Tidings to the Sick and Lame

Whereas there is lately come into these Parts, a very honourable, truly, [sic] wise and learned Physician, by Name *Dr. Pedanto;* who by his great Travels in Forraign Kingdoms, can speak Five and thirty several Languages; and

39. See Varty, p. 73; Bond, pp. 75–76; M. D. Anderson, *Animal Carvings in British Churches* (Cambridge, Eng., 1938), p. 14. H. W. Janson disagrees, however: *Apes and Ape Lore* (London, 1952), pp. 233–234, n. 80.

having been Physician to three Emperors, seventeen Kings, thirty nine Dukes, infinite other Great Lords, and Persons of Quality, hath attained the fine Art of Healing, equal to the Knowledge of *Hippocrates* and *Galen,* and far beyond the Skill of any other yet known in the World at this day. This Physician hearing of the great Fame of this renowned Kingdom, having Travelled far to see it, is now desirous to shew his great Skill in this place. Therefore proposeth to all Diseased Persons whatsoever, to Cure the *Running* of the *Reins* (by Artists called the *Gonorrhea*) the *Pox, Gout, Scurvey, Dropsie,* and all other Distempers whatsoever, internal or external, whether curable or not. And all this for a very reasonable Reward, requiring nothing before the Cure be fully performed.

(p. 49)

Besides this likeness of jargon between Scoto and Pedanto, another interesting parallel to the play is the fox's relation to Zani the ape, who helps disguise Reynardine and steals the necessary instruments for him from the peddler (as in the iconography) but ultimately become his rival and betrays him, only to destroy himself. This immediately brings to mind Scoto's helper "Zan Fritada," Nano the dwarf, who actually describes himself as "a pritty little ape" (III.iii.12–14); and the likeness is strengthened by a passage in Jean de Condé's "Renart Mestres de l'ostel le Roy," in his early fourteenth-century *Dit d'entendement*, in which a young ape, a young dog, and a young cat entertain Reynard with songs, pulling faces, and stupidities whose main art, as the poet remarks, is mocking at others, like the entertainments of Volpone's three freaks.[40] Not that Jonson knew either text, of course, but there may well have been some tradition behind his idea of the fox's apish entertainers. Moreover, the rivalry between Reynardine and Zani which results in Zani's destruction can be related also to Mosca; and, when it is considered along with images of the ape tending the sick fox and others (to be mentioned below) of the fox aided by an ape while preaching, it suggests that the tradition of the fox's ape helper [41] may have been one

40. See Flinn, *"Roman,"* p. 353. Mosca's identification of the three freaks as Volpone's children (I.v.46–49) may relate to the convention that Reynard had three children: see, for example, the three peeping cubs in Illustration 7.

41. There is an early fourteenth-century Latin tale in which the ape is portrayed as the fox's chamberlain, receiving his guests as Mosca receives Volpone's (see Flinn, *ibid.,* pp. 693–695; Varty, p. 65); and Stith Thompson records a folktale (W.152.1) of the fox destroying his food rather than share it with an ape, like Volpone's behavior at the end of the play.

influence on the Mosca role too. Varty devotes a whole section (chap. 5, pp. 60–67) to the relation between the fox and the ape; and, besides the possible relationship to Mosca, the accomplice who becomes a self-defeating rival, and to the apish entertainer Nano, there are also certain likenesses to the Would-be subplot of *Volpone,* with the imitative "ape" qualities transferred to parrots. Certainly, Lady Pol, besides her relation to the fornicating she-wolf, is apelike in her attendance at Volpone's sickbed; and her penchant for noisy pedantry and unsolicited advice is much like the characterization of the ape Dame Rukenauwe, Reynard's aunt, who takes over his defense with long-winded references to Seneca, Solomon, Avicenna, and Aristotle in chapter 29 of Caxton's translation and in chapter 37 gives him equally extended advice on how to fight Isengrin, citing a nonsensical spell.[42] There is no real equivalent to Sir Pol, however, though Rukenauwe's husband, Martin, is a bishop's clerk proud of his influence and his knowledge of official secrets.

Much more certain than these ape resemblances are likenesses to the literary and iconographic tradition of Reynard as fake preacher. Anti-clericalism is a persistent theme of the Reynard literature, particularly in later versions, and one of Reynard's most frequent disguises is as a mendi-cant friar (cf. Varty, chap. 4, "The Fox Religious," pp. 51–59). The theme appears early in two episodes of *Ysengrimus:* one where the fox, pretending to be a pilgrim on the road to Rome, tries to trick a cockerel; the other where, pretending to be a member of a convent, he persuades Isengrin to become a monk so that he himself can seduce the she-wolf. The cockerel incident is later elaborated into Chantecler's paean for his lost hens in Branches II and V^a of the *Roman,* and appears subsequently in *Reinaert,* the Caxton version, and in Branch V of *Renart le Contrefait.* Isengrin as monk is expanded in Branch III of the *Roman.* The false pilgrimage turns up again at the end of Branch I, and later in *Reinhart Fuchs* and *Reinaert I;* while in *Reynard in the Chancery* the fox pro-fesses to have become a hermit. In Branch VI of the *Roman,* after Reynard is beaten by Isengrin, he is rescued by Friar Bernard on condi-tion that he become a monk, but is then ejected for eating the monastery capons; and in Branch XII he and Tibert the cat dress up as monks and conduct vespers, till Reynard arranges for the cat to be caught ringing

---

42. Caxton, pp. 129–132, 167–169.

the bells. Volpone's perverse matins is in the tradition of this latter episode.

The clerical satire becomes much more elaborate in the continuations of the *Roman, Renart le Bestourné, Renart le Nouvel, Renart le Contrefait,* and especially in *Le Couronnement de Renart,* where the fox joins two mendicant orders simultaneously, hears the dying lion's confession, and, becoming king himself, teaches "renardie" to the college of cardinals with the pope's blessing. In the *Couronnement* he also delivers an elaborate sermon to the court, and in Book 8 of *Renart le Contrefait* (version A) he preaches an interminable sermon in the guise of a friar to a congregation of little birds, but is forced to flee by the appearance of Isengrin, the cuckold.

In iconography Reynard is usually depicted as wearing clerical dress; and by far the most popular of these depictions—in fact, the most common of *all* the fox images—are representations of him preaching, usually from a pulpit, to a congregation of domestic fowl: he often has a dead bird or two tucked into his cowl; sometimes there is a helper, another fox or, more frequently, an ape, behind the pulpit; and in at least one example the congregation consists of women, not birds—recalling Jacque de Vitry's comment on Renart's attempt to persuade a wren to give him the kiss of peace (in Branch II) as representing priests who preach only to seduce women. "If the fox preach," says Robert Greene, " 'tis to spie which is the fattest goose." [43]

As in the case of the fox feigning death, there are far too many examples of the fox preaching to list them all. Some of the most interesting for our purposes are misericords in Bristol Cathedral (Varty #44, plate 73) and Beverley Minster (Varty #11, plate 86), each of which shows the fox with an ape helper, the latter dated as late as 1520;[44] a related example is a misericord in St. George's Chapel, Windsor, where the preaching fox is supported by an ape bowman taking aim at a goose in the congregation (Varty #192, plate 88). Flinn (*L'Iconographie,* p. 54) adds an interesting variant from the façade of the *hôtel de ville* in Saint Quentin, where Reynard preaching to fowl is imitated by a monkey on

43. Flinn, *L'Iconographie,* p. 49; Greene, *Works,* ed. A. B. Grosart (London, 1881–1886), IX, 228.

44. See Illustrations 11 and 12.

Illustration 11. Fox, with Ape Helper, Preaching to Geese, from misericord (N. 5. 1520), in Bristol Cathedral. (Photo: D. R. Maxted)

Illustration 12. Fox, with Ape Helper, Preaching to Geese, from misericord (N. 4. 1520), in Beverley Minster, Yorkshire. (Photo: J.C.D. Smith)

the other side of the façade. There are three examples where the second animal is another fox, not an ape: Lincoln Cathedral (Varty #114, plate 64), the Benedictine Church at Kempen in Germany (Flinn, *L'Iconographie,* p. 49, with plate facing p. 50), and St. Fiacre-du-Faouet in Brittany (Flinn); one where it is apparently a cock—the Priory of Christchurch, Hampshire (Varty #70, plate 75); and one where it is an ass—St. Botolph, Boston, Lincolnshire (Varty #26, plate 65). Two other especially interesting specimens are a carving in Holy Trinity, St. Austell, Cornwall, where the congregation is composed of women, not fowl (Varty #154, plate 67); and a carving on the choirstalls at Amiens, where Reynard is preaching to a richly dressed vixen, or she-wolf, who is showing her dugs (Flinn).[45] In the light of this widely disseminated image and the stories and images of Reynard pretending to be a doctor, it is certain that the mountebank scene in *Volpone,* far from being the inorganic, overextended episode it has sometimes been called, would have seemed a familiar, almost inevitable scene to its original audience. And the same may be argued for another incident whose organic usefulness has sometimes been questioned, Volpone's burst into song in the seduction of Act III, scene vii.

IV. Reynard the Musician and Reynard Victorious

For the tradition of fox as musician,[46] the iconography is even more important than the literary sources, because, though Reynard does feature

45. Other English examples listed are: MS illuminations in the *Smithfield Decretals* and *Queen Mary's Psalter;* stained glass at one time in St. Martin's, Leicester; carvings at Abington Manor, Northampton; St. Mary's, Beverley, York-shire; Blackburn Cathedral; St. Michael's, Brent Knoll, Somerset; Canterbury Cathedral; Ely Cathedral; All Saints, Gresford, Denbighshire; Parish Church of Hexham, Northumberland; a sixteenth-century example in the Old Halfmoon Inn, Ipswich (Varty #106, plate 83); St. Laurence, Ludlow; St. Mary's, Nantwich, Cheshire; St. Petroc, Padstow, Cornwall; Ripon Cathedral. There is an even fuller list for the Continent: see Flinn, *L'Iconographie, passim* (especially for France); L. Maeterlinck, *Le genre satirique, fantastique et licencieux dans la sculpture flamande et wallone* (Paris, 1910), pp. 76, 176; Wright, pp. 78–80; and for German exempla, Doris Lamke, *Mittelalterliche Tierfabeln und ihre Beziehungen zur bildenden Kunst in Deutschland* (Greiswald, 1937).

46. See Varty, chap. 7, "The Fox Minstrel," pp. 76–80.

as a minstrel in Branch I^b of the *Roman de Renart,* one of the beast epic's oldest sequences written about 1185, he does so in a very different context from the seduction of Celia. In this branch Reynard is outlawed after Noble's attack on his castle and, jumping through a window, lands in a dyer's vat which stains him yellow. Thus disguised, he passes himself off to Isengrin as an English minstrel, persuades the wolf to steal a viol, then leaves him in the musician's house to be beaten and mutilated. After practicing on the viol, Reynard goes home to find his wife, the vixen Hermeline, about to marry a cousin, Poncet the badger, on the assumption that she is a widow. Reynard sings at the celebration but that evening lures Poncet into a trap which kills him; then, revealing his identity, he beats Hermeline and turns her out of the house. A noisy quarrel follows between Hermeline and Reynard's ex-mistress, the she-wolf; but both marriages are saved by the fortuitous appearance of a saintly pilgrim.[47] Another episode occurs in Guillaume Tardif's elaboration of Laurence Valla's fable "De vulpe et capite quodam" (itself a version of Aesop's "The Fox and the Mask"—cf. Handford, p. 11) in *Les Apologues de Laurent Valla, suivis des ditz moraulx* (1495).[48] In this fable Reynard, posing as a hermit, goes to a musician to learn how to play an instrument, preferably the harp, but finally decides on a choir of cocks and hens instead. More pertinent to the *Volpone* situation, perhaps, is Reynard's love song to Queen Fière in Jean de Condé's "Renart mestres de l'ostel le Roy" (Flinn, *Roman,* p. 352), which itself is a reflection of the more than sixty songs printed, with music, in *Renart le Nouvel.*

Minstrels are criticized in Branch VII of *Renart le Contrefait* as leading people to hell by their misuse of music, and it is this aspect more than the illustration of any particular incident which is behind most of the iconography of the fox as musician. As a theme this goes right back to classical Greek and Latin literature, and it became particularly popular in the late Middle Ages.[49] Flinn (*L'Iconographie,* p. 88) notes that Dürer

---

47. For analogues to the fabliaux and folklore, see Foulet, p. 356, and Sudre, pp. 250–272.

48. Cited in Flinn, *"Roman,"* p. 467; Varty, p. 78.

49. See chap. 21 in Bond, pp. 171–175, and E. Curtius, *European Literature and the Latin Middle Ages,* trans Willard R. Trask (New York, 1953), pp. 95–97.

represents "Temptation" in his *Hours of Maximilian* by a picture of Reynard playing a flageolet before a cock and some hens; and he records three other interesting examples of the image on the Continent: a fourteenth-century wall painting from the chapel of Plaincourault near Poitiers in Berry, which shows Reynard playing a viol to a cock and other fowl (*L'Iconographie,* plate 4, facing p. 42); a bas-relief in the cathedral of Bâle of a fox playing the viol to another, unidentifiable beast (*ibid.* pp. 17–18); and an illustration in the manuscript of Aquinas's *Summa* at Segovia Cathedral in which Reynard plays a church organ with another fox watching (or pumping?) from behind the organ. Varty lists nine English exempla: two of the most interesting are a twelfth-century carving from St. Nicholas, Barfreston, Kent, of a fox playing a harp while a woman does a back somersault (Varty #3, plate 117); and a misericord from Chichester Cathedral on which a fox plays a harp while an ape dances (Varty #67, plate 118).[50] Two of the other examples show foxes playing bagpipes, two show foxes playing flutes, and one has a fox playing a trumpet; and there are two examples (Varty, plates 114, 115) in which a fox plays a viol for two other foxlike creatures to dance, which pretty clearly represents the events of Branch I[b]. In all then, Volpone's burst into song at III.vii.165 ff. would scarcely come as a surprise to spectators familiar with this tradition of the fox as perverter of music. And, according to Topsell,[51] the fox was also notorious for his unpleasant voice, which might add an extra dimension to the satire, and perhaps to the staging too.

Finally, there is the problem of tone, particularly at the conclusion. Jonson himself feared that the end of *Volpone* was too severely moral for comedy, yet its seriousness is qualified by Volpone's punning reaction to his sentence and his impertinent epilogue asking the audience to dissociate itself from the court by applause. A similar problem of tone is endemic to the beast epic, which all commentators see as a tug-of-war between an anarchic identification with the fox and a satiric condemnation of the evils and institutions he represents, with the latter predominating in the later versions till Reynard becomes increasingly a

---

50. See Illustrations 13 and 14.
51. Edward Topsell, *The History of Foure-footed Beasts* (1658 ed.), p. 175.

Illustration 13. Human Somersaults to Fox's Harping. A 12th-century carving from St. Nicholas, Barfreston, Kent. (Courtauld Institute of Art: A47 / 4238)

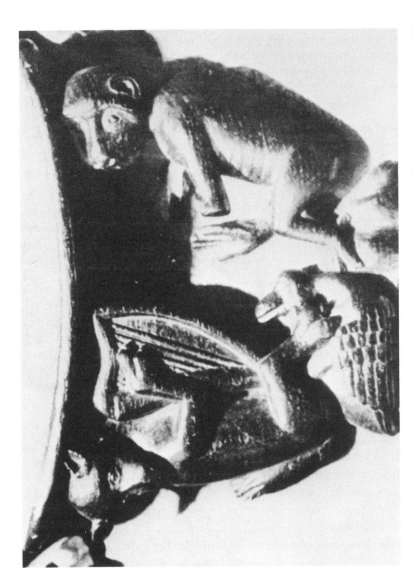

Illustration 14. Ape Dances to Fox's Harping. Misericord (S. 20. 1330) from Chicester Cathedral (Courtauld Institute of Art: B36 / 1323)

symbol for the devil himself—and comic élan is quite lost. As a historian of
French literature puts it:

Renart n'était pour les premiers poètes qui l'ont chanté qu'un joyeux fripon,
dont la malice incorrigible rebondissait de farce en farce: tant de bonne
humeur se dégageait de sa personne . . . que personne ne lui gardait rancune
de ses tours: il avait les lecteurs pour complices. Mais [plus tard] . . . on le
prend au serieux, voire au tragique: . . . on le peint comme étant l'ami du
Mal. L'interprétation allégorique s'en mêlant, il devient le Mal en personne,
et l'Hypocrisie. En lui s'incarnent tous les vices du siècle.[52]

Volpone also goes through this arc but his balance is more complex,
neither wholly farcical at the beginning nor wholly repudiated at the end.
The somber view of a whole civilization corrupted by "renardie" with
which the later versions of the *Reynard* conclude is the position from
which Jonson's play begins, but the somberness is lightened by vitality.
Volpone's aubade about the power of money is a dynamic version of the
complaint at the end of *Le Couronnement de Renart* that "Argent" controls everything except death, or the conclusion of Caxton's *History of
Reynard the Fox:*

There is nothing beloved nor known in the court nowadays but money. The
money is better beloved than God. For men do much more therefor. For
whomsoever brings money shall be well received and shall have all his desires,
is it of lords or ladies or of any other. That money does much harm. Money
brings many in shame and dread of life and brings false witness against true
people to get money. It causes uncleanness of living, lying, and lechery
(p. 185).

Volpone's first speech says these things in a different tone.

Similarly with the fox's malice. The character of Reynard is developed
in the beast epic beyond the sly selfishness of the fox of Aesop and the
bestiaries to a delight in savage mischief and malice for their own sake
—what Flinn calls "son penchant inné vers le mal, . . . sa perversité et
sa méchanceté qui ne connaissaient pas de limite" (*Roman,* p. 689).
This malice is acceptable insofar as most of the fox's victims are no better
than himself: it satirizes and condemns the corruption of others—as, for
example, in Volpone's criticism of Corbaccio's vices of age (I.iv.144 ff.).

52. Joseph Bedier and Paul Hazard, *L'Histoire de la littérature Française il-
lustrée,* rev. ed. (Paris, 1949), I, 53.

But a more negative aspect appears in Reynard's habit of jeering, his rubbing in of defeat with taunting words, which is clearly related to Volpone's "jig," that fatal last trick of taunting the disappointed legacy-hunters in disguise as a "commendatori" or sergeant.[53] In the epic as in the play, this jeering sometimes leads to the fox's downfall: as early as *Ysengrimus* the cock escapes from Reynard's mouth by encouraging him to insult his pursuers—a trick best known to English readers from Chaucer's *Nonnes Preestes Tale,* and similarly he loses Couart the hare when he stops to jeer at Noble's court at the end of Branch I of the *Roman.* To an audience familiar with the Reynard tradition, then, Volpone's last trick would come with a much greater sense of appropriateness than it did to Dryden, who thought Volpone's motive was merely money.

There is a similar ambiguity in the punishment at the end. There is never much sense that Reynard's enemies deserve to win: Noble is venal, Isengrin brutal, and the innocent and harmless fowl and hare lack all Reynard's "personality"—his energy and excitement. There is always a sense of disproportion as well as rightness, therefore, in the scenes of Reynard's punishment; and this finds iconographic expression in the familiar images of the birds hanging the fox, which, as Thomas Wright noted over a century ago, are related to the popular medieval motif of "le monde bestourné," the world upside down or turned topsy-turvy.[54] Moreover, though he is taken to the scaffold and even sometimes left for dead, Reynard never really dies. As Foulet points out (p. 391), the basic problem for all the Reynard authors was how to condemn the fox without losing him as a hero, and their solution was a series of postponed fatalities. In Branch I Reynard escapes right from the gibbet, to go on a pilgrimage which he discards as soon as he is safe; in I[a] he is rescued by his wife with gold; in II–V[a] he evades Isengrin's plot with the mastiff, Roenel; in IV Friar Bernard rescues him from Isengrin on condition he become a monk, but he is then evicted for eating the monastery capons; in X he escapes condemnation by posing as a doctor; in XVII he feigns

---

53. Renart also claims to be a sergeant in Branch XXIII of the *Roman de Renart,* to excuse his killing of Coupée, the hen, but this has no other resemblance to the *Volpone* situation.

54. Wright, pp. 88–91; see also Bond, pp. 74–75. Varty lists six English examples (see his #12, 45, 52, 119, 120, and 226), and Bond cites three more. See Illustration 15.

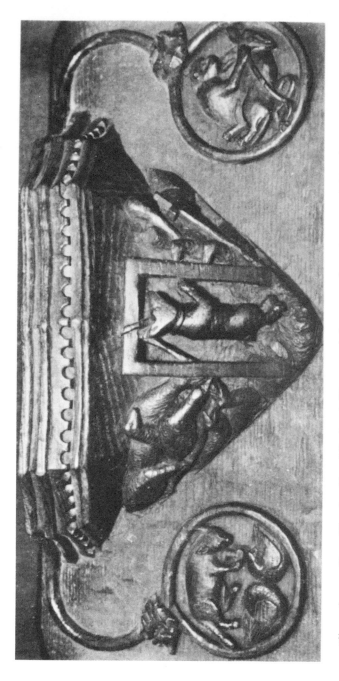

Illustration 15. Geese Hanging Fox. Misericord (N. 4. 1520) from Beverley Minster, Yorkshire (Photo: D. R. Maxted)

death three times; in XXIII he escapes by promising the king a rich marriage; in XXVII (as recorded in *Rainardo e Lesengrino*) by promising to adopt an honest profession; and in *Reinaert I* and Caxton by "confessing" to hidden treasure which leads the court off on a wild goose chase. In no version is the fox finally quelled; so an Elizabethan audience might be expected to take the point of Volpone's survival, as he spoke the epilogue: the fox survives because he represents something permanent in all of us, a corruption which is closely linked to our vitality. The balance was nicely caught by the poet Rutebeuf:

> Renart est mort
> Renart vit
> Et Renart regne—

"Reynard is dead, Reynard lives, and Reynard reigns."

V. Conclusion

What then can we conclude? It is impossible to prove any sort of direct influence, of course; but it is clear that many details of Jonson's plot are closer to well-known aspects of the Reynard epic than was realized. Its original audience would *almost certainly* have recognized behind the play the familiar episodes of the fox feigning sickness and death to lure scavengers, and catching the crow's wife; the fox's attempt at rape, and double trial before a venal and savage court, where his defense is a plea of age and an attack on his accuser's chastity; and the combination of fox as false doctor and lecherous preacher behind the episode of Scoto the mountebank. They *probably* would have recognized the fox's downfall through his malicious urge to jeer; his misuse of song in the seduction scene; and his survival in the epilogue to claim the audience's guilty sympathy. Just *possibly,* they might have connected the fox's traditional association with entertaining, imitative, and competitive apes with the roles of Nano, Lady Politic Would-be, and Mosca; and Volpone's "dying" entrance to the first trial with the "Funeral Procession of Reynard."

If such recognitions are plausible, three things follow (besides the recognition that Jonson is once again combining classical and native influences). The play is much more tightly unified than we have hitherto realized, with the "episodes" of Scoto and Volpone's song especially more meaningful. The tonal balance between anarchic comedy and satire is more complex, but also for its original audience more familiar, with the epilogue an essential and expected finale, and with recognition of likeness to the beast epic reducing the play's brutality to a more acceptable dimension. And, lastly, the original staging may well have recalled some of the most familiar scenes of the widespread fox iconography; at all events, it would have been less likely for the staging to present men with some characteristics of animals—as has been the tendency in modern productions—and more likely for it to follow beast-epic convention and present the characters as recognizable animals who behave like men.

Shakespeare's Troilus and Cressida and the Monumental Tradition in Tapestries and Literature

JILL L. LEVENSON

W HEN SHAKESPEARE WROTE his great, unloved play about Priam's Troy (ca. 1601–1602), his audience knew the plot and characters primarily from two sources: literature and wall hangings. From studies such as Kimbrough's, we already know a good deal about the origins and transmission of the literary tradition on which *Troilus and Cressida* depends for its satiric impact.[1] But the pictorial tradition remains to be explored; it too influenced the Elizabethans' conception of the fable and, consequently, their response to the play.

Medieval and Renaissance tapestries that picture the Troy legend captured the imaginations of their viewers not by formulating a bold, new version of the tale, but by re-creating ancient and medieval literary

1. Robert Kimbrough, *Shakespeare's "Troilus and Cressida" and its Setting* (Cambridge, Mass., 1964). See also Robert K. Presson, *Shakespeare's "Troilus and Cressida" & the Legends of Troy* (Madison, Wisc., 1953); John S. P. Tatlock, "The Siege of Troy in Elizabethan Literature, Especially in Shakespeare and Heywood," *PMLA*, XXX (1915), 673–770; and the discussions of sources in the New Variorum edition, ed. Harold N. Hillebrand (Philadelphia and London, 1953), and in the Cambridge edition, ed. Alice Walker (Cambridge, Eng.), 1957.

narratives visually. Produced collectively, and received by a large and varied audience, these storied textiles configure in striking images a widely accepted conception of the legend. Whatever their immediate sources, the extant wall hangings all reflect the famous narrative tradition established by Benoît de Sainte-Maure in the twelfth century with his *Le Roman de Troie*. Like Benoît's long, embellished, and aesthetically impressive recital, they conceive Troy's debacle as "l'histoire riche e granz," and they depict it in compositions that are monumental, filled with opulent details, and intellectually engaging.

Familiarity with the Troy tapestries and the literary tradition they preserve sharpens our sense of how Shakespeare debunks the fundamentally respectful medieval and Renaissance attitudes toward the legend of the second Troy. We recognize by now the uniqueness and effect of Shakespeare's approach to tradition in *Troilus and Cressida*: ". . . his entertainment depended on the audience's recognition that this was the Troy story with a difference;" [2] and scholars have explained, by anatomizing the play, how it reduces particular characters, episodes, and themes from classical, medieval, and Renaissance literature. In an attempt to supplement and corroborate existing studies, this article will focus upon the distinguishing features of the monumental tradition and the ways in which Shakespeare minimizes or otherwise distorts them in *Troilus and Cressida*.

I

As an art form both practical and luxuriant, medieval and Renaissance tapestries were the ideal means for popularizing the legend of Troy with the splendor and majesty that characterize Benoît's *Le Roman de Troie*.

2. Walker, ed., p. xlv. Scholars who share Professor Walker's view of Shakespeare's approach include: R. A. Foakes, "*Troilus and Cressida* Reconsidered," *UTQ*, XXXII (1963), 150–154, and *Shakespeare: The Dark Comedies to the Last Plays: From Satire to Celebration* (London, 1971), pp. 45–46 and 60–61; L. C. Knights, "'Troilus and Cressida' Again," *Scrutiny*, XVIII (1951), 154; A. P. Rossiter, *Angel with Horns: Fifteen Lectures on Shakespeare*, ed. Graham Storey (London, 1961), pp. 130–131.

Despite their costliness, they entertained an audience vast and diverse. As displays of wealth and station, they insulated, adorned, and partitioned the homes of the nobility. They decorated churches; accompanied journeys and military campaigns; and "invaded the streets." In discussing medieval French tapestry, Roger-Armand Weigert describes the public role of the pictured textiles throughout Europe: "They took their place in the urban scene as temporary backcloths for public ceremonies. Without regard for the appropriateness of the subject represented, religious and secular tapestries were hung indiscriminately along the routes of processions, on the occasions of royal entries, receptions for notable visitors, and popular festivals. There are few descriptions of public ceremonies . . . which fail to make a reference to some choice tapestry."[3] In addition, many members of the working classes had regular contact with these splendid cloths. Since the Middle Ages and the Renaissance produced more tapestries than the largest homes or lengthiest streets could exhibit, the majority of the hangings remained in storage attended by guards, servants, and menders. When tapestries peregrinated, craftsmen and carters waited upon them. These pictured cloths enjoyed a following sizable, varied, and appreciative enough to sustain J. Duverger's conclusion that "the tapestry weaver created . . . the frame for the events of both public and private life."[4]

In Shakespeare's England in particular, tapestries won tremendous popularity. Those who admired these expensive wall hangings but could not afford them substituted painted cloths. In numerous documents of the period, references to tapestry and its imitations indicate their widespread use. Harrison's *Description of England* (1577–1587) makes an

3. Roger-Armand Weigert, *French Tapestry,* trans. Donald and Monique King (London, 1956), p. 24.

4. For information about the wide and varied audience of medieval and Renaissance tapestries, see: Roger-A. D'Hulst, *Flemish Tapestries from the Fifteenth to the Eighteenth Century,* foreword by H. Liebaers, historical account by J. Duverger, trans. Frances H. Stillman (Brussels, 1967), p. xiii; Geneviève Souchal, *Masterpieces of Tapestry: From the Fourteenth to the Sixteenth Century,* introd. Francis Salet, trans. Richard A. H. Oxby (Greenwich, Conn., 1974), pp. 16–17; W. G. Thomson, *A History of Tapestry from the Earliest Times until the Present Day,* rev. ed. (London, 1930), pp. 244–245 (Thomson explains the way Henry VIII in particular preserved his huge collection of tapestries); Weigert, p. 24.

observation typical of many documents: "In the days of Elizabeth, the walls of our houses on the inner side are either hanged with tapestry, arras work, painted cloths wherein either divers histories, or herbs, beasts, knots, and such like are stained."[5] In addition to comments like Harrison's, frequent mentions of pictorial hangings in inventories, wills, and the belletristic literature of the period testify to the currency of woven and painted cloths as wall decorations.

From the fourteenth to the seventeenth centuries, tapestries frequently entertained their vast European audience by narrating stories, a practice which George Leland Hunter extols as their "mission."[6] In highly detailed scenes, they wove complicated narratives based on literary sources which ranged from parables to contemporary dramas. And like the literature that they re-created visually, they played a considerable part in familiarizing medieval and Renaissance Europe with religious, secular, and legendary history. They engaged their viewers in the stories they told by means of the features which together distinguish them from other graphic art forms and make their narrations impressive and memorable. Monumental, they appeared splendid at a distance; detailed, they proved full of surprises at close sight. Their bold use of color and the flat unrelieved treatment of their subjects intensified their narrations. Having engaged its spectators, the grand and multifarious world of storied tapestry challenged their powers of comprehension. "Any picture, by its very nature, remains an appeal to the visual imagination; it must be supplemented in order to be understood."[7] In reading a narrative tapestry, the observer had to discern a sequence of events and its implications from an immense composition of figures and details. He had to discover the chronology of episodes, the relationships among characters, the causal

5. Small but useful collections of these documentary references appear in Frederick Hard, "Spenser's 'Clothes of Arras and of Toure,'" *SP*, XXVII (1930), 162–185, and in John Humphreys, *Elizabethan Sheldon Tapestries* (London, 1929), pp. 9–10. Harrison is quoted in Humphreys, p. 9.

6. George Leland Hunter, *Tapestries: Their Origin, History and Renaissance* (New York, London, Toronto, 1912), p. 279.

7. E. H. Gombrich, *Art and Illusion: A Study in the Psychology of Pictorial Representation,* Bollingen Series XXXV, 5, 2d ed., rev. (New York, 1961), pp. 242–243.

links between incidents, and the themes which informed the action. A storied tapestry which attracted and held its viewers' attention offered not only pleasure but also edification. Analogous with other medieval and Renaissance forms of artistic expression, pictorial wall hangings instructed the mind with counsel and warnings, biblical and allegorical precepts, and didactic reference to classical fables; they represented the ideas most cherished by their epochs.[8] In England they exerted a particularly strong influence on Elizabethan conceptions of classical myths: ". . . paintings were less familiar than on the continent, tapestries were common, . . . Whatever the popularity of Ovid and the mythographers, they could not altogether counteract the effect of a tapestry on the wall. . . ."[9]

Resplendent and complex by virtue of their composition, tapestries and Benoît's version of the Trojan War inevitably merged. Among traditional subjects for tapestries, the account of the second Troy remained enormously popular from the Middle Ages through the seventeenth century. What we know about these magnificent wall hangings rests on three kinds of evidence: extant tapestries, the scholarship of art historians, and references to tapestries in such documents as inventories, accounts, and instructions. In many ways this evidence proves less plentiful than that which exists for studies of Troy literature. Although numerous wall hangings survive, probably more have disappeared; and analyses of the iconography of extant tapestries have occupied few art historians. Yet the evidence provides a substantial base for careful speculation. Documentary material, for example, establishes both the frequency of the subject and the particular aspects of it treated in either individual hangings or whole sets. Among other things it reveals that Henry VIII possessed more than two thousand pieces, dozens of them depicting the Nine Worthies, Hector, the history of Helen and Paris, and the siege of Troy; that some of these crown tapestries about the Trojan legend lasted until the reign of

8. For data about narration in tapestries, I am indebted to: N. Y. Biryukova, text and notes, *The Hermitage, Leningrad: Gothic & Renaissance Tapestries,* trans. Philippa Hentgès (London, 1965), pp. 11 and 14; Hard, p. 164; A. F. Kendrick, *Catalogue of Tapestries* (London, 1914), p. 14; and *2000 Years of Tapestry Weaving: A Loan Exhibition* (Hartford, Conn. [?], 1951 [?]), p. 6.

9. Douglas Bush, *Mythology and the Renaissance Tradition in English Poetry,* rev. ed. (New York, 1963), p. 80.

Charles I; and that many sets which related the complete story of the war existed during the sixteenth century in England, Scotland, Sweden, Portugal, and France.[10]

These three kinds of testimony not only indicate that the matter of Troy appeared very often in tapestries throughout Europe during the Middle Ages and Renaissance, but also inform us as to the various ways in which wall hangings formulated the subject. From the beginning of the period, artists both epitomized the entire story in sets and extracted from it individual characters for presentation in either single tapestries or sets. In short, whereas the fragmentation of the narrative in literature happened on occasion during the Middle Ages and constantly during the Renaissance, abridgment invariably prevailed in the pictorial hangings. Obviously, the graphic art had to summarize the account in one way or another; it could not indulge in what J. Huizinga calls the "quantitative method" of the large medieval romances.[11] Further, in the extant tapestries, we see the story realized in modes ranging from Gothic to Mannerist. Naturally, as artistic styles changed over three centuries, so did the iconography of the large textiles. But throughout tapestry's gradual transition from medieval to Renaissance guise, none of the successive styles ever totally displaced any of the others. Weigert remarks on this phenomenon: the history of tapestry was "affected by constant and imperceptible variations, inevitable time-lags in the adaptation of new aesthetic ideals. . . ."[12] Just as the medieval literary conception of the Troy legend stood firm during the English Renaissance, so Gothic tapestries on Trojan War subjects retained their appeal through the sixteenth and seventeenth centuries. (Hence, Sir Sidney Colvin argues that a Gothic wall hanging on an episode from the Troy saga inspired Shakespeare's "piece / Of skillful painting, made for Priam's Troy, . . ." in

10. See Thomson's abridged version of the inventory of Henry VIII, pp. 245–260; the published inventories of Charles I in *Abraham van der Doort's Catalogue of the Collections of Charles I,* ed. and introd. Oliver Millar, *The Thirty-Seventh Volume of The Walpole Society* (1958–1960); and the evidence collected by J. P. Asselberghs, "Les Tapisseries flamandes de la Cathédrale de Zamora," diss., Université Catholique de Louvain, 1964, p. 144.

11. J. Huizinga, *The Waning of the Middle Ages* (New York, 1954), p. 280.

12. Weigert, p. 89.

The Rape of Lucrece [ll. 1366–1582].)[10] By the time Shakespeare wrote *Troilus and Cressida,* then, the Trojan story in tapestry flourished in a wide variety of versions and styles; in comprehensive synopses and character sketches; in Gothic, Renaissance, and Mannerist garb. Finally, the extant tapestries and some art historians make it absolutely clear that the majority of wall hangings about the Trojan War depended upon the medieval literary formulation of the tale: "None of these tapestries depicting antique stories shows—any more than the mediaeval literary versions which were used as their sources—any influence of classical art, classical form, or classical culture and customs."[14]

Whatever their style or choice of subject from the matter of Troy, tapestries that represented the legend were almost invariably large, detailed, opulent, and to different degrees, symbolic. This point should become apparent in the following pages, which survey the ways in which medieval and Renaissance wall hangings treated the Trojan legend, and briefly describe both the dimensions and compositions of individual tapestries.

To begin with, when artists singled heroes and heroines out of the story, they treated them either symbolically or objectively. In the many tapestries that celebrated the Nine Heroes or Nine Heroines, therefore, Greek and Trojan characters often resided majestically among pagan, Hebrew, and Christian Worthies embodying chivalric ideals. Helen and Penthesilea appeared among the ladies, and Hector frequently took a place among the conquerors. The chivalric theme of the *Neuf Preux,* systematized ca. 1310 by Jacques de Longuyon in his *Voeux du Paon,* imposed its orderliness upon the woven pictures. In the fourteenth-century set made for Jean, Duke of Berry, for example, each of three tapestries (more than twenty-one feet wide and approximately sixteen feet high apiece) portrays three heroes surrounded by smaller figures in an architectural frame (see illustration 1). Among the models of knighthood sits Hector, identified by his armor and accouterments, and

13. (Sir) Sidney Colvin, "The Sack of Troy in Shakespeare's 'Lucrece' and in Some Fifteenth-Century Drawings and Tapestries," in *A Book of Homage to Shakespeare,* ed. Israel Gollancz (Oxford, 1916), pp. 88–99.

14. Betty Kurth, "Masterpieces of Gothic Tapestry in the Burrell Collection," *The Connoisseur,* CXVII (1946), p. 8.

Illustration 1: The Gothic Hector Tapestry (ca. 1385). The Metropolitan Museum of Art, The Cloisters. Collection, Gift of John D. Rockefeller, Jr., 1947

ensconced imposingly on a Gothic throne in a highly wrought Gothic niche. Bearded and crowned, dressed in medieval garments and armor, this static Hector unmistakably emblematizes "all honour, longing to chivalry, . . ." Enhancing his stature, the little people around him appear like figures attached to a ducal castle of the fourteenth century: warriors, primarily, and a lady holding a flower.[15] In addition to the *Neuf Preux* tapestries, others which expressed abstract themes incorporated figures from the Troy story. An early sixteenth-century set, the allegorical *Triumphs of Petrarch,* illustrates the idea of Fame by depicting Menelaus, Priam, Paris, and Pyrrhus crowded among other famous personages. Another set, the "Triumph of Cupid," Gothic in style but perhaps contemporary with the "Triumph of Fame," includes among its victims of love Helen and Paris.[16]

Far less emblematic than the Heroes and Triumphs compositions, numerous biographical tapestries portrayed in some detail episodes from the fabled lives of individual characters. In certain cases, a single wall hanging conceived the personage by conflating several events in which he played a major role. Thus, a Flemish tapestry dating ca. 1510–1515 pictures Ulysses by fusing together four of his adventures within a space twelve feet high and over twenty-one feet wide. (see Illustration 2, and details in Illustrations 3, 4, and 5).[17] On the right side of the piece, Ulysses and Diomedes, ambassadors for the Greeks, stand before Priam and Paris in a consultation that occurs early in the siege. The central portion shows the theft of the Palladium by Ulysses and Antenor, a deed that precipitated the razing of Troy. In the upper left corner, Ulysses pretends madness in a fruitless attempt to avoid taking part in the war; in the lower left corner, he discovers Achilles hiding out among the

---

15. Precise information about this set has been put forth by James J. Rorimer and Margaret B. Freeman in both an article and a pamphlet. I have used the article, "The Nine Heroes Tapestries at the Cloisters," in *Medieval Tapestries at the Cloisters* (New York, 1949), pp. 7–15, which includes the quotation about "honour, longing to chivalry" from a fifteenth-century poet in *The Flower and the Leaf* on p. 8.

16. See Kendrick, pp. 33–37, and Thomson, pp. 183–185.

17. See Illustration 2, and details in Illustrations 3, 4, and 5. This tapestry is on display at the Royal Ontario Museum in Toronto, where information about its size, origin, and subject matter is available.

Illustration 2. The Ulysses Tapestry, Flemish (1510–1515). Royal Ontario Museum, Toronto

Illustration 3. The Ulysses Tapestry, detail. Royal Ontario Museum, Toronto

Illustration 4. The Ulysses Tapestry, detail. Royal Ontario Museum, Toronto

Illustration 5. The Ulysses Tapestry, detail. Royal Ontario Museum, Toronto

daughters of Lycomedes, king of Scyros. Medieval in its unsequential disposition of scenes, this Renaissance work stresses in its arrangement of incidents the wiliness of Ulysses and the treachery of the Greeks. Through its central episode, it highlights the general depravity that caused the war and its tragic consequences.

Whereas this single tapestry intensively summarizes a character, extant sets of wall hangings draw individual figures with leisurely strokes. Of the series devoted to personages from the Troy legend, early sixteenth-century sets about Helen and Paris survive in whole pieces and fragments.[18] Magnificent and full of ceremony, the extant works about Helen in particular characterize the art of the court during the golden age of Brussels tapestry. In these elegant sets, each piece deals with a single event, and the series in their entireties present receptions, corteges, marriages. Contributing to the general splendor, "De beaux personnages, somptueusement vêtus, s'y meuvent calmement dans de riches palais." The designers selected episodes for "leur statisme": the wedding of Helen and Paris; Helen before Menelaus.[19] In their exquisite elaboration of those episodes, they celebrated the Trojan legend.

Finally, innumerable sets of storied tapestries synopsized events of the whole Trojan War. From Asselberghs's summary account of these, based on documentary evidence and surviving fragments from the fourteenth through the sixteenth centuries, their frequency and stylistic variety appear obvious.[20] The range of their variation can be gauged by examining two elucidative works: the illustrious fifteenth-century Tournai series; and a late sixteenth-century tapestry which survives apparently from a set and represents a style that prospered in Brussels from the last third of the sixteenth century through the first half of the seventeenth (see Illustrations 6, 7, and 8 and the detail in Illustration 9).[21]

18. Apparently Hector, Helen, and Paris inspired many sets of wall hangings. According to Asselberghs, pp. 143–144, Paris thrived especially in the first half of the sixteenth century: "Celui-ci semble bien être le personnage principal des tapisseries de cette première moitié du siècle`. . ." (p. 143).

19. *Ibid.,* pp. 142–143.

20. *Ibid.,* pp. 140–146.

21. Whereas the Tournai set has received much attention from art historians, information about the sixteenth-century Brussels tapestries is scarce. My knowledge about the later wall hangings derives from Asselberghs, pp. 144–146, and from

Illustration 6. A Fragment from the Tournai Series (ca. 1472–1474). Hector and Andromache. The Metropolitan Museum of Art, Fletcher Fund, 1939

Regaling the great courts of medieval and Renaissance Europe with their magnificence, the eleven tapestries comprising the Tournai set include no less than five hundred figures in their enormous expanse (each piece measured approximately fifteen feet high and thirty feet wide). Documentary references, three groups of drawings, and many extant fragments of the wall hangings furnish scholars with enough evidence to reconstruct the cycle's history. In the most comprehensive study of this remarkable set, Asselberghs establishes that it was produced from the same cartoons at least four times between 1468 and 1493, and that its

Michael Stettler, *"Das Trojanische Pferd: ein Brüsseler Wandteppich,"* in *Festschrift für Werner Abegg* (Bern, 1973), pp. 229–262. (I am especially indebted to Stettler for much of my analysis of the Brussels tapestry.)

Illustration 7. A Fragment from the Tournai Series (ca. 1472–1474). Battle Scene with Centaur. The Metropolitan Museum of Art, Fletcher Fund, 1952.

earliest owners included Charles the Bold, Duke of Burgundy; Henry VII of England; Charles VIII of France; and Ferdinand I of Naples. Not surprisingly, he discovers signs of its influence in tapestries relating "la 'geste' troyenne" until ca. 1530.[22] Like Asselberghs, other art historians believe that the Tournai series depends upon a literary source. For this inspirational position, they propose a number of candidates: for instance, the first French translation of Guido de Columnis's *Historia Destructionis Troiae* (1287); a fourteenth-century French prose version of Benoît; Jacques Milet's fifteenth-century "play," *Mystère: L'Istoire de la destruction de Troye la Grant*. They concur, however, that whatever immediate source the designer used, the tapestries reflect—at a distance but faithfully —Benoît's *Le Roman de Troie*.

22. Widely discussed, this set receives its most comprehensive treatment in Asselberghs's dissertation and in an article he derived from the dissertation, "Les Tapisseries tournaisiennes de la Guerre de Troie," *Revue belge d'archéologie et d'histoire de l'art*, XXXIX (1970), 93–183. The dissertation provides an extensive bibliography of scholarship on these tapestries.

Illustration 8. The Brussels Series. The Destruction of Troy. Abegg-Stiftung, Bern

Illustration 9. The Brussels Series. The Destruction of Troy, detail. Abegg-Stiftung, Bern

   The style of the series illustrates late fifteenth-century taste. Each piece includes several scenes and many characters, the action explained by French and Latin verses at the top and bottom of the wall hanging. Lacking perspective, the huge, complex scenes teem with particulars, and the detail ". . . intensifies the surface effect of the tapestries and binds together all the individual forms into one big two-dimensional unity." [23] Although somewhat haphazard, the arrangement of the architecture clearly divides episodes. In addition, the disposition of the figures and juxtaposition of contrasting colors render the tableaux intelligible. [24]

23. Dora Heinz, *Medieval Tapestries*, trans. J. R. Foster (New York, 1967), p. 10.
24. James J. Rorimer, "A Fifteenth-Century Tapestry with Scenes of the Trojan War," *Bulletin of the Metropolitan Museum of Art*, XXXIV (1939), 226.

Greeks and Trojans, distinguished from one another only by the names woven into their garments, wear very elaborate late fifteenth-century costumes and arms. No thread of humor or frivolity relieves the solemnity of these narrative tapestries.

An English architect who sketched part of one set in 1799 had little admiration for its narrative achievement: "As to the story relating to the siege of Troy, that is a matter of indifference, . . . and but for the name of the several characters engaged in the history written on their dresses, we might conclude the representation related to some eventful period of our own history, . . . "[25] But Asselberghs points out how carefully the tapestries organize subject matter, their scenes composed to clarify and interpret one another. The central scene of the eighth tapestry, for example, follows directly from the central scene of the seventh. In the latter, set in a temple, the Trojans celebrate the anniversary of Hector's death at Achilles' hand, while Achilles falls in love with Polyxena, his half-closed eyes turned toward her. The crucial scene that occurs in the eighth tapestry takes place in the same edifice; it shows the result of Achilles' infatuation with Hector's sister, his death at the hands of Paris.[26] Clearly, the designer of this series demanded a close reading of his narrative, which relates what the verses on the eleventh tapestry describe as "listore miserable / De la cite digne de grant renom . . ." Through his delineation of one furious medieval melee after the other, he stresses the horror and devastation of the war. With his gorgeous details—harness pendants shaped like fruits, a brocaded tent, brocaded trappings on Hector's horse, little bells on Achilles' tunic,[27] an exquisite artificial tree (derived from Benoît)—he pays his tribute to the city worthy of great renown. Although the siege proper occupies the largest portion of his tableaux, intermittent scenes of consultation hint the war's causes and the concluding exhibition of the sack of Troy declares its effect.

Unlike the Tournai set, the Brussels tapestries about Priam's Troy have

25. Quoted in H. C. Marillier, "The Tapestries of the Painted Chamber; The 'Great History of Troy,' " *Burlington Magazine for Connoisseurs,* XLVI (1925), 36.

26. Asselberghs, "Les Tapisseries flamandes," pp. 77–78, and "Les Tapisseries tournaisiennes," pp. 112–114.

27. William H. Forsyth, "The Trojan War in Medieval Tapestries," *The Metropolitan Museum of Art Bulletin,* XIV (1955), 80, stresses these details in his description of parts of the set owned by the Metropolitan Museum of Art in New York.

been rarely published or discussed by art historians. However, in his recent study of six Brussels pieces, Michael Stettler has closely examined one woven hanging which seems to have come from a late sixteenth-century series. Depicting the destruction of the city by means of the treacherous horse, this tapestry fuses within its rectangular dimensions (twelve feet high by sixteen feet wide) several related scenes. Comparable to the Ulysses wall hanging and the Tournai series, it presents simultaneously in the Gothic fashion: the adventures of Sinon at the end of the war (left top, close to center); the havoc wrought by the device of the wooden horse (right top); battle scenes (middle area, forefront, and right foreground); the penetration en masse of the Greeks (left top, corner); and some additional incidents. The events derive from Aeneas's account of the destruction of Troy in the second book of Virgil's *Aeneid,* a classical text to which the Middle Ages and Renaissance often referred for purposes of embellishing with incidents the medieval story of the second Troy. Wherever the action abates in the tapestry, the space admits architecture, tents, flowers, and trees. The border of the piece, including some features Renaissance in style, contains ornamentation (such as leaf-work and urns), allegorical figures, and a central medallion with a consultation scene, the vista of Troy, and representation of part of the Greek army. In its conflation of incidents and its employment of color and detail, this tapestry remains in the Gothic mode of the Middle Ages. But its border edges toward the Renaissance, and its eccentric use of perspective leaps into Mannerism. Whereas fifteenth- and early sixteenth-century tapestries tended to place the theme of the picture centrally, in this work the wooden horse appears in the upper right quarter of the field, half turned away from view. In every way, the designer arranged the action to lead the beholder's eyes to this horse as the principal motif. And this focus gives the wall hanging a satirical cast. Our eyes rest finally on the rump of the horse, directed there by human figures: an oversize warrior, two banner carriers, the body of a fallen soldier. At the heart of the composition, this bizarre image points the absurdity of the horrific episode.

From the general statements and the illustrations offered to this point, we can describe with some precision the distinguishing features of medieval and Renaissance Troy tapestries. Large and imposing, the woven pictures recount the tale in whole or in part with a sense of immensity and often of grandeur. They offer rich detail which, like the descriptions in medieval literary narrative, comments upon the lost brilliance of antiquity. Though the late sixteenth century indulges at least once in black comedy, most tapestries give the story and its characters dignified presentation. All provide the action with a philosophical dimension, thus demanding thoughtful observation. The storied works require a great deal of intellection, and even the simpler symbolic portrayals of individual characters ask the viewer to link legendary figures with moral and ethical ideas. Because art historians have not fully mastered the iconography of these pictorial cloths, we cannot say with certainty that the designers repeated only the familiar literary version, that they made no innovations. But we can deduce the ultimate source of most of the tapestries: the medieval literary conception of the Trojan War; and we can argue that the woven pictures transmit that conception faithfully. Although the graphic art could not reproduce the entire narrative structure of the literature, it could set forth the characters and episodes, themes and points of view with much of their medieval complexity. In the last analysis, tapestries from the fourteenth to the seventeenth centuries generally re-create selected parts of the grand medieval narrative of Troy's fall, and in their opulence and splendid decorative power they sustain the spirit of Benoît's *Le Roman de Troie*.

II

Having isolated the distinctive characteristics of the monumental tradition as they appear in tapestries—a sense of immensity, grandeur, rich detail, action with a philosophical dimension—we can now locate their analogues in Benoît's *Le Roman de Troie*. By analyzing the narrative structure of the epic romance, we shall discern literary features which large, pictured textiles could and did accommodate easily, features which account for Benoît's version of the Troy fable being the most popular source for storied tapestries about the Trojan War. We shall discover that what the graphic art form achieves by means of large expanses of space, color and symbolic details, and positioning of figures, Benoît accomplishes by prolonging his narrative in time (it occupies over thirty thousand octosyllabic lines), using description, juxtaposing and repeating significant episodes, and placing events in a medieval context.

Benoît fashioned his action with a philosophical dimension from the plots he found in two journalistic forgeries: *De Excidio Troiae Historia* by Dares the Phrygian (composed in the early sixth century A.D.) and *Ephemeris Belli Troiani* by Dictys of Crete (composed in the fourth century A.D.). Inherent in these dynamic and well-made plots was a point of view for the action. Both Dares and Dictys had offered a lucid, uncomplicated chain of events that emphasized cause and effect; both traced circumstantially the destruction of Troy. From beginning to end their plots alternate councils with acts of violence; men gather together for rational discussion of political and military issues, and their deliberations inevitably result in decisions that antagonize their foes and provoke anarchy. As this sequence of events thrusts forward to its foregone conclusion—the obliteration of Troy and the reduction of the Greek forces to a wandering band—its very career acquires significance. The repeated displays of counsel issuing in disaster, of rationalization instigating folly, reveal that men destroy themselves when they act on the belief that their rational faculties curb their impulses and control history.

Like the accounts of Dares and Dictys, Benoît's romance proceeds in a "pattern of descent," [28] from the building of Priam's Troy to the destruction of the city and the dispersal of the Greeks. Similarly, Benoît arranges events in a sequence of causes and effects, of deliberations that almost always result in disorder: plunder, rape, warfare, treachery, and the ruin of a civilization. But *Le Roman de Troie,* unlike its terse predecessors, dwells upon the antecedent councils and their consequent anarchy, and as a result, we shall see, it illuminates itself by providing three points of view for the action rather than one.

Deliberation bulks large in Benoît's work for two reasons. The first and more fundamental grounds itself in sheer number; *Le Roman de Troie* incorporates into its epic text approximately fifty incidents of counsel. Consultation accounts for nearly everything that occurs: the creation of

28. For this phrase and its definition (which links it with sacred myth), see Robert Scholes and Robert Kellogg, *The Nature of Narrative* (New York, 1966), p. 224.

Troy; the rape of Helen; the arrangement of embassies, the procuring of food and other supplies for the Greek army; the tactics by which Trojans and Greeks wage the war; the death of Hector; the sack of Troy. In effect, the participants in this calamity rationalize every stage of its progress in an effort to survive with honor. And by means of this incessant deliberation, they demoralize themselves and promote acts of destruction.

The second reason derives from the manner in which Benoît presents his many incidents of counsel. In contrast to Dares and Dictys, who recorded debates and their issues concisely, Benoît portrays at length and in detail the course of most consultations. A representative and significant deliberation takes place at the beginning of the narrative (ll. 3651–4031):[29] the Trojan council which determines that Paris shall make an expedition to Greece to avenge the wrongs perpetrated by the Greeks against Troy. Although Priam is enraged, like a typical medieval ruler he uses a tone of persuasion (not command) in addressing the nobles assembled.[30] In a speech of almost one hundred lines, he circumstantially assesses the humiliations inflicted by the Greeks upon the Trojans and the Trojan resources for effective reprisal, and he urges the assembly to adopt a resolution of war. Responding to Priam's address, his sons, one by one, offer their opinions. Hector, sensible, estimates the powers of the Greeks and predicts that a war could be disastrous for the Trojans; but Paris, on the basis of his notorious vision, counsels vengeance against the Greeks. Although Deiphobus approves Paris's advice, Helenus warns that if Paris abducts a Greek lady, "Senz mort, senz dolor e senz peine / N'en porra eschaper uns sous, . . ." (ll. 3966–3967). Helenus's words completely silence the assembly until Troilus speaks, mocking the silence, Helenus, and priests. Troilus presses the Trojans to take revenge for the shames the Greeks have caused them, and the entire gathering approves his suggestion: "A cele parole ot grant bruit: / 'Mout a bien dit,' ço dient tuit" (ll. 4019–4020). And thus Priam appoints Paris and Deiphobus to expedite "l'Enlèvement d'Hélène."

29. Benoît de Sainte-Maure, *Le Roman de Troie,* ed. Léopold Constans, Société des Anciens Textes Français, 6 vols. (Paris, 1904–1912). References in my text to Benoît's poem are to the line numbers on the left margin in this edition.

30. M. V. Clarke, *Medieval Representation and Consent* (London, New York, Toronto, 1936), p. 249, mentions tone of address of medieval rulers in council.

This council, "full of tongue and weak of brain," reveals much about Benoît's conception of the Troy story. Like the rest of *Le Roman de Troie,* this episode transfers events, via Dares and Dictys, from antiquity into the ethos of a feudal society. Hence, we witness not a Trojan council but a medieval assembly. Benoît locates the irrationality and impulses that produced the Trojan War in a contemporary political and social context. He makes the remote immediate, the general detailed.

Behind the procedures of Priam's consultation, behind the unanimous agreement with which it concludes and the ultimate disregard of reasonable arguments, lies the medieval doctrine of consent: "what touches all must be approved by all" ("quod omnes tangit ab omnibus approbetur").[31] That doctrine, the legacy of the Roman Empire to medieval Western Europe, determined the conduct of both secular and ecclesiastical parliaments during the Middle Ages. As J. Roland Pennock explains: "The concurrence of all, the unanimity principle, seems universally to have been considered the ideal for positive action . . . Typically, there was no fixed, mechanical formula for determining when a decision could be made, but unanimity was sought even if it could be obtained only by the process of wearing down and shouting down the dissenters . . ."[32] The Middle Ages did not recognize majorities and minorities in its voting procedures: "The majority device receives the interpretation: 'the minority must follow the majority.' That is to say, the minority must withdraw its objection and agree with the majority, in order that a unanimous 'common will' may be settled upon."[33] According to the principle of unanimity, the councils in Benoît's *Le Roman de Troie* conclude with everyone agreeing to undertake a particular course of action and therefore with the unspoken acquiescence of characters who might have voiced dissenting views during the progress of the parliament. In the Trojan consultation cited above, for example, the irrational biases of Priam, Paris, and Troilus override the sensible arguments of Hector and Helenus, and finally the entire assembly shouts its approval of Paris's absurd plan.

31. *Ibid.,* p. 249.

32. J. Roland Pennock, "Majority Rule," in *International Encyclopedia of the Social Sciences,* IX, 536.

33. John Gilbert Heinberg, "Theories of Majority Rule," *American Political Science Review,* XXVI (1932), 454.

The authenticity of Benoît's councils heightens their significance. For the doctrine of consent which they embody served the Middle Ages not only as a practical determinant of decision-making policies, but also as a social ideal:

It served to express the permanent need of ultimate social unity, to give formal acknowledgment to the truths that the whole is greater than its parts and that a house divided against itself cannot stand.

. . . high value has always been set on the idea of an unanimous judgment, as it not only carries with it the compulsion of authority, but is the outward sign of that permanent harmony which ought to be the basis of all united action.[34]

Clearly, the two services of the doctrine closely meshed: the ideal expressed itself through the policies; the procedures attempted to apply the ideal in the workaday world. It follows, then, that the conception of social harmony is intrinsic to the operations of the assemblies in *Le Roman de Troie,* an unspoken and ironic commentary upon their transactions. By making his parliaments contemporary, Benoît persistently draws our attention to the human limitations that prevent the idea of social harmony from realization as a fact and ensure that it remains nothing more than an "outward sign." His Trojans and Greeks agree unanimously upon every decision that they make; yet their decisions arise not out of a united, reasoned effort to achieve a common goal for the good of all, but out of the disparate, selfish, shortsighted exertions of individual men striving for individual ends. Only in their organization and ultimate concord do Benoît's assemblies recall the ideal that governed the functions of medieval councils. The formal debates that produce decisions prove to be rhetorical exercises in rationalizing the destructive appetites of irresponsible men. Persuasive arguments rely not upon logic but upon the zeal and determination of the speaker. Inevitably, the vigor of a Troilus or a Paris triumphs over the judiciousness of a Hector or a Helenus.

Benoît and many of his followers frequently attribute the tragic falling out of events in the Troy story to Fortune. When councils heedlessly mock sensible advice and prudent warnings, the medieval writers conclude, like Benoît, that hostile powers undermine human efforts to behave circumspectively: "Mais Fortune nel voleit mie, / Que trop lor esteit

34. Clarke, pp. 343 and 336.

enemie" (ll. 4165–4166). However, the notion of Fortune does not explain events in these stories; it simply describes them in a figurative way. The storytellers invoke Fortune after they have demonstrated hubris,[35] and the reader comes away from their narratives not shaking his puzzled head over the vagaries of Fortune, but nodding his sober recognition of myopic ego's fond pageant.

Benoît's presentation of councils in *Le Roman de Troie* typifies his narrative technique, a technique that characterizes the best-known derivatives of his poem and distinguishes the later medieval versions of the Troy story from the accounts of Dares and Dictys. Benoît did not, of course, originate his approach to classical material; medieval artists generally relocated tales from antiquity in the Middle Ages. His contribution to the Troy legend resulted from the literary sleight by which he made an orthodox and somewhat unsophisticated narrative method yield thought-provoking commentary on the events he recounted. In the narratives of Dares and Dictys, the emergent pattern of occurrences had served almost alone as gloss upon individual episodes. In Benoît's *Le Roman de Troie,* the pattern and its service remain, but in addition the medieval political and social context acts as interpreter, and the reader gains immediate access to the implications of particular incidents. Benoît and his followers demand more intellection of their audiences than Dares and Dictys did. By viewing the Trojan War as a contemporary event, they add a philosophical dimension to the story which insistently challenges the reader's judgment.

Like the councils, the anarchy that they generate weighs substantially in *Le Roman de Troie*. The poem gives a detailed account of internecine encounters peripheral to the war proper: the rape of Helen with its attendant violence; the Greek capture and sack of Tenedos; Achilles and Telephus's attack on Mysia to acquire supplies for the Greek army; the razing of Troy. And to the twenty-three battles that comprise the Trojan War itself, the poet devotes thousands of lines and a wealth of circumstance.

Benoît has transferred the battles, with the rest of his tale, into the Middle Ages. His descriptions of warfare borrow from two closely related medieval traditions: military practice and narrative custom. In the

---

35. Cf. Charles Moorman, "Malory's Tragic Knights," *MS*, XXVII (1965), 123.

first place, battles in *Le Roman de Troie* bear comparison with feudal warfare. Greeks and Trojans, transformed into *les chevaliers,* fight with the arms and accouterments of medieval knights. In the manner of their prototypes, they engage in conflict without the benefit of strategy or tactics, legal or logistic formulas. C. W. C. Oman's sketch of typical feudal warriors applies as well to Benoît's fighting heroes: "When the enemy came into sight, nothing could restrain the western knights; . . . the mailclad line thundered on, regardless of what might be before it." [36] Since military strategy had yet to appear in medieval Europe, warfare remained a primitive art and consisted primarily of frontal attacks that failed to exploit the advantages of mobility and speed.[37] Authentically, the battles in *Le Roman de Troie* begin with frontal attacks. The battalions having been organized by one prominent knight or another, either the Greeks fall on the Trojans or the Trojans fall on the Greeks. In fact and in the poem, frantic melees that last for hours or days follow the initial assault, melees in which striking feats of arms win more acclaim than any hints of strategic acumen.

Oman limns a tragicomic cartoon of medieval warfare: "An engagement . . . was [often] nothing more than a huge scuffle and scramble of horses and men over a convenient heath or hillside." [38] A sense of this confusion pervades Benoît's *Le Roman de Troie:* individual heroes bustle to recover their horses while surrounded by foes; a charge against the enemy dazes and fragmentizes them; the battlefield, mobbed with knights, presents a spectacle of fierce and bloody disorder. But Benoît does not allow chaos to run unchecked. For control he employs the literary device of "themes," devices that Albert C. Baugh defines as "recurring features of . . . description or narrative which are treated according to an established pattern . . ." (for instance, the arming of a knight).[39] Themes characteristic of oral composition appeared also in medieval romances, and the most extended theme described a fight, an encounter

36. C. W. C. Oman, *The Art of War in the Middle Ages:* A.D. *378–1515,* rev. and ed. John H. Beeler (Ithaca, N.Y., 1953), p. 59.

37. *The Ancient Art of Warfare,* produced under the direction of Jacques Boudet (London, 1966), I, 328.

38. Oman, pp. 60–61, describes the "fearful melees" of medieval warfare.

39. Baugh's detailed discussion of "themes" appears in "Improvisation in the Middle English Romance," *PAPS,* CIII (1959), 425–427.

between two knights or a battle that comprised a series of such encounters. Baugh has studied the fight theme and collected forty-nine
elements which recur often enough to indicate that they belonged to a
general narrative stock. Several of the motifs that he lists occur repeatedly
in Benoît's descriptions of battles: for example, no. 18, "He unhorses his
opponent"; no. 25, "He cleaves opponent to the saddle, chin, etc."; no. 26,
"He cuts the body, etc. in two." Unlike the Homeric formulas for these
occasions, which allow warriors to engage each other in wide-ranging,
provocative, and moving conversation, the medieval variety depends on
third-person pronouns and reduces in large measure the emotional impact
of confrontations. In *Le Roman de Troie,* therefore, the total chaos of
medieval warfare again and again subsides, leaving in the forefront of the
narrative an encounter between two heroes which takes place in an orderly, formulaic manner. Some of the formulas enhance the stature of
individual knights to colossal proportions: Benoît often applies no. 44,
"The hero slays many," and no. 43, "None could stand against him
(them)," to figures like Hector and Troilus; frequently thousands of
knights surround the famous warriors (using nos. 39 and 44, Benoît
largely exaggerates the sizes of the two hosts; he seems unrestrained by
any sense of historical accuracy); the heroes carve paths for themselves
out of their dilemmas by killing incredible numbers of foes (nos. 43, 44,
and 46 help the poet to make this point).

   In his delineation of the Trojan War, therefore, Benoît regularly dis-
engages scenes of individual and often heroic combat from the drama of
general melee; he brings less chaos out of more chaos in a process that
gives his narrative a definite rhythm. This cadence contributes to the total
rhythm of the battle segment of the work, which continually alternates
periods of combat with periods of truce. During the truces, the violent
busyness of war abates, and the opposing forces decorously indulge their
grief and vanity. Both sides bury their dead, devoting themselves to
lamentation which punctuates the action with reminders of the tremendous losses that gradually and irrevocably deplete the Greek and
Trojan nations. Courtly love affairs bloom and soon canker, rotting into
deceit and death. Faithful, Briseïda parts from her lover Troilus during
the second truce, but she betrays him for Diomedes during the third and
eighth pauses in the war. Achilles grows infatuated with Polyxena, with-
draws from the siege (sixth truce), and for love of her, walks into a

deathtrap set by Hecuba and Paris (ninth truce).[40] Chivalric and wordy, these romantic tales ensconced in the truces suggest that courtly love, like courtly councils, simply glosses passion with rhetoric. Finally, while arms are suspended, military councils take place which ensure the prolongation of the war.

By turning the Trojan War into an extended medieval siege with accompanying truces, and by using artfully the literary device of the fight theme, Benoît characteristically interprets events as he relates them. The tableau of the war in all of its horrific confusion repeatedly becomes the backdrop for scenes of individual heroism. In these scenes, true chivalry —at least, courage and nobility—finds its only domicile in *Le Roman de Troie*. And that domicile, the brief and fleeting scenes, proves fragile. As the battles continue, the encompassing chaos relentlessly swallows up moments of personal bravery; lamentation swells again and again over the deaths of great warriors; passion, incessant, warps mind and spirit. In this progress of events, the forces of confusion and waste manifest themselves almighty, constantly undermining our passing impressions of heroism. The scenes of glory that we have witnessed serve in the end to help us realize the magnitude of the triumphant forces and of the tribute they demand.

Thus Benoît's arrangement of events illuminates itself in three different yet complementary ways. The poem proceeds through a sequence of causes and effects, antecedent councils and their consequent anarchy, and this sequence performs the same function in *Le Roman de Troie* as it had in the narratives of Dares and Dictys. In addition, Benoît's use of medieval contexts provides a running commentary upon events. Finally, the Trojan War segment demonstrates purposeful, rhythmic repetition in the presentation of encounters and truces. Moreover, that enormous episode reiterates not only its own incidents and ideas, but also material from the assemblies that preceded the war proper. We can justifiably define the action that includes the twenty-three engagements of the war as the most devastating effect of the ratiocinative procedures incapsulated in the early parliaments. Benoît has so organized and portrayed the

40. For an extensive discussion of the love stories in *Le Roman de Troie*, see R. M. Lumiansky, "Structural Unity in Benoit's *Roman de Troie*," *Romania*, LXXIX (1958), 410–424.

engagements that, when he focuses upon this tragic result, his readers never forget its causes. The impulses disguised by rhetoric in the councils —greed, lust, aggression—surface in the bloody commotion of war, an image that assaults all the senses as it externalizes the tumult of passion. They surface also in the romantic scenes. For the folly of Achilles and the shortsightedness of Troilus recall in general the conditions that prevailed in the assemblies and in particular the ardor of Paris, furbished with rhetoric, which persuaded the Trojans to ravish Helen. In the wartime councils, the echoes of earlier parliaments ring obvious. The effect of this kind of repetition, Benoît's third method for commenting upon his text, has been described by Harold Toliver: ". . . every continuous narrative of any dimension finds ways to circle back upon itself in the rhythms of meditation, description, and narration. In the restatement of motifs it practices something akin to musical structure: it retrieves its own internal past and prepares for themes and images that lie ahead. . . ."[41]

From every point of view, *Le Roman de Troie* reveals that hubris, a mortal constant, erodes rare men and eminent civilizations. An exhibitor of folly, it adopts both the plot and the implications of its sources. Yet Benoît wears his rue with a difference. Whereas Dares and Dictys spent their narratives relating the process of destruction, Benoît emphasizes not only the process but also the grandeur of the culture destroyed. The poet creates no human monuments to the splendor of antiquity; he depicts his heroes and heroines cursorily with brief portraits, a few epithets, and gestures noble and ignoble.[42] Instead, he epitomizes the accomplishments of the ancients in his descriptions of marvelous things.

These descriptions, which occupy much of Benoît's attention, characterize the French *roman* of the twelfth and thirteenth centuries.[43] Ed-

41. Harold Toliver, *Animate Illusions: Explorations of Narrative Structure* (Lincoln, Nebr., 1974), p. 169.

42. Samples of the portraits in *Le Roman de Troie* appear in ll. 2927–2962 and ll. 5093–5582. Among the personages of the poem, Briseïda, an exception, is characterized in some detail (see her monologue, ll. 20237–20340).

43. G. D. West, "The Description of Towns in Old French Verse Romances," *FS*, XI (1957), 50–59, supports the scholarly hypothesis that there might have been a doctrine for the use of description available to writers of early French verse romances.

mond Faral explains their usage. "Cette description porte sur des objets très divers, des êtres et des choses: . . . Elle est destinée à exciter l'admira tion; elle prétend enchanter l'imagination du lecteur; . . . le merveilleux est installé au milieu de leurs descriptions."[44] More specifically, Hugo Buchthal elucidates the descriptions in *Le Roman de Troie*: "They reflect the idea that antiquity was a period of prodigious science and culture, which employed the finest and most precious materials, and knew and appreciated the secret qualities and magical virtues of things."[45]

When his account of Priam's Troy opens, Benoît pays tribute to the ancient city with an extensive and detailed recital of its architecture, decorations, and pastimes (ll. 2993–3192). His resplendent descriptions of things—from walls and towers to painted windows to games of chess— crystallize in visual images his conception of a peerless culture: "C'onques en terre n'ot cité / Que la resemblast de beauté / Ne de grandor ne de largece / Ne de plenté ne de richece" (ll. 2995–2998). Although Benoît did not invent his description—graphic representations of towns enjoyed popularity in French romances from ca. 1150–1300[46]—he makes ingenious use of it. He introduces his tragedy with a magnificent portrayal of that which rash pride will immediately jeopardize and finally destroy, a city that symbolizes in his brilliant depiction the summit of man's creative achievement.

As *Le Roman de Troie* advances, descriptions frequently halt the ac- tion: accounts of remarkable tombs, a sumptuous *Chambre de beautés, les automates* (that is, mechanical devices in the shapes of plants, animals, and people, which create the illusion of being real), *objets d'art,* unusual clothing, and precious stones.[47] These images call to mind the initial pic- ture of Troy and its symbolic meaning. While he narrates the deteriora- tion and fall of Troy, therefore, Benoît continues to accent emblematically the imaginative genius of both Trojans and Greeks. By means of this

44. Edmond Faral, "Le Merveilleux et ses sources dans les descriptions des romans français du XIIᵉ siècle," in his *Recherches sur les sources latines des contes et romans courtois du moyen âge* (Paris, 1913), pp. 307–308.

45. Hugo Buchthal, *Historia Troiana: Studies in the History of Mediaeval Secu- lar Illustration,* Studies of the Warburg Institute (London, 1971), p. 4.

46. See West, "Description of Towns."

47. See Faral's essay, pp. 305–388, for a helpful, detailed catalogue of these descriptions.

counterpoint, he stresses the calamitous waste that results when the lower
faculties of mind prevail over the higher.

The monumental literary conception of the Trojan War which Benoît
created in his immense, complex, and richly descriptive poem was still
vital when Shakespeare wrote *Troilus and Cressida*. It thrived not only
in tapestries but also in literary works descended from Guido de Columnis's *Historia Destructionis Troiae* (1287), a Latin recasting of *Le Roman
de Troie* into prose.[48] To illustrate this general statement, let us consider
for a moment two variations of the tale especially pertinent to this study:
John Lydgate's *Troy Book* (composed between 1412 and 1420) and William Caxton's translation of Raoul Lefevre's version into *The Recuyell of
the Historyes of Troye* (printed ca. 1474). Both of these English books
circulated widely not only during the late Middle Ages but also during
the sixteenth century: Lydgate's poem made its journey in a large number
of manuscripts and a few prints; Caxton's prose version traveled in several printed editions.[49] The two works share the same narrative structure,
and as they circulated, they popularized a single formulation of the Troy
legend. (According to Douglas Bush, Caxton's work probably exerted
the greater influence: "Far more than any other book the *Recuyell* established the Elizabethan conception of the Trojan story.")[50] That formulation, faithful to Guido's, retains the narrative pattern introduced by
Benoît. In addition, like Guido, Lydgate and Caxton preserve in their
narratives the descriptions created by Benoît which emphasize the devastation resulting from arrogance and passion. Lydgate in particular lav-
ishes details on the descriptions of things; his portrayal of Priam's Troy
at the beginning of his poem (Book II, ll. 479–1066) rivals Benoît's in its
appreciation of the city: "So fresche, so riche, and so delitable, / Þat it

48. The English Renaissance reprinted and read not only Lydgate and Caxton,
but also their sources and analogues: Dares, Dictys, "Pindarus Thebanus," Guido,
and Joseph of Exeter (Bush, p. 29).

49. For a detailed account of the Lydgate manuscripts and prints, see Henry
Bergen, ed., *Lydgate's Troy Book,* EETS-ES, no. 126 (London, 1935 [for 1920]),
pt. 4, pp. 1–84. H. Oskar Sommer describes the Caxton prints in his edition of
Caxton's *The Recuyell of the Historyes of Troy* (London, 1894), I, lxxxii–cvii.

For quotation from Lydgate, I refer in my text to Bergen's edition (EETS-ES,
no. 97 [London, 1906], pts. 1–3).

50. Bush, p. 31.

alone was incomperable / Of alle cites þat any mortal man / Sawe euer ȝit, sithc þc world bcgan" (ll. 585–588).

Through these two medieval works, Benoît's concept of the Troy fable as a whole persisted constant; that is, during the English Renaissance, Lydgate's *Troy Book* and Caxton's *Recuyell* stood firm as sequential, cause-and-effect, all-inclusive compilations of the events that led to the fall of Priam's Troy. Throughout the epoch, these accounts remained, intact and authoritative, the background against which all new versions of the tale could be viewed and understood. Because the compilations served this purpose, English writers could expect their audiences to fill in narrative lacunae by reference to the medieval story and to respond with surprise and even reflection to any fundamental change in the format of the tale.

III

Shakespeare's *Troilus and Cressida* must have confronted its Elizabethan audience like a cranky genius: neurotic, brilliant, and offensive. That it deflated the grand medieval conception of the Trojan War would not in itself have seemed eccentric. By the turn of the century, writers like Peele and Greene had already reduced somewhat the magnificent old fable. But their reductions appear less deliberate attempts to undermine tradition than the inevitable results of recasting parts of the full-scale medieval account into shorter recitals: dramas, poems, romances, ballads, discourses. Shakespeare, however, undermines the monumental tradition deliberately and with a vengeance. And if moderate deflation of the legend had become a familiar literary phenomenon, wholesale debunking was something new.

With originality, vigor, and apparent glee, Shakespeare minimizes and otherwise skews those features that comprise the stately Troy narrative of the Middle Ages: immensity, opulence, and action with a philosophical dimension. As we have seen, the world of the ancients appeared vast and splendid in both tapestries and the grand medieval romances. The heroes and heroines of legend impressively occupied large expanses of space in the wall hangings and line after imposing line in the enormous literary recitals. The Middle Ages emphasized that this world abounded in nonpareils: Ulysses the wiliest; Achilles the strongest; Helen the most beautiful; Nestor the oldest; Hector the most chivalrous; Antenor the most treacherous. Through lustrous details in costume and scenery, tapestry insisted that antiquity produced in rich abundance extraordinary people and things, and literature made the same statement by means of description and, to a lesser extent, brief verbal portraits and distinctive epithets. In their versions of the Trojan War, the Middle Ages presented huge tableaux filled with personages of great stature.

Shakespeare contracts monumental tableaux into an unattractive miniature. In a less than subtle manner noticed often by critics, he transforms heroes and heroines to fools and whores: "Here is such patchery, such juggling and such knavery!" (II.iii.70-71).[51] In a manner so subtle that scholars neglect it and audiences realize only its effect, he diminishes the uniqueness of each character. To make legendary figures seem interchangeable, commonplace, and therefore few, he relies primarily upon the simple device of comparison. Throughout the play, characters appraise one another's merits or demerits in relative terms: for example, Cressida is set against Helen (I.i.43-45, 76-78); Troilus against Hector (I.ii.55-91, 116-118); Troilus against Paris (I.ii.99-111, 239-240); Greek ladies against Trojan ladies (I.iii.273-301); Helen against Hesione (II.ii.77-80); Menelaus against Paris (IV.i.53-68). From these comparisons, few differences emerge, and often the balancing procedure makes a pair of characters appear ridiculous, corrupt, or stupid in proportions remarkably equal:

PARIS

And tell me, noble Diomed, faith, tell me true, . . .
Who, in your thoughts, merits fair Helen most,
Myself or Menelaus?

DIOMEDES

Both alike: . . .
He, like a puling cuckold, would drink up
The lees and dregs of a flat taméd piece;
You, like a lecher, out of whorish loins
Are pleased to breed out your inheritors.

51. For analysis of Shakespeare's *Troilus and Cressida,* I refer in my text to Walker's edition.

Both merits poised, each weighs nor less nor more;
But he as he, the heavier for a whore.

(IV.i.53–68)

In addition to making direct comparisons among themselves, characters draw other kinds of connections which efficiently reduce two figures to a single absurdity. So Agamemnon expects that Ulysses' speech will offer more "music, wit and oracle" than Thersites' (I.iii.70–74), and Ajax mistakes Thersites for Agamemnon (III.iii.259–262). Thersites in particular huddles together pairs of heroes: for instance, Achilles and Patroclus ("With too much blood and too little brain, these two may run mad;" [V.i.47–48]); Achilles and Ajax ("They set me up in policy that mongrel cur, Ajax, against that dog of as bad a kind, Achilles"; [V.iv,11–13]); Troilus and Diomedes ("What's become of the wenching rogues?" [V.iv.31–32]). In something of an understatement, he summarizes at one point: "Agamemnon is a fool; Achilles is a fool; Thersites is a fool, and, as aforesaid, Patroclus is a fool" (II.iii.58–59). No character lays absolute claim to any trait outstandingly admirable—or ludicrous:

PANDARUS

. . . At whose request do these men play?

SERVANT

. . . at the request of Paris my lord, who is there in person; with him, the mortal Venus, the heart-blood of beauty, love's indivisible soul.

PANDARUS

Who, my cousin Cressida?

SERVANT

No, sir, Helen. Could you not find out that by her attributes?

(III.i.29–37)

In effect, Shakespeare transforms a panorama of heroic Greeks and Trojans to a narrow scene of redundant character types. By having these dramatic figures mimic one another—as Patroclus does Agamemnon and Nestor, and Ajax does Achilles (see I.iii.146–196)—he intensifies the audience's sense of repetition and folly. Occasionally, he limns group portraits (or cartoons) which blend several legendary characters into one silly entity: thus Priam's family dissolves in mirth over a banal joke

(I.ii.143–170), and the Greek leaders vie for a kiss from the bawdy Cressida (IV.v.17–52).

With a variety of devices, then, Shakespeare rolls triteness in a ball and tears it through the iron gates of tradition. The world of *Troilus and Cressida* admits neither extraordinary people nor fabulous creatures and things. The details and descriptions that played so significant a role in the medieval accounts of Troy virtually disappear in the play. In a fleeting reference, Shakespeare disposes of the centaur: ". . . the dreadful sagittary / Appals our numbers;" (V.v.14–15). Sumptuous armor adorns only one knight, the anonymous Greek pursued by Hector at the action's close; and it not only conceals a "Most putrefièd core" but also costs both warriors their lives. As for "Troye la grant," only its walls, towers, and gates survive in a few matter-of-fact allusions (for example, Prologue, ll. 15–17; I.i.2; I.iii.12, 278; II.ii.47; II.iii.8–9) and a prediction by Cressida which reduces the ancient city to stones decomposing (III.ii.185).

Thus Shakespeare minimizes two distinctive features of the monumental tradition; he contracts immensity to a span and turns all-embracing opulence into an occasional symbol of mutability and decay. In his treatment of the third characteristic—action that reflects upon itself philosophically—he rearranges material from Caxton's version[52] of the grand literary compilation to change radically the points of view from which the narrative illuminates itself. When tapestries and short literary narratives epitomized the full-scale medieval recital, they preserved the essential qualities of its action: clearness, and irony tempered by pathos and admiration. But Shakespeare's plot design, like the Mannerist composition of the Brussels tapestry described above (p. 62), effects the treatment of familiar themes "from unexpected points of view and eccentric angles."[53] His reworking of the tale also directs our attention to the horse's crupper, the absurdity inherent in disaster. Shakespeare sum-

52. Although scholars continue to debate the play's immediate sources, on the whole they concur that Shakespeare relied mainly on Caxton. Presson offers the only important dissenting view: that Shakespeare was influenced to a large extent by Chapman's Homer. His painstaking arguments have not convinced other scholars.

53. Quoted from Frederick B. Artz, *From the Renaissance to Romanticism: Trends in Style in Art, Literature, and Music, 1300–1830* (Chicago and London, 1962), p. 117.

marizes the entire medieval account dramatically,[54] a feat that Thomas Heywood would attempt approximately ten years later. Heywood's chronological arrangement of episodes would result in a conventional and pedestrian recounting of the matter of Troy; Shakespeare's unchronological organization, forcing us to find directions by indirections, places the old story in a new light.

Troilus and Cressida disorients its audience from the start. With allusions to the medieval concept of the war's origins—the assembly of sixty-nine Greek princes at Athens, the Greek attack on Tenedos—the Prologue makes us ready for a customary account of the destruction of Troy: a series of well-known events causally related. The tone of the Prologue, of course, immediately implies that the play will deviate from the popular legend in spirit, and after twenty-six lines it becomes clear that the play will depart from the norm not only in tone but also in narrative format. It will bound over ". . . the vaunt and firstlings of those broils," (l. 27), the initial councils, embassies, and battles, "Beginning in the middle;" (l. 28). Because of the references to Caxton in the first score of lines, we expect to land in the midst of the war proper: a battle, an encounter between two heroes, a council of war. But the play leaps into a love episode.

In the traditional story, as we have seen, affairs of the heart flourished and withered during truces. When the battles paused, passion articulated itself in courtly gestures and rhetoric; and the romantic subplots underscored an idea central to the primary war plot, that men demoralize themselves in the process of formally rationalizing their impulses. Shakespeare stresses the same idea, but he does not set it forth with such neatness and decorum. His drama does not begin during a truce; Troilus's ardor chafes him as battle is being waged outside the walls of Troy. Moreover, this scene dispenses with chivalrous demonstrations of undying love. Troilus's exchange with Pandarus, which belabors among other things a baking image charged with sexual innuendoes (ll. 13–28),[55] makes it plain that love wounds the young knight with a sensual sting.

Thus we unexpectedly meet Troilus, itchy with desire, as the action of

54. The play frequently recalls past events and predicts the future of the war: for recollections of the war's inception, see, for instance, the Prologue and Paris's speeches in II.ii.; for predictions, Cassandra's passages in II.ii. and V.iii.

55. For analysis of the scene's use of culinary terms, see Beryl Rowland, "A Cake-Making Image in *Troilus and Cressida*," *SQ*, XXI (1970), 191–194.

Troilus and Cressida begins. Through his portrayal, the opening scene sketches the play's central theme in a manner that characterizes the plot as a whole. Standing at the pivot of Act I, scene i, Troilus embodies what Robert Burton calls "concupiscible and irascible appetites," the "manifold desires" which, immoderate, allow a man no rest.[56] Trapped by his armor and by the battle surging around him which his armor represents, Troilus expresses the disquiet, the egotism, the impulsiveness which perpetuates the violence that presently baffles him. Medieval writers had juxtaposed chivalric warfare and courtly love in parallel lines, as two distinct, pernicious products of concupiscence. But Shakespeare draws a circle with excessive appetite as the center, armed conflict as the circumference, and romantic love as an inner circle concentric with war. In his play, battles —like love—become an extension of the ticklings of flesh and spirit; they designate the outermost limit of incontinence. Like most boundaries, they sometimes prove a source of frustration, but generally they offer the ultimate means for fulfilling unreasonable cravings. Not surprisingly, three alarms and a brief conversation with Aeneas persuade Troilus to enter the fray that he had earlier avoided. His skittish temperament uncurbed, Troilus cavorts from fantasies of sex to the fields of war (ll. 115–117). In his responses, the first scene traces a path between center and circumference, between appetite and its manifestation in sexual scheming and bloody violence.

This pattern, the tracking in radius vectors of appetite's various semblances, repeats itself in every scene of the play. According to Burton's categories of appetites, Shakespeare uses as points of departure three "of the chief, and most noxious in their kind": "that exorbitant appetite and desire of honour, which we commonly call ambition"; "self-love, pride, and inordinate desire of vain glory or applause"; and love of the opposite sex (p. 280). He stresses their manifestation not only in affairs of war and love, but also in councils. Instead of the medieval narrative format, the linear sequence that trimly alternated assemblies, engagements, and truces, Shakespeare's arrangement conflates battles, peace, and consultation in an action that perpetually shifts its focus between appetite and romantic entanglements, formal arguments, or military operations. Al-

56. Robert Burton, *The Anatomy of Melancholy,* introd. Holbrook Jackson (London and New York, 1932), I, 280. Other references to Burton in my text will be to this edition.

though Aeneas refers in Act I, scene iii, to ". . . this dull and long-continued truce" (l. 262), in fact the war pauses for only one day in *Troilus and Cressida* (during Act IV), and throughout that day, Greeks and Trojans anticipate a battle to begin early the next morning. Hence, councils and love affairs take place simultaneously with armed conflict, all three belonging to the same orb of folly. Having meshed events traditionally successive, Shakespeare explores the connections among them. Again and again he follows the course that links indulgence to war, war to indulgence.

Vacillation between notions of physical violence and physical pleasure marks the scenes in *Troilus and Cressida* that treat the three love affairs of the medieval story (see Act I, scene ii, for the first representative instance). In the works of Benoît and his followers, these romances served as decorous interludes between the frantic acts of war. Shakespeare strips them of propriety, and they appear brazen in the substance of his plot. Like Troilus, Paris and Achilles entertain whims both sexual and military; they dart from bed to battlefield in their minds and in fact. Paris, satiating himself with Helen in Act III, scene i, remembers that he ". . . would fain have armed today" (ll. 137–138) and prepares eagerly to greet the Trojan heroes coming back from their bloody toil (ll. 149–155). Achilles' dreams of glory conflict with his love of Polyxena. Of the three beloved ladies, Polyxena alone does not appear in the drama. She nevertheless plays a role similar to that of the cloying Helen and the shrewd Cressida. Sometimes in a literal and always in a figurative way, these women disarm the Greek and Trojan heroes, exposing the lust common to deeds of love and valor.[57]

Shakespeare's scenes of council in *Troilus and Cressida*—ludicrous displays of self-indulgence—also measure the route from concupiscence to war.[58] Epitomizing the ubiquitous consultations of the medieval

57. David J. Houser discusses "Armor and Motive in *Troilus and Cressida*," *RenD*, N.S. IV (1971), pp. 121–134.

58. These councils have been often analyzed. Particularly helpful readings appear in: F. Quinland Daniels, "Order and Confusion in *Troilus and Cressida* I.iii," *SQ*, XII (1961), 285–291; E. M. W. Tillyard, *Shakespeare's Problem Plays* (London, 1950), pp. 54–70; D. A. Traversi, " 'Troilus and Cressida,' " *Scrutiny*, VII (1938), 311–317; Gladys D. Willcock, "Shakespeare and Rhetoric," *E&S*, XXIX (1943), 57–59.

accounts, Act I, scene iii, and Act II, scene ii, condense innumerable incidents of irrational behavior into two councils. Rather than a sequence of events, these assemblies constitute a block of action toward the beginning of the drama, a lengthy static period occupied with formal arguments that illustrate derisively every kind of self-delusion and *amour-propre*. Hence the Greek council, much of it invented by Shakespeare, commences with a ceremonious and finally hollow discussion of a theme recurrent in the play: the values that survive the stresses of time and circumstance; and it ends by promoting one "of the chief, and most noxious" kinds of desires, the excessive pride that stimulates violence and disorder. Whereas the Greeks in consultation subject one another to persuasive monologues, the Trojans engage in debate. Based on the Trojan council summarized above (pp. 65–66), the burlesque version in Act II, scene ii, proceeds with far less decorum. Here Priam's sons do not speak in chronological order; and they insult one another openly. Further, the medieval doctrine of consent does not dignify Hector's reversal at the conclusion of the argument. Under no social or political compulsion to submit, Hector joins the ranks of the capricious. If he throws bad rationalizations after good, his brothers Troilus and Paris produce only nonsense. In this scene, Shakespeare makes explicit what the medieval narrators had implied: that facile ratiocinations are the trappings of restless passion. Addressing Troilus, Hector asks: ". . . is your blood / So madly hot that no discourse of reason, / Nor fear of bad success in a bad cause, / Can qualify the same?" (ll. 115–118). In a later speech, he no longer questions but declares:

> The reasons you allege do more conduce
> To the hot passion of distempered blood
> Than to make up a free determination
> 'Twixt right and wrong: for pleasure and revenge
> Have ears more deaf than adders to the voice
> Of any true decision . . .
>
> (ll. 168–173)

Although Priam (ll. 142–145) and Helenus (ll. 33–36) corroborate Hector's view, this council ends as the Greek one had, encouraging appetite to indulge itself in warfare.

The exhibit of man thinking at the start of the play lacks the poignant irony of the medieval assemblies. Uninformed by the doctrine of consent, an anachronism by the late sixteenth century, the councils in *Troilus and Cressida* aspire in no way to an ideal of social harmony. They simply show the rhetorical means by which men in groups influence one another to find politically acceptable channels for socially destructive impulses. Similarly blunt, the exhibit of man fighting which concludes *Troilus and Cressida* comprises a sequence of individual encounters devoid of valor. Chasing one another over the stage, the heroes of legend hardly beat a trail of glory. We witness instances of pettiness, sexual rivalry, cowardice, and barbarism—conduct that argues more powerfully than any of Thersites' detractions the utter futility of the Trojan War.

In their narratives, the composers of the medieval Troy story had distinguished man thinking from man fighting from man loving. These three conditions, all originating in immoderate desire, nevertheless comported themselves with varying degrees of dignity. Even the love affairs now and then allowed an impressive display of faithfulness. The councils, thrusting toward unanimity, strove blindly for an ideal. On the battlefield, individual knights exercised courage and magnanimity. The source of these conditions in the end undermined their dignity. Whenever thwarted, appetite grew furious, its rage more and more destructive. Gradually it turned council, warfare, and love into treacherous intrigues that razed Troy and slaughtered multitudes of Greek heroes. In effect, the Middle Ages held an ambivalent view of the legend. They articulated both the ignominy inherent in Troy's fall and the idealism intrinsic to antiquity's noble achievements. The lamentations and rich descriptions which punctuated the medieval narratives emphasized that the ancient heroes not only aspired to laudable values but sometimes personified worthiness. From the perspective of the Middle Ages, therefore, the ruin of Troy constituted a disaster of great moment; it qualified to rank as a tragedy.

Despite its old age, the medieval Troy story in Shakespeare's version has not the thinnest patina of tragedy. The action of *Troilus and Cressida* blurs the distinctions among acts of war, consultation, and love. None of the three evinces dignity; all conspicuously display the excessive appetite that is their common source. Melding them together in his plot, Shakespeare stresses their likenesses. His characters turn instantaneously from love to war, from war to love, from council to love and war, because each condition supplies the same immediate though temporary relief of immoderate and "manifold desires." As the characters rush from one distraction to another, the play sprints to and fro between cause and effects, concupiscence and its expression in sexual indulgence, consultation, or warfare. Constantly changing its focus, the skittish narrative signifies and produces confusion. Within it, the dazed heroes aspire to nothing more than quick satisfaction of their impulsive cravings. Only the mad Cassandra grieves for the passing of Troy; otherwise no one mourns for anyone or anything. Neither eulogies nor rich descriptions honor the Greeks and Trojans. Instead, the railing of Thersites, "intellectual power deserted by all grace," brutally mocks the vanity of human wishes. Blotting the extraordinary from his account, Shakespeare harps on the appetites that wring folly and pain from the human heart, and translates idealism into a chimera that inspires empty rhetoric.

But a description of Shakespeare's formulation of the Troy story is not a description of the total effect of his play. Whatever variations he rings on the monumental tradition, the medieval legend—its characters, events, themes, and dignity—remains the grand referent of *Troilus and Cressida*. In the audience's minds, then, the two always stand juxtaposed: the old version, splendid, stately, ordered, and tragic; the new, mundane, undignified, confusing, and burlesque. Shakespeare's fable defies the medieval classifications of episodes and characters, and the medieval idealization of antiquity. In turn, the Troy legend of the Middle Ages in its formal composition and its commemorations of noble thoughts and deeds challenges his cynicism. Together they suggest a vast range of perspectives from which to view human conduct and history. The Middle Ages celebrates the mind's potential occasionally to reach beyond itself toward values worthy of reverence and mourns the loss of a civilization that allowed indulgence to topple its lofty spirit. Shakespeare, anatomizing the psyche, insists that the lowest faculties always subject reason and will. In combination, the two versions measure the breach between the ideals we value and the deeds we accomplish, and in the process they betray nostalgia for the imaginary kingdom where heroic virtues almost flowered.

Richard II *and the Perspectives of History*

ERNEST B. GILMAN

SHAKESPEARE, like his fellow poets of the earlier seventeenth century, associated the word *perspective* not with the painter's *perspectiva artificialis* alone—that is, with the Albertian rules for representing three-dimensional space to which we chiefly connect the word in its literal sense—but also with what I will call the "curious perspective."[1] The Renaissance was fascinated by pictures and devices that created surprising, often paradoxical, effects by manipulating the conventions of linear perspective. The curious perspective is a miscellaneous category including

[1]. I borrow the term from the title of Jean François Niceron's treatise on distorted perspectives, *La Perspective curieuse* (Paris, 1638), and from Hobbes, who reminds D'Avenant of a particularly ingenious "perspective": "I believe (Sir) you have seen a curious kind of perspective, where, he that looks through a short hollow pipe, upon a picture conteining diverse figures, sees none of those that are there painted, but some one person made up of their parts, conveighed to the eye by the artificiall cutting of a glass" (*The Answer of Mr. Hobbs to Sr. William D'Avenant's Preface before Gondibert,* in *Literary Criticism of Seventeenth-Century England,* ed. Edward W. Tayler [New York, 1967], p. 290). For a lavishly illustrated survey of anamorphic art, see Jurgis Baltrušaitis, *Anamorphoses* (Paris, 1969).

distorted, "anamorphic" images, sometimes hidden within regular images, that resolve themselves when seen from unusual points of view or in refracting lenses or mirrors of varying shapes (flat, cylindrical, conical); landscapes which, turned on their side, become faces; reversible portraits (Illustration 2); and, more broadly, the *trompe l'oeil* illusionism of *camerae obscurae,* and the other marvels made possible by the new optics. Thus Cleopatra has a reversible portrait in mind when she says of her two-faced Antony, "Though he be painted one way like a Gorgon, / The other way's a Mars" (II.v.116–117); Orsino thinks of optical trickery when, seeing Viola and Sebastian together at last, he marvels, "One face, one voice, one habit, and two persons! / A natural perspective, that is and is not" (V.i.208–209); and France's bantering with Henry V turns on a joke about hidden landscapes:

KING

. . . and you may, some of you, thank love for my blindness, who cannot see many a fair French city for one fair French maid that stands in my way.

FR. KING

Yes, my lord, you see them perspectively, the cities turned into a maid; for they are all girdled with maiden walls that war hath never ent'red.[2]

(V.ii.311–316)

Our own ability to see *Richard II* "perspectively" may be somewhat clouded unless we look more closely than students have thus far[3] at Shakespeare's most elaborate use of the perspective image, for it proposes in effect that the play itself is to be regarded as a kind of perspective device.

2. All quotations from Shakespeare are taken from *The Complete Works,* ed. Peter Alexander (New York, 1952). For examples of other poets using "perspective" in this sense, see Jonson's *Alchemist,* III.ii.382 ff., and Herbert's "Sinne (II)." See also my "Marvell and Velázquez in Perspective," *JGE,* XXVI, no. 4 (Winter 1975), 269–279.

3. The fullest treatment of "perspectives" in *Richard II* that I have seen is in Claudio Guillén, "On the Concept and Metaphor of Perspective," *Comparatists at Work,* ed. Stephen G. Nichols, Jr. and Richard B. Vowles (New York, 1968), pp. 28–90. Guillén is mainly concerned with the theme of the visualization of grief.

I

At the end of Act II, scene i, we have just seen Richard leave for the Irish wars and Northumberland tell the other disaffected nobles that the exiled Bolingbroke is about to land at Ravenspurgh. In a moment Green will report the chilling news to the queen, but before he rushes in the queen confides in Bushy that she feels the weight of some unknown grief, nameless and yet heavier to bear than the mere sadness of Richard's absence:

> Yet again methinks
> Some unborn sorrow, ripe in fortunes womb,
> Is coming towards me, and my inward soul
> With nothing trembles. At something it grieves
> More than with parting from my lord the King.
>
> (II.ii.9–13)

Bushy's reply ingeniously plays on the scholastic distinction between substance and shadow, something and nothing, to invent a consolation for grief that he—if not the queen with her premonition, or the viewer with his experience of the previous scene—will find convincing:

> Each substance of a grief hath twenty shadows,
> Which shows like grief itself, but is not so;
> For sorrow's eye, glazed with blinding tears,
> Divides one thing entire to many objects,
> Like perspectives which, rightly gaz'd upon,
> Show nothing but confusion—ey'd awry,
> Distinguish form. So your sweet Majesty,
> Looking awry upon your lord's departure,
> Find shapes of grief more than himself to wail;
> Which, looked on as it is, is naught but shadows
> Of what it is not. Then, thrice-gracious Queen,
> More than your lord's departure weep not—more is not seen;
> Or if it be, 'tis with false sorrow's eye,
> Which for things true weeps things imaginary.
>
> (II.ii.14–27)

Bushy would have the queen believe she has "nothing" to fear. In this he is precisely, if ironically, correct. The play will demonstrate that having "nothing" to fear is hardly a consolation. This "heavy nothing," this "nameless woe," will soon become substantial enough when Green arrives:

QUEEN

So, Green, thou art the midwife to my woe,
And Bolingbroke my sorrow's dismal heir.
Now hath my soul brought forth its prodigy;
And I, a gasping new-delivered mother,
Have woe to woe, sorrow to sorrow join'd.

(II.ii.62–66)

For Richard the "shadows" of what is not—the foreshadows of the nothing ahead—are even more ominous. Like Lear (reduced, says the Fool, to "Lear's shadow," "an O without a figure"), Richard will have to endure the loss of his power, his crown, the very name of king, finally his life. "Are you contented to resign the crown?" asks Bolingbroke in the deposition scene (IV.i.200). Richard's "Ay, no; no, ay; for I must nothing be" (l. 201) is the properly ambiguous response of a "great minor poet" always sensitive to a quibble.[4] For if he is "contented"— willing—to resign, he is then certainly not contented in the other sense, substantially the king, full with the royal authority. Bolingbroke is now full, Richard empty, and in an equally empty ceremony the crown changes hands in token of the shifted weight of political power. And in the moments before his murder in the keep of Pomfret Castle, Richard struggles with his contradictory thoughts, none of them "contented":

Sometimes am I king;
Then treasons make me wish myself a beggar,
And so I am. Then crushing penury
Persuades me I was better when a king;
Then am I king'd again; and by and by
Think that I am unking'd by Bolingbroke,
And straight am nothing. But whate'er I be,
Nor I, nor any man that but man is,

4. In Mark Van Doren's phrase, *Shakespeare* (New York, 1953), p. 68. The Pelican editor glosses line 201: " 'yes, no; no, yes,' but also 'I, no; no, I' " (p. 659 n.); the line is also *heard* as, "I know no I." For this and other insights I am indebted to Professor E. W. Tayler.

> With nothing shall be pleas'd till he be eased
> With being nothing.
>
> (V.v.32–41)

These thoughts are "still-breeding" (l. 8), endlessly generating yet still-born, barren, and thus the last paradoxical echo of the queen as a "gasping new-delivered mother" of the "nothing" in fortune's womb.

All this is beyond Bushy's ken, for in Act II, scene ii, the irony of Bolingbroke's return, of the empty shadow becoming the terrifying substance, is directed against his attempt to explain (away) the queen's sorrow. By the time he loses his head and is "grav'd in the hollow ground" (III.ii.140), he will have learned the meaning of a "nothing" grief, but now he is made to speak more than he knows: while he argues that Richard's leaving can be understood unambiguously if one only regards it from the right point of view, his analogy with the curious perspective suggests that there are several possible points of view, and further that it is not as simple as it seems to choose the "right" way of looking.

Bushy maintains that there is only a single "true" grief falsely multiplied into twenty "imaginary" shadows by the tears in sorrow's eye, as if by a multifaceted refracting lens. These deceitful perceptions are "like perspectives," anamorphic pictures, which *"rightly* gaz'd upon, / Show nothing but confusion—ey'd *awry,* Distinguish form" (italics mine).[5] But how are they "like"? which is the deceitful point of view? The conceit in these lines turns on a punning reversal in the usual meanings of the words I have emphasized. "Rightly" here means, "at right angles," "directly," and hence the *wrong* way to look at an anamorphic image; the right way is to look "awry," that is, obliquely. The queen finds too many "shapes of grief . . . to wail" because (in line 21) she looks "awry" upon her lord's departure—but which way is that? If the second "awry" in line 21 carries on the metaphor of lines 18–20 and means "obliquely but technically correct for an anamorphic picture," then Bushy is saying: It is a mistake to look obliquely and thereby to distinguish multiple shapes of grief. Look at it "as it is" (i.e., "rightly"—straight on, and in this case

---

5. II.ii.19 is variously punctuated in different editions of the play—a detail that reflects the difficulty of the conceit. See Matthew Black, ed., *Richard II,* The Variorum Shakespeare, (Philadelphia, 1955), XXVII, 137.

correctly) and you will see that what you fear is just (needless) confusion and (empty) shadows. But if "awry" in line 21 means "wrongly" in the usual sense, then Bushy's advice becomes: You look wrongly to look rightly (i.e., straight on) at your lord's departure and find there delusive shapes of grief. See it instead "as it is" (i.e., obliquely) and realize that the terrifying confusion in the direct point of view is in fact naught but the harmless shadows of one limited grief.

In the best tradition of the Variorum editor and his predecessors, I have attempted to cut a logical path through the forest of puns in Bushy's speech.[6] However, with this prose version to guide us, we run the risk of not seeing the forest for the footnotes: to untangle the knotted complexities of the text is to overlook its effect on the reader or the playgoer. In our actual experience of Bushy's speech the crisscrossing double meanings of "rightly" and "awry" make the passage itself like an anamorphic perspective that conflates two images into one and requires of the witness the kind of mental juggling act Tesauro would have approved as the touchstone of a witty conceit. This is the same experience Stanley Fish describes in his reading of the "shifting relationships" in the final couplet of Herbert's "The Crosse":

Reading these lines is like looking at a gestalt figure in which first one and then another pattern emerge from the same physical (here verbal) components . . . until finally there is only one pattern made up of two declarations which, if they were laid side by side, would be perceived as mutually contradictory, but here, occupying the same linguistic space, they constitute a triumph over discursive language.[7]

I have singled out Bushy's speech because both the notion of a double perspective and the experience of seeing double that Fish describes are central to the play. Shakespeare's use of the painter's "perspective" as a metaphor for the understanding is one of the earliest in English. The word was common in English before the seventeenth century, as Claudio Guillén points out, in a more literal sense that referred first to the rules

6. Black, pp. 137–138, note on l. 22.

7. *Self-consuming Artifacts* (Berkeley, Calif., 1972), p. 188. The lines from Herbert are: "And yet since these thy contradictions / Are properly a crosse felt by thy Sonne, / With but foure words, my words, *Thy will be done*" (Hutchinson ed., p. 165).

and devices of optics and later to the artificial perspective of the artist.[8]
Through the Christian association of optics with magic, pagan sooth-
saying, and the vanity of appearances on the one hand, and the pictorial
illusionism of the artist's perspective on the other, the perspective metaphor was often used to figure a deception of the eye and mind, as in
Drummond of Hawthornden's "All we can set our eyes upon in these
intricate mazes of Life is but Alchimie, vain Perspective, and deceiving
Shadows."[9] In the seventeenth century perspective provides a metaphor
for cognition as well as illusion. It contributes a vocabulary for speaking
of the mind's point of view as an observer of its own contents or the
facts of experience; like the figures in a painting, the objects of knowledge are "seen" at various distances or in different aspects in a conceptual
space, as in Bacon's metaphor: "We have endeavored in these our
partitions [of the *Advancement*] to observe a kind of perspective, that
one part may cast light upon another."[10] Similarly the perspective conceit
in Ben Jonson's sonnet "In Authorem" demonstrates that those who fail
to appreciate Nicholas Breton's verse must be looking at it from the
wrong point of view:

> Looke here on *Bretons* worke, the master print:
>> Where, such perfections to the life doe rise.
> If they seeme wry, to such as looke asquint,
>> The fault's not in the obiect, but their eyes.

8. Guillén, pp. 43–47. See Shakespeare's Sonnet 24: ". . . perspective it is best
painter's art" (l. 4).

9. *Cypress Grove* (1623), cited in Guillén, p. 42. Cf. Bacon: "It hath been an
opinion that the French are wiser than they seem, and the Spaniards seem wiser
than they are. . . . It is a ridiculous thing . . . to see what shifts these formalists
have, and what prospectives to make superficies to seem body that hath depth and
bulk," *Essays* (1625) quoted in Guillén, p. 43.
In Nashe's *The Unfortunate Traveller,* Jack Wilton witnesses Cornelius Agrippa
conjuring in a "perspective glass," a magical device that appears on stage in
Greene's play, *Friar Bacon and Friar Bungay.* On the deceptions of the painter's
perspective illusions, Nicholas Hilliard's formulation is typical: "painting [uses]
perspective . . . by falshood to expresse truth. . . . For perspective, to define it
brefly, is an art . . . for a man to express anything in short'ned lines and shadowes,
to deseave both the vnderstanding and the eye," "Nicholas Hilliard's Treatise
Concerning 'The Arte of Sinning,'" *First Annual Volume of the Walpole Society*
(Oxford, 1912), p. 20.

10. *The Advancement of Learning,* II.viii.1.

> For, as one comming with a laterall viewe,
>   Vnto a cunning piece wrought perspectiue,
> Wants facultie to make a censure true:
>   So with this Authors Readers will it thriue:
> Which being eyed directly, I diuine,
> His proofe their praise, will meete, as in this line.[11]

In the later seventeenth century the perspective metaphor becomes important for Leibniz as a way of imagining the unity of the universe from a divine point of view beyond the multiplicity of our individual perceptions. In the *Monadologie* he compares the universe with a city whose aspect changes with the observer's point of view, "comme multipliée perspectivement," but which is nonetheless the same city.[12] The varieties of individual experience are thus seen as valid, though partial "perspectives" on a perfect whole, and a metaphor based on the anamorphic perspective serves him, in another place, as an assurance of universal harmony:

C'est comme dans les inventions de perspective, òu certain beaux dessins ne paraissent que confusion, jusqu'à ce qu'on rapporte à leur vrai point de vue, ou qu'on les regarde par le moyen d'un certain verre our miroir. . . . Ainsi le déformités apparentes de nos petits mondes se réunissent en beautés dans le grand, et n'ont rien qui s'oppose à l'unité d'un principe universellement parfait.[13]

Shakespeare's metaphor has the same form as Liebniz's but none of the philosopher's rational delight in the certainty of our knowledge or his assurance that the world we seek to understand is perfect and harmonious. In *Richard II* the painter's anamorphic "perspectives" lend the playwright not just a local metaphor but, as I hope to show, a conceptual model for seeing the chronicle of English history. We must see the play, like the queen her "nothing" grief, both "rightly" (awry) and "awry" (rightly)—as a wedged contrariety that contains two opposed points of view, neither offering the consolation of complete certainty, but both nec-

11. Ben Jonson, *Works,* ed. C. H. Herford and Percy and Evelyn Simpson, 11 vols. (Oxford, 1952), VIII, 362. The poem was originally printed before Breton's *Melancholike Humours* (1600).

12. *Monadologie,* No. 57, in P. Janet, ed., *Oeuvres Philosophiques de Leibniz* (Paris, 1900), I, 716, cited in Guillén, p. 53.

13. Cited in Guillén, pp. 55–56.

essary for a fuller, if paradoxical, apprehension of a truth beyond our logical reach. This perspective is akin to the Shakespearean "mode of vision" which Norman Rabkin, borrowing a term from Einsteinian physics, calls "complementarity." The term, coined by Niels Bohr and popularized by Robert Oppenheimer, describes the theoretical necessity to regard light as both wavelike *and* corpuscular according to the experiment one is performing. For Rabkin this is analogous to the literary technique which is certainly not Shakespeare's alone, but his preeminently, of "presenting a pair of opposed ideals . . . or groups of ideals and putting a double valuation on each." [14] But we need not ally Shakespeare with such distinguished if historically remote colleagues from the pure science faculties when the playwright offers us a comparison closer at hand in the curious perspective.

II

Before putting the play in that perspective, we might pause over an example of anamorphic painting, the finest one of the style done in England: Holbein's *The Ambassadors* (Illustration 1). [15]

The figures in Holbein's double portrait are French envoys to the court of Henry VIII, Jean de Dinteville and Georges de Selve. Between them

14. *Shakespeare and the Common Understanding* (New York, 1967), pp. 20 ff.

15. Chambers in 1891 suggested Holbein as a possible source of Shakespeare's lines (Black, p. 137 n.). William Heckscher also mentions Holbein in connection with the metaphor in *Richard II* on pp. 10, 21 of his "Shakespeare in his Relationship to the Visual Arts: A Study in Paradox," *RORD*, xiii–xv (1970–1971), 5–73. An anamorphic portrait of Edward VI (now in the National Gallery) is known to have been displayed in Whitehall in Shakespeare's time. It is possible that *The Ambassadors*, of which the Edward portrait is a kind of technical imitation, also hung there earlier in the sixteenth century. The "ambassador" Dinteville took his portrait back to France; it remained there until 1787, when Lebrun bought it and resold it in England to a dealer. The National Gallery acquired it in 1890.

Henry VIII employed Holbein in the reconstruction of Whitehall, which is known to have housed other works by the artist including the great fresco of Henry with his parents and Jane Seymour that was destroyed in the fire of 1698: see James B. Shaw, "The Perspective Picture: A Freak of German Sixteenth-century Art," *Apollo*, VI (1927), 213. My discussion of Holbein is indebted to Baltrušaitis and to G. H. Villiers, *Hans Holbein: The Ambassadors* (London, n.d.).

Illustration 1. Hans Holbein, *The Ambassadors* (1533). Reproduced by courtesy of the Trustees, The National Gallery, London

they represent the temporal and spiritual arm of the French legation—Dinteville, on the left, is Seigneur de Polisy and Selve the Bishop of Lavour—with the poise, solidity, and magnificence that characterize Henry in Holbein's famous portrait of 1540. Dinteville is the more imposing figure in his black velvet surcoat lined with ermine and set off with rose-red satin sleeves. The gold neck chain carrying the badge of the order of St. Michael and the ornate golden sheath of the dagger in his right hand emphasize the gorgeous variety of color and texture in Dinteville's costume. Although Selve's purple brocaded robe is more subdued and his pose less commanding, he makes almost as forceful an impression: the two share an authoritative but wary look that joins the studied poise of men who know their own importance in the public eye with the shrewd, critical detachment of practiced courtiers in a foreign land.

In Holbein's composition their authority rests symbolically, as their elbows do in fact, on a table displaying the tools of mastery over the liberal arts. The lower shelf contains, on the side near Selve, a lute and open hymnal, and on the other side, the more practical instruments of worldly managements suited to Dinteville—a terrestrial globe showing the papal line of demarcation between Spanish and Portuguese possessions in the New World, a T-square and compasses, and a partially opened book that can be identified as Peter Apian's "Well-grounded Instruction in all Merchant's Arithmetic." The objects on the "higher" shelf, including an astrolabe, a solar clock, and a celestial globe, complete the symbolization of the four arts of the quadrivium by adding astronomy to arithmetic, geometry, and music. Pictorially, the collection stresses the interrelationship of the arts by balancing the lute against the celestial globe, upon which all earthly harmony depends, and the celestial globe against the earthly to point the analogy between the "upper" and "lower" spheres of knowledge represented on the two shelves. There may also be an allusion to the *perspectiva artificialis,* that other liberal art which the Renaissance had added to the inherited list: Holbein's lute is shown in almost the exact position as the lute Dürer had chosen a few years earlier as the subject of his woodcut demonstrating a precise mechanical method of perspective drawing.[16]

16. *Unterweysung der Messung* (1525), reproduced in H. W. Janson, *History of Art* (Englewood Cliffs, N.J., 1967), p. 392.

Such still-life objects are of course common in late Renaissance painting, either as the subjects of smaller works such as inlaid panels or as
significant background for other figures.[17] Here these objects, meticu-
lously detailed, lighted, and foreshortened, are at once emblems of the
worldly knowledge associated with the ambassadors and in themselves
a center of attention nearly as prominent as the main figures. The heavy
table and the men flanking it form a single rectangular grouping welded
by the horizontals of the shelves and the verticals of the figures, fully
defined in surface and volume, convincingly represented to the eye. These
men and the world at their command are, we tell ourselves, palpable,
undeniably, "there."

So far, if we are looking "rightly," we experience the painting as an
affirmation of the solidity and power of human achievement—of the
instruments of policy, measurement, and exploration displayed before us,
of the men who use them, and of the artist's power to image both in his
own medium. Still we must reconcile this view with several small but
disturbing details. The lute has one broken string, which in the iconographical tradition changes it from an emblem of harmony to an emblem
of discord.[18] Richard has the emblematic significance of a broken string
in mind during his prison soliloquoy:

> Music do I hear?
> Ha—ha—keep time! How sour sweet music is
> When time is broke and no proportion kept!
> So is it in the music of men's lives.
> And here have I the daintiness of ear
> To check time broke in a disordered string;
> But, for the concord of my state and time,
> Had not an ear to hear my true time broke.
> I wasted time, and now doth time waste me. . . .
>
> (V.v.41–49)

The open book next to Selve is a Lutheran hymnal whose pages hint at
another harmony beyond the discord of the earthly lute: Luther's German translation of the "Veni Creator Spiritus," "Kom Heiligen Geyst," is

17. See Fabrizio Clerici, "The Grand Illusion: Some Considerations of Perspective, Illusionism, and *Trompe-l'oeil,*" *Art News Annual,* XXIII (1954), 98–180,
esp. pp. 135–141, 152–157.

18. See Alciatus, *Emblemata* (1531).

legible on the left, and on the right is the introduction to his shortened version of the Decalogue, in which Luther urges obedience to the divine law above all. We might also notice a tiny silver crucifix in the upper left corner (almost obscured by the folds of the curtain), an even smaller death's-head device in Dinteville's cap, and this: the decorative pattern of the floor places the scene unmistakably in the sanctuary of West-minster Abbey, though our view of the church is hidden behind the green drapery in the background.

It has been suggested that the discordant string alludes to the failure of the League of Cognac in 1533, which ended seven years of fragile alliance between England and France, or that Selve is shown with a copy of Luther's hymns because the French cleric was dedicated to healing the religious schism, itself the most strident discord of the age. Still there is the suggestion in these nearly submerged details of sacred imagery that the scene before us is somehow discordant and deceptive in its very solidity (the empty lute case can just be seen under the table). These men posed like acolytes on either side of the altar of human competence —in a kind of compositional parody of a religious scene—only conceal a truth that may be found on the altar behind the curtain.

That suggestion becomes part of the viewer's experience of the painting when he regards it "awry," in the perspective required by the anamorphic streak in the foreground. Seen from the right edge of the painting, the streak resolves itself into a skull. This bit of visual trickery, in part a clever signature ("holbein" means "hollow bone"), takes on a special significance in relation to the main theme of the work: it is a *memento mori* and an emblem of *vanitas* posed against a vital image of worldly prowess. Holbein had earlier used the death's-head device in the woodcut *Death's Coat of Arms* (1526), where, placed between two robust figures, it gapes out its somber reminder.[19] *The Ambassadors* achieves the same effect more forcefully by creating the second point of view, for as the skull takes shape the rest of the painting becomes as blurry and indistinct as the streak was before. The "right" view goes "awry" as the wry view turns into a visual demonstration *de incertitudine et vanitate scientiarum et artium atque excellentia verba Dei.*[20] These wittily superimposed images

19. Reproduced in Baltrušaitis, p. 101.
20. From the title of Cornelius Agrippa's *Declamatio* (1530).

join the two sides of Holbein's career. The secular portraitist and official recorder of the glories of the Tudor court controls one perspective, but the other is in the charge of the painter of the Basel altarpieces, the designer of the *Dance of Death* woodcuts, and the illustrator of Luther's Bible and Erasmus's *Praise of Folly.*

As Holbein celebrates and negates the two ambassadors, so the same ambiguity extends to the painting itself, which asserts both the power of perspective to create an illusion of reality and the emptiness, the *vanitas,* of that illusion.[21] That duplicity carries with it a similar process of loss and gain in the role of the viewer. The shifting perspectives undercut *his* authority as the ideal observer, but substitute a different kind of knowledge—an awareness of the reach and limitations of his own perceptions, and a disillusioned understanding that things are and are not what they seem.

III

That *Richard II* is capable of yielding the same understanding is a mark of its greater maturity over the first tetralogy and its kinship with the later tragedies. Compared with the limitations of the *Henry VI* plays —their episodic structure, their one-dimensional characters like Talbot, their vigorous heroics and unclouded patriotism—*Richard II* represents not only a considerable technical advance but a deepened insight into the problems of history and human motivation. Even *Richard III* seems crudely conceived beside it, despite the brilliance of the hunchback king's Machiavellianism, which sustains the play. As Richard III bustles from one hateful villainy to the next, and finally to a bloody dog's death in Bosworth field, the play moves toward its swift and untroubled resolution, reenacting a key chapter in the official Tudor explanation of English history. The Wars of the Roses, according to the chronicler Hall, showed "What mischiefe hath insurged in realmes by intestine devision . . . by domestical discord & unnatural controversy"; but this controversy

21. Agrippa had included perspective as one of the deceptions of the arts and sciences because it deals with false appearances.

by the union of Matrimony celebrate and consummate betwene the high
and mighty Prince King Henry the seventh and the lady Elizabeth his moste
worthy Quene, the one beeying indubitate heire of the hous of Lancastre,
and the other of Yorke was suspended and appalled in the person of their
most noble, puissant and mighty heire King Henry the eight; and by hym
clerely buried and perpetually extinct.[22]

The lesson of Henry's victory was plain: "that all men (more clerer than
the sonne) may apparently perceive, that as by discord greate thyngs
decaie and fall to ruine, so the same by concord be revived and erected."
As the wars had issued from a breach of harmony, the union of Henry
and Elizabeth "erected" fallen England to a state of sacramental in-
tegrity exemplified not only by "man & woman in marriage" but by the
union of the "Godhed to the manhod," for in Christ "manne was joyned
to God whiche before by the temptacion of the subtle serpent was from
hym segregate and divided." The defeat of Richard III, the last and most
vicious fomenter of discord, was nothing short of an act of redemption,
a national resurrection.

So in Shakespeare's play England awakes from Richard's "dead mid-
night" to a new morning under Richmond, whose prayer at the end has
the full moral weight of the play behind it:

> . . . as we have ta'en the sacrament,
> We will unite the white rose and the red.
> Smile heaven upon this fair conjunction,
> That long have frown'd upon their enmity!
> What traitor hears me, and says not amen?
> England hath long been mad and scarr'd herself;
>
> . . . .
>
> All this divided York and Lancaster,
> Divided in their dire division,
> O, now let Richmond and Elizabeth,
> The true succeeders of each royal house,
> By God's fair ordinance conjoin together!
> And let their heirs, God, if thy will be so,
> Enrich the time to come with smooth-fac'd peace,
> With smiling plenty, and fair prosperous days!
>
> (V.v.18–23, 27–34)

22. Edward Hall, *Union of the two Noble and Illustrate Families of Lancastre
& Yorke* (1548), quoted in Geoffrey Bullough, *Narrative and Dramatic Sources
of Shakespeare* (London, 1960), III, 16–17.

Richard II returns to the origins of the division and also records the over-
throw of a king and the installation of a new regime. But where
Richard III has its moral poles clearly marked—on one side Richard,
"determined to be a villain," and on the other the pious Richmond, a
captain of the Lord and a minister of chastisement—*Richard II,* without
abandoning the framework of the Tudor myth, confronts the ambiguities
inherent in the orthodox interpretation of English history.

These ambiguities arise first of all from the chroniclers' attempt to impose a providential design on the historical record. Richard II, though
not malicious of heart, suffered from the "frailties of wanton youth,"
ruled willfully rather than justly, and gave himself overmuch to his
pleasures. To this extent, and because he had been unlawfully used at
Richard's hand, Bolingbroke's revolt could be justified, and Holinshed
could discern the "providence of God" at work in the deposition. Nevertheless, Bolingbroke was the "first author" of discord; as Henry IV he
and his line were "scourged afterwards as a due punishment unto re-
bellious subjects." [23] This paradox was sharpened by the elaboration,
under Elizabeth I, of the doctrine of the king's divinity. In the late
fourteenth century the historical Richard had ruled as *primus inter pares.*
At the deposition, as reported in Holinshed, the Bishop of Carlisle is concerned only with the injustice of passing judgment on a king in his
absence. But Shakespeare's Carlisle, influenced by the concept held by
late Tudor political theology of the king's divine right, argues Richard's
immunity from human judgment: "What subject can give sentence on his
king? / And who sits here that is not Richard's subject?" (IV.i.121–122). [24]

The claims of divine right were elaborated in a series of homilies issued
by the crown from 1547 on. Distributed to every parish in the kingdom,
the homilies taught the duty of passive "obedience to Rulers and Magis-
trates" as the Lord's deputies on earth, and the sinfulness of rebellion
even against an evil king: "Shall the subjects both by their wickedness
provoke God for their deserved punishment, to give them an undiscreet
or evil prince, and also rebel against him, and withal against God, who

23. Hall, quoted in Bullough, p. 68; Raphaell Holinshed, *The Chronicles of
England* (1587), III, quoted in Bullough, pp. 402, 409.
24. Lily Cambell, *Shakespeare's "Histories"* (San Marino, Calif., 1947), p. 206.

for the punishment of their sins did give them such a prince?"[25] This theological doctrine of the king's divinely ordained rule was reflected in English law, as Ernst Kantorowicz has shown, in the concept of the "king's two bodies."[26] Possessed of an immortal "body politic" (in effect the "body" of the state, with its citizenry the "members" and the king its "head") as well as a perishable "body natural," the king combined within himself the divine and the human—in a union analogous to the church's status in canon law as a *corpus mysticum,* and ultimately based on the dual nature of Christ.

The potential paradox of a king who both enjoys the special sanction of divinity and suffers the infirmities of the flesh did not trouble the Tudor jurists. In fact the ambiguity of this legal fiction was an asset in that it permitted the courts to argue with equal validity the divine or the human aspect of kingship according to the case before them. But applied retrospectively to an event like the deposition of Richard II, the doctrine of the king's divinity could only complicate the Tudor myth. If, despite his unfitness for rule, Richard stood above human judgment, then his deposition and murder by a subject could be nothing but the most impious treachery. Indeed, a "deposition" engineered by the sword could only be futile since the crown is an alienable possession that only separates itself from the king's person upon the death of his natural body, whereupon it invests itself in the proper successor. Nor can Richard the man effectively consent in his own deposition, even to preserve the nothing that is left him without the name of king, for the king cannot act against his own interest—"what the king does in his Body politic cannot be invalidated or frustrated by any Disability in his Natural Body." Yet that deposition must have fallen into God's larger plan, and the mantle of divinity must have passed to the usurper—especially if the usurper was to be the paternal ancestor of the Tudor line. From a providential point of view the glorious union of the white and red roses required the deposition of Richard II as prologue, just as Christ's salvation required the Fall of Adam. The Tudor lawyers had emphasized the seamless unity of

25. *Anglican Homily XXIII* (1573), in Bullough, p. 378. See Alfred Hart, *Shakespeare and the Homilies* (Melbourne, 1934).

26. Ernst Kantorowicz, *The King's Two Bodies: A Study in Medieval Political Theology* (Princeton, N.J., 1957).

the king's dual nature, "a Body natural and a Body politic together indivisible . . . incorporated in one Person." [27] But the dramatist's concern lies with testing the fit between the physical and the metaphysical, between human action and providential design, in a case where the king's two bodies are violently separated.

When Richard is dethroned his royal identity is shattered like the mirror in the deposition scene, the glass that reflects, as Kantorowicz says, only the "banal face and insignificant *physis* of a miserable man, a *physis* now devoid of any *metaphysis* whatever." [28] He is left with a self defined only by deprivation and the fear of death; for Richard as for Holbein, the splendor of power dissolves into the imagery of the grave, of the "hollow crown" where death keeps his court. Deprived of the power of action and reduced to Bolingbroke's "Jack of the clock" (V.v.60)—an automaton ticking off another man's hours—Richard falls backs on a desperate theatricality, on acting. Kingship becomes a role for Richard to play as he becomes the mere "shadow" of a substantial king. (In the Renaissance the word *shadow* included "actor" among its many meanings.)

It is the hopeless attempt to reconstruct the shattered fragments of his identity that turns Richard into a witty poet as well. Critics have regarded Richard's strained, punning language as a sign of the play's immaturity. The later Shakespeare, like Berowne in *Love's Labor's Lost,* would forswear "Three-pil'd hyperboles, spruce affectation, / Figures pedantical," the "summer-flies" of a style full of "maggot ostentation" (V.ii.407–409). *Richard II* has been soberly pronounced "a qualified achievement in the consciously artificial manner." [29] But this judgment fails to realize that artifice is Richard's only resource, that his language is excessive and conceited because it must stretch itself around the paradox of a king unkinged. Richard seizes obsessively on the words spoken to him and splits them in two. His language sets "the word itself / Against the word" (V.v.13–14), for only a double language, painfully aware of the opposite meanings lurking in words, is adequate to Richard's own double condition:

27. Edmund Plowden's *Reports,* in Kantorowicz, pp. 7 ff.
28. Kantorowicz, p. 40.
29. R. F. Hill, "Dramatic Techniques and Interpretation in 'Richard the Second,' " in J. R. Brown and B. Harris, ed., *Early Shakespeare,* Shakespeare Institute Studies (New York, 1966), p. 121.

BOLINGBROKE

Go, some of you convey him to the Tower.

KING RICHARD

O, good! Convey! Conveyers are you all,
That rise thus nimbly by a true king's fall.

(IV.i.316–318)

Richard's "conveyers" become both "royal escorts" and "thieves," as his
"still-breeding thoughts" are both fertile and stillborn, and his anguished
"Ay, no; no, ay" a knotted pun of conflicting impulses. Bolingbroke can
afford to be, as Richard calls him, a "silent king" (IV.i.290), or, when
he speaks, a skilled but conventional rhetorician concealing as much as
he reveals: "Henry Bolingbroke / On both his knees doth kiss King
Richard's hand . . ." (III.iii.35–36). His real meanings have no need for
public utterance because they are attached to actions and backed with
the weight of political power. Compared with Richard's frantic ostentation, Bolingbroke's reticence is powerful enough to topple a king without
his once declaring his intentions. Bolingbroke not surprisingly has little
patience with Richard's wordplay, but Richard persists in ruling the only
realm where he still holds sway, persists in hammering his verbal subjects
into linguistic models of his own paradoxical state.

But the effort is unavailing: Richard can never fashion his splintering
words into a language that will reestablish connections. His final attempt
to "compare / This prison where I live unto the world" (V.v.1–2)—to
rejoin the shrunken kingdom of his own natural body to the greater
world from which he has been severed—must fail. The only solution to
his grief is the dissolution of the metaphysical and the physical in death:
"Mount, mount, my soul! thy seat is up on high; / Whilst my gross flesh
sinks downward, here to die" (V.v.111–112).

By setting Shakespeare's king next to Holbein's ambassadors, I have
hoped to suggest that Richard's character and language must be seen
from the two points of view of the curious perspective, generated, in
Richard's case, by his double nature as king and man. In him the perspectives of imperishable authority and fragile mortality are joined in an
unstable union, a discord, that requires us to see both the crown and the
hollowness at its center. One analogue for Richard's character may be
found in mortuary sculpture which presents two reposing figures of the

Illustration 2. Reversible Portraits. Esme de Boulonnois, *Il Faut Mourir* (17th century). The Metropolitan Museum of Art, the Elisha Whittelsey Fund, 1949

deceased, one fully fleshed and lifelike on the lid of a carved tomb and the second, a skeletal corpse, inside the tomb.[30] Another visual model that conflates the two aspects into a single figure is the reversible perspective portrait like the seventeenth-century French woodcut entitled *Il Faut Mourir* (Illustration 2). I would like to propose further that our need to see Richard rightly and awry extends to our experience of the play as a whole.

The "seeing" with which I have been concerned so far is a kind of

30. Reproduced in Kantorowicz, Figures 28, 30, 31.

intellectual balancing act in the presence of a double character speaking a double language. But of course we see a play in the literal sense as well: whether in performance or in the mind's eye, the drama depends upon our visual experience more directly than the lyric or the novel—which may or may not call up relevant imagery for the individual reader. The composition of figures on stage and the rhythm of their movement and gesture are crucial to what Michael Goldman terms the "energies of drama." [31] The play's sequence of visual imagery forms a pattern of understanding comparable to our experience of a painting, and it is worth special attention in *Richard II* because of the formal, posed quality of its court scenes. [32]

IV

The first four scenes of the play alternate between public ceremony and private conversation. The public scenes, Bolingbroke's challenge (I.i) and the aborted combat (I.iii), are visually identical: two opponents take their place on either side of King Richard, who (with the viewer) must make a choice between them. The characters' movement on stage, like their language, is restricted to the few ritual acts prescribed by the solemn occasion. Standing "face to face / And frowning brow to brow" (I.i.15–16), Mowbray and Bolingbroke throw down the gage in turn and accept the other's challenge. In Act I, scene iii, the locale has shifted to the lists at Coventry, where there are perhaps more "Nobles" in attendance, the combatants are now armed, and a Marshall replaces Gaunt as an interlocutor between them and the king; otherwise this scene echoes the first in both its balanced composition and rigid formality. With Richard in the center (whether on a balcony above the "field" or on the platform stage), Bolingbroke and Mowbray enter from either side and "orderly proceed" to announce their name and cause, profess their loyalty to the king, and receive the lance. They are posed in a formal tableau that is all the more static because the action we suppose will issue from

31. *Shakespeare and the Energies of Drama* (Princeton, N.J., 1972).

32. For studies in this vein, with differing emphases, see Mark Rose, *Shakespearean Design* (Cambridge, Mass., 1972) and Ann Haaker, *"Non Sine Causa:* The Use of Emblematic Method and Iconology in the Thematic Structure of *Titus Andronicus,"* RORD, XIII–XV (1970–1971), 143–168.

all this ceremony is frustrated. Having refused to be reconciled, they will now not be permitted to fight:

LORD MARSHALL

Sound trumpets; and set forward combatants.
[*A charge sounded*]
Stay, The King hath thrown his warder down.

KING RICHARD

Let them lay by their helmets and their spears,
And both return back to their chairs again.

(I.iii.117–120)

The judicial forms of challenge and combat are intended to make conflicting claims manifest, a part of the public record, and to resolve them by the certain test of battle. Yet here nothing happens and no judgment is rendered except for Richard's apparently capricious decision to suspend the contest and banish both parties. It is left for the smaller scenes to reveal what lies hidden in the public spectacle. Richard explains his verdict publicly as a precaution against shedding kindred blood in civil strife, but in Act I, scene iv, he tells Aumerle that his private motive for the banishment lay in the fear of Bolingbroke's ambition and popularity. We know further from Gaunt in Act I, scene ii, that Richard is already spotted with kindred blood for his complicity in the murder of the Duke of Gloucester—that when Bolingbroke accuses Richard's agent Mowbray of spilling Gloucester's blood, "Which blood like sacrificing Abel's, cries / . . . To me for justice and rough chastisement" (I.i.104, 106), it is the king himself who stands guilty by proxy of committing the sin of Cain. The public scenes appear to be richly significant with all the trappings of history; but counterpointed against what is said out of public hearing, they become opaque. Their color and detail, their rhetoric, their very factuality, form an ornate surface concealing the truth beneath it. The high ceremony is there not merely to recreate a nostalgic picture of a lost medieval order, as Tillyard believed, but to suggest that history itself—for all its high-stomached language—is an inarticulate dumbshow.

I have emphasized the visual composition of Act I, scene i, and Act I, scene iii, because the same pattern recurs at three other points in the play, twice in the deposition scene, Act IV, scene i, and again in Act V, scene iii. Schematically, the three principal figures on stage—in Act I, scene i, and Act I, scene iii, Bolingbroke, Richard, and Mowbray—form a kind of triptych with the central character in the judgment seat:

This is a scenic equivalent for the Gardener's judicial image of Bolingbroke and Richard "weighed" in the balance (which in production the Gardener will certainly make a living emblem by extending his arms like a pair of scales):

> Their fortunes both are weigh'd.
> In your lord's scale is nothing but himself,
> And some few vanities that make him light;
> But in the balance of great Bolingbroke,
> Besides himself, are all the English peers,
> And with that odds he weighs King Richard down.
>
> (III.iv.84–89)

In each recurrence a dual judgment is to be made, that of the character at the fulcrum about the two contenders in the balances, and that of the viewer about the scene itself. These scenes together form a larger set of balances that weigh the crucial dilemma of the play.

At the beginning of Act IV, scene i, when Bolingbroke has the power if not the crown, the "woeful pageant" of deposition opens with a formal challenge between Bagot and Aumerle over which the new king must preside. The captured Bagot is called to testify what he knows of "noble Gloucester's death; / Who wrought it with the King, and who perform'd / The bloody office of his timeless end" (ll. 3–5). He accuses Aumerle, who is brought forward and told to "look upon that man" (l. 7) as Bagot levels his charge:

> In that dead time when Gloucester's death was plotted
> I heard you say 'Is not my arm of length,
> That reacheth from the restful English Court
> As far as Calais, to mine uncle's head?'
> Amongst much other talk that very time
> I heard you say that you had rather refuse

The offer of an hundred thousand crowns
Than Bolingbroke's return to England;
Adding withal, how blest this land would be
In this your cousin's death,

(ll. 10–19)

Visually and thematically, the scene reenacts the challenge in Act I, scene i, and Act I, scene iii, which also concerned responsibility for Gloucester's death, with different actors in the key positions:

Though Aumerle denies the charge, it seems at first that the balance has tipped decisively against him as three other witnesses line up on Bagot's side: Fitzwater supports Bagot's testimony from personal knowledge ("I heard thee say, and vauntingly thou spak'st it, / That thou wert cause of noble Gloucester's death"), Percy throws down the gage to defend Fitzwater's honor, and "Another Lord" adds his own gage to the pile as he declares Aumerle forsworn and treacherous (IV.i.36–37, 44–48, 52–56). At this moment, however, Surrey steps in as an eyewitness to the conversation between Aumerle and Fitzwater: "My Lord Fitzwater, I do remember well / The very time Aumerle and you did talk" (ll. 60–61). Fitzwater acknowledges that Surrey was there and looks to him for support, whereupon Surrey flatly contradicts Fitzwater's accusation and the two fall into a quarrel of their own:

FITZWATER

'Tis very true; You were in presence then,
And you can witness with me this is true.

SURREY

As false, by heaven, as heaven itself is true.

FITZWATER

Surrey, thou liest.

SURREY

Dishonourable boy!

(ll. 62–65)

Since this is Surrey's first appearance in the play we have no voucher for his honesty or, indeed, for Fitzwater's, Bagot's, or Aumerle's. With one eyewitness for each side, the case reaches an impasse that can only be broken by calling yet another witness—for now Fitzwater remembers having "heard the banish'd [Mowbray, Duke of] Norfolk say / That thou, Aumerle, didst send two of thy men / To execute the noble Duke at Calais" (ll. 80–82). Bolingbroke is willing to have the conclusive witness repealed; but Norfolk, he is told, has died in exile, and he has no choice but to leave all these differences unresolved—"under gage" until some future "days of trial" which are never appointed in the course of the play (ll. 105–106).

This episode, inconclusive and apparently unrelated to the deposition that follows, is nevertheless reconstructed with some care out of a few details in Holinshed's chronicle. There Sir John Bagot is reported to have given a deposition containing "certeine evill practises of king Richard" and affirming Richard's "great affection" for the Duke of Aumerle. Bagot also testified to a private conversation with Mowbray in which the latter, having denied any part in Gloucester's death, named Aumerle as the one who carried out the king's murderous wishes. The next day, according to Holinshed, Fitzwater appealed Aumerle for treason and "twentie other lords also . . . threw downe their hoods, in pledge to prove the like matter against the duke of Aumerle." Bolingbroke then licensed the return of Mowbray to answer the charges against him and learned of Mowbray's death.[33] While Holinshed makes no mention of anyone speaking *for* Aumerle, who in his account stands condemned on all sides, Shakespeare deliberately adds the character of Surrey to balance the scales, and further makes Aumerle's case depend on the unobtainable testimony Mowbray carried with him to the grave. With these changes Shakespeare creates a scene where a matter of historical judgment becomes ambiguous: Surrey and Fitzwater see the past from conflicting points of view, and neither we nor Bolingbroke can decide which is "right" and which is "wry." That "dead time when Gloucester's death was plotted" is not just past but dead as Mowbray is dead—silent and beyond recall. Like one of Richard's double words, the past has split into opposites that cannot be reconciled.

33. In Bullough, pp. 409–410.

By its parallelism to the earlier judgment triptychs, this scene makes
the question of Gloucester's murder all the more uncertain (given that
Richard wanted it done, who carried it out? Mowbray? Aumerle?) and
reminds us of the stasis and concealment, the inconclusiveness, of the
history open to public view. The scene's importance as a prelude to the
deposition becomes clear if we realize one obvious but vital aspect of our
own relationship to this history play. Bolingbroke's vantage point on
the history of Bagot and Aumerle is analogous to our vantage point on the
history of Richard II and Henry IV: we are spectators at a reenactment,
an attempted resuscitation, of a dead past, but the replica is necessarily a
death mask and not the living flesh. Because we cannot see more than
the preserved public face, we can never attain the certainty of knowing
the private heart.

That limitation first of all gives special point to Carlisle's speech, which
follows next. "What subject can give sentence on his king?" warns not
merely against the offense of judging God's deputy but against the
presumption of judging at all. If Bolingbroke cannot in conscience give
sentence on two of Richard's underlings, how can he give sentence on
Richard? The same caution must apply to the audience's judgment of
the deposition. For Richard, acting as the stage manager of his own
deposition, will maneuver Bolingbroke into the same position Bagot
and Aumerle were in a moment before. Taking the crown (from York
or one of the officers who has carried it into the room), Richard invites
Bolingbroke to "seize" it, and the figures hold the pose, each with a
hand on the crown between them, while Richard speaks:

> Give me the crown. Here, cousin, seize the crown.
> Here, cousin,
> On this side my hand, and on that side thine.
> Now is this golden crown like a deep well
> That owes two buckets, filling one another;
> The emptier ever dancing in the air,
> The other down, unseen, and full of water.
> That bucket down and full of tears am I,
> Drinking my griefs whilst you mount up on high.
>
> (IV.i.181–189)

Richard's conceit of the crown as a "deep well / That owes two
buckets" echoes the Gardener's scales as a figure of the shifting fortunes

of the two men and the difficulty of the judgment we have to make
between them. The banishment of Bolingbroke and Gaunt's prophetic
denunciation of Richard in Act I had been followed by an announcement
of Bolingbroke's return. Now the deposition of Richard and Carlisle's
prophetic denunciation of Bolingbroke are followed (at IV.i.326–334) by
the laying of a plot against the new king. As the beginning of the new
regime reenacts the end of the old, our judgment is suspended in an
equilibrium that carefully balances their competing claims.

The final triptych occurs in Act V, scene iii, where Henry must decide
between two suppliants. On one side Aumerle (seconded by his mother)
begs the king's forgiveness for his part in the conspiracy which has just
come to light; on the other Aumerle's father, the Duke of York, urges the
king to condemn Aumerle for treason:

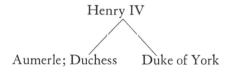

Henry IV

Aumerle; Duchess   Duke of York

An uncle to both Richard and Bolingbroke, York had been torn between
them but finally bound his allegiance to the new king so securely that—
even though Henry is inclined to be lenient—he now demands his own
son's death. Henry, angry as he is with Aumerle, is also half amused at
these proceedings, for the old duke and his persistent wife make a faintly
ridiculous pair (ll. 79–82); and what is held up for ridicule in the warm
light of Henry's generosity is York's vindictive code of "honor" and
"dishonor" which places political loyalty over the natural affection of
fathers for their children:

> **YORK**
> Mine honour lives when his dishonour dies,
> Or my sham'd life in his dishonour lies.
> Thou kill'st me in his life; giving him breath,
> The traitor lives, the true man's put to death.
>
> (ll. 70–73)

Henry chooses mercy over this harsh brand of justice, and his forgiveness
is as complete as Aumerle's guilt. York urges him to say his pardon in

French—to "say 'pardonne moy'" (l. 119)—but the king refuses to
quibble. He will not "set the word itself against the word" (l. 122) but
will rather speak it plainly, "I pardon him, as God shall pardon me"
(l. 131); and to leave no doubt he grants the duchess's plea that he speak
it twice:

DUCHESS

Speak it again.
Twice saying 'pardon' doth not pardon twain,
But makes one pardon strong.

BOLINGBROKE

With all my heart
I pardon him.

(ll. 133–136)

Balanced against the play's opening triptych, this scene completes one
view of the historical process—let us call it the "right" view—that justifies
the deposition morally and metaphysically, suggesting (as York had
earlier put it) that "heaven hath a hand in these events" (V.ii.37). In the
first act Richard had ruled in a case of treason and, to keep his own guilt
hidden, had dispensed not justice but vengeance on both parties. By
exiling and then dispossessing Bolingbroke of his inheritance, he had
taken "from Time / His charters and his customary rights" and so broken
the chain of "fair sequence and succession" by which he could claim his
own authority. (II.i.195–196, 199). In this view Bolingbroke, as Henry IV,
has rejuvenated the political order by putting time back into joint; he has
created a "new world" (Fitzwater, IV.i.78) and a "new spring of time"
(York, V.ii.50). Richard has the blood of Abel on his hands. Like the
Gardener he is "old Adam's likeness," and his fall signified a "second fall
of cursed man" (III.iv.73, 76). Although at the deposition Richard had
played the role of a betrayed Christ—"Did they not sometime cry 'All
hail!' to me? / So Judas did to Christ" (IV.i.169–170)—this was nothing
but a shadowy performance, for the substance of divine kingship had
passed to another man. Now when Henry pardons Aumerle the duchess
correctly proclaims him a "god on earth," and leads her son off stage with
the words, "Come, my old son; I pray God make thee new" (V.iii.136,
146). The old Aumerle is forgiven under a new dispensation of mercy,
and his pardon is the emblem of a regenerate kingdom. In short the

"right" view is that English history recapitulates spiritual history as a redemptive movement from sinfulness to grace.

If the play ended here it would be another version of Richard III, moving from "Richard's night to Bolingbroke's [= Richmond's] fair day" (III.ii.218), but the concluding three scenes establish the second, "wry" point of view. First Exton and a servant remain on stage:

EXTON

Did'st thou not mark the King, what words he spake?
"Have I no friend will rid me of this living fear?"
Was it not so?

SERVANT

These were his very words.

EXTON

"Have I no friend?" quoth he. He spake it twice,
And urg'd it twice together, did he not?

SERVANT

He did.

(V.iv.1–6)

Having just twice spoken the words of pardon, Henry (evidently before the scene with Aumerle) had already twice spoken the words of treachery and murder. Having just refused to set the word itself against the word in a French pun, Henry now presents us with a far more disturbing contradiction—which is echoed a moment later in the language of Richard's prison soliloquy. For among Richard's discontented thoughts, the

thoughts of things divine, are intermix'd
With scruples, and do set the word itself
Against the word,
As thus: "Come little ones"; and then again,
"It is as hard to come as for a camel
To thread the postern of a small needle's eye."

(V.v.12–17)

Weighing his own fate, Richard is caught on the dilemma of reconciling the scripture's promise of mercy with its threat of retribution. The same dilemma confronts the spectator in the juxtaposition of Act V, scene iii, and Act V, scene iv, which presents the equivalent (and equivocal) problem of interpreting King Henry:

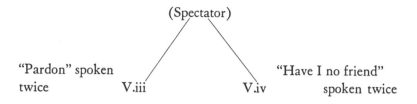

Henry's final action in the play, the banishing of Exton, completes the "wry" perspective by recalling the allusion to Abel in Act I, scene i: "They love not poison that do poison need, / Nor do I thee. . . . With Cain go wander thorough shades of night" (V.vi.38–39, 43). Exton is Henry's man as Mowbray was Richard's, and through these exiled surrogates both the deposed king and his successor bear the guilt of a kindred murder. In the "wry" view English history recapitulates the sin of Cain, recording a cycle of homicide rather than a spiritual progress.

These two perspectives together comprise the play's two bodies, a spiritual and a physical nature paradoxically incorporated in one dramatic form. The play is bracketed by two opposing structural symmetries, corresponding to two opposed patterns of meaning, which may be represented schematically:

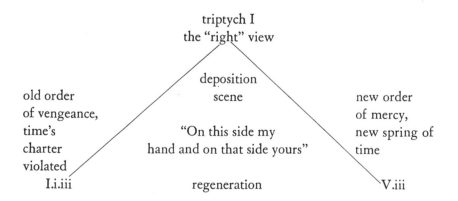

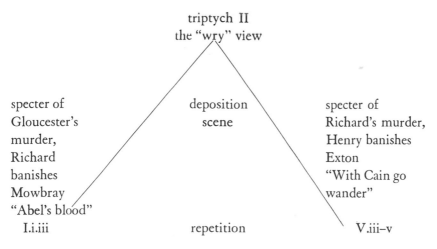

triptych II
the "wry" view

specter of   deposition   specter of
Gloucester's   scene   Richard's murder,
murder,   Henry banishes
Richard   Exton
banishes   "With Cain go
Mowbray   wander"
"Abel's blood"
    I.i.iii   repetition   V.iii–v

In our experience of the play, the "right" and "wry" points of view are superimposed in a way that forces us to hold both configurations in mind. As the model of a double character generates a witty double language, it also imbeds two modes of explanation in the same historical event, or rather discovers in one event two necessary, if logically incompatible, meanings. The play neither endorses nor denies the Tudor myth but builds on its premises to show that the providential theory of the king's double nature necessarily requires a complex kind of doublethink for which the curious perspective is the visual model. Confronted with these shifting patterns of meaning, the witness can have no unequivocal point of view. Instead he is put in the difficult role of balancing conflicting but equally valid perceptions. He must see both the "controlling majesty" of kingship and the vanity of the "hollow crown."

"Anticke Pageantrie": The Mannerist Art of Perkin Warbeck

MICHAEL NEILL

W HEN HAVELOCK ELLIS wrote of *Perkin Warbeck* that it was "an exception to every generalization that may be arrived at concerning [Ford's] work," he expressed what has since become a standard view of the play.[1] With the exception of those who have tried to impose a Burtonian interpretation of Perkin,[2] most critics have tended to see it as a straightforward revival of "chronicle history" and to discuss it in terms of the political arguments appropriate to that genre.[3] More

---

1. See, for instance, Una Ellis-Fermor, *The Jacobean Drama* (London, 1947), p. 233; H. J. Oliver, *The Problem of John Ford* (Melbourne, 1955), p. 99; M. C. Bradbrook, *Themes and Conventions of Elizabethan Tragedy* (Cambridge, Eng., 1935), p. 260; Havelock Ellis, ed., *John Ford* (*Five Plays*) (London, 1888), p. xiii; Peter Ure, ed., *Perkin Warbeck,* The Revels Plays (London, 1968), pp. xlix–l; all citations from *Perkin Warbeck* are from this edition.

2. See S. B. Ewing, *Burtonian Melancholy in the Plays of John Ford* (Princeton, N.J., 1940); G. F. Sensabaugh, *The Tragic Muse of John Ford* (Stanford, Calif., 1944); L. L. Babb, "Abnormal Psychology in John Ford's *Perkin Warbeck,*" *MLN,* LI (1936), 234–237.

3. See especially Irving Ribner, *The English History Play in the Age of Shakespeare,* rev. ed. (London, 1969), pp. 299 ff.; D. K. Anderson, Jr., "Kingship in

recently, however, Peter Ure and Jonas A. Barish have given attention to an aspect of the work which accords more easily with the manneristic self-consciousness of the rest of Ford's drama—its treatment of the player-king.[4] And Ure's analysis of the "moral elegance" with which the play embodies the ideal of "civility" suggests a significant connection with what might be called the "moral aesthetic" of *The Lovers Melancholy* and *The Broken Heart*.[5] In fact, I would suggest that *Perkin Warbeck,* with its celebration of the actor as hero and its elevation of style as an absolute moral principle, has a particularly close relation to *The Broken Heart* as a second example of that peculiarly Fordian genre defined by R. J. Kaufmann—the "tragedy of manners."[6] In this regard it is perhaps significant that *Perkin* should have followed *The Broken Heart* in being the second of Ford's plays to carry on its title page Ford's anagram, *"Fide Honor";* for the idea of honor, the subject of Tecnicus's choric oration in Act III of *The Broken Heart,* becomes of even more crucial importance here. In this, perhaps the latest of his major plays, Ford completes the strange metamorphosis, begun in his other tragedy of manners, by which the honor of the neo-stoic noble man is realized in the *maniera* of a consummate courtier, in an actor's display of bravura style.

I. Traditional Honor and the Style of the Courtier

In the dedication of *Perkin,* with a flourish of mannerist wit, Ford makes a complimentary allusion to his treatment of honor in the play. After dutifully listing Newcastle's titles of honor, he gracefully reminds his lordship that "Eminent titles may indeed inform who their owners are, not often what" (p. 5)—only of course to emphasize the earl's dis-

---

Ford's *Perkin Warbeck,"* ELH, XXVII (1960), 177–193; and M. C. Struble's introduction to *A Critical Edition of Ford's Perkin Warbeck* (Seattle, Wash., 1926). Cf. also D. L. Frost, *The School of Shakespeare* (Cambridge, Eng. 1968), p. 120.

4. Ure, pp. liv–lxxxiii; Jonas A. Barish, *"Perkin Warbeck* as Anti-History," *Essays in Criticism,* XX (1970), 151–171; cf. also Anne Righter, *Shakespeare and the Idea of the Play* (London, 1962), p. 137.

5. Ure, p. lvi.

6. R. J. Kaufmann, "Ford's 'Waste Land': *The Broken Heart,"* RenD, N.S. III (1970), 167–187.

tinction in matching the real to the ideal. But in *Perkin* itself the gulf between the "who" and the "what" of eminence is not so easily bridged.[7] The play opposes the ethos of traditional honor, represented by the ancient nobility of the English and Scottish realms, to the self-sufficient politics of Renaissance individualism—Henry's Machiavellian pragmatism on the one hand, and Perkin's stoical histrionism on the other. Writers on honor of course had often debated the relative importance of gentle birth and gentle deeds in making the noble man, but the two were generally regarded as inseparable. Henry and Perkin are, by contrast, representatives of a world in which personal prowess no longer has any necessary connection with inherited social status. If Henry's master in this is Machiavelli, Perkin's is Castiglione, whose *Courtier* is recognizably a denizen of the *Prince's* court. Castiglione, in fact, may be regarded as the first of the virtuous Machiavels, producing a compendium of courtly arts for a rising breed of ambitious careerists—"a new man in his kind of trade," as his translator, Thomas Hoby, put it with unwitting felicity.[8] Where the traditional idea of honor defined a man's rights, duties, and obligations in firmly social terms, Castiglione is concerned to offer only, in Rosalie Colie's phrase, "a handbook of self-making."[9] The Courtier, that politician of *politezza,* is bound to his Lord solely by the ties of mutual interest; he cultivates his arts firstly as a means to advancement, and secondly as a defense against the vagaries of fortune in a ruthlessly competitive society. Central to this ideal is the notion of style (*maniera*) which gives it its self-consciously theatrical character: like the artists to whom he is so frequently compared, the Courtier is to

7. The phrase is echoed on three significant occasions in the play. In Act I, scene ii, Huntley successfully urges his daughter to "Consider whose thou art, and who" (l. 103); but at the end of the play Oxford's "Remember, lady, who you are" (V.iii.111) provokes her to a defiant definition of "what" she and Perkin are (ll.112–121). Compare Perkin's recollection of "who I was" (II.i.75)—a claim to "eminent titles" which the last act renders irrelevant.

8. See Baldassare Castiglione, *The Book of the Courtier,* trans. Sir Thomas Hoby (London, 1948), p. 2. For evidence of Ford's interest in Castiglione, see F. M. Burelbach, "The Truth in John Ford's *The Broken Heart* Revisited," *N & Q,* XXXII (1967), 211–212.

9. R. L. Colie, *Paradoxia Epidemica* (Princeton, N.J., 1966) p. 361; a similar point is made by R. B. Hinman, " 'The Apotheosis of Faust' in *Metaphysical Poetry,"* Stratford-upon-Avon Studies 11 (London, 1970), p. 169.

cultivate an artificial following of nature, always taking care, however, to conceal his artifice with an appearance of negligent ease. Admiration for the Courtier's performance (or the artist's *dimostrazione*) will thus depend on a kind of paradoxical consciousness: a simultaneous appreciation of the delicate artifice which improves on nature, and of the further artifice which is used to conceal the first, making it appear like nature unadorned once more. Performer and audience become collaborators in a perspective show of willingly enjoyed deceits. One senses that the indignation of Fletcher's punctilious courtier-heroes or of the Caroline précieux at any trespass on their honor is partly motivated by aesthetic outrage at a refusal to collaborate in the display; but it is a violation of the artifice which, if allowed to persist, will call their whole being in question. The man of honor has *become* his style.[10]

In *Perkin Warbeck,* from the moment when Lambert Simnel's voluntary degradation is cited to show "the difference between noble natures / And the base born" (I.i.67–68), the assumptions and vocabulary of chivalric honor are much in evidence. Henry, James, and Perkin alike publicly assume the inalienability of greatness from "birthright," and both the English and Scottish courts contain a retinue of feudal nobles whose sense of dignity and of social rights and obligations reflects a thoroughly traditional ideal of honor. However, the progress of the action forces a reassessment of this ideal, confronting not only the audience but also certain of the characters with the fact that it contains insoluble contradictions. In the end we have to choose between the pragmatic kingship of Henry and the histrionic royalty of Perkin; and it is significant that, in posing this choice, Ford should now choose to make Simnel the touchstone not of Henry's nobility, but of Perkin's, and that the measure of their difference should no longer be action, but "language" (V.iii.55).

The existence of a disjunction between chivalric ideals and political reality becomes most obvious in Henry's court, since here all ideals are subject to the overriding interest of a prince—a monarch whose rule depends less on "right" than "subsidies" (III.iv.84–86). The old nobility,

10. The final degradation of this ideal is seen in a Restoration fop, like Wycherley's Sparkish, whose "honour" is indistinguishable from his "parts" (*The Country Wife*, II.i.270–271).

Surrey, Oxford, and even Daubeney, are demonstrably of less importance than conniving politicians like Durham, Urswick, and Hialas; and their ability to realize their ideals in action is circumscribed by the practical requirements of politics. Surrey responds warmly to the chivalric romanticism of James's challenge in Act IV, scene i, for which he wins the envious regard of his peers (IV.iv.10–23). But although his answer is composed in the proper style of compliment demanded by the code of honor, it has nevertheless to be qualified by the proviso that "In affairs / Of princes, subjects cannot traffic rights / Inherent to the crown" (IV.i. 47–49). Oxford, who characteristically swears his loyalty to Henry's title "By Vere's old honours" (II.ii.24), is if anything even more conscious than Surrey of his nobility: offering his "service" to Katherine in Act V, scene i, he presents himself as the very embodiment of inherited honor (ll. 85–99). Yet both his honor and the sovereign's "royalty" which it represents are muddied by the discourtesy he displays in the final scene as part of Henry's politically necessary attempt to discredit the Pretender. Perkin's own aphorism in Act V, scene iii, sarcastically points out the subservience of honor to power in such a world: "Possession of a crown ne'er wanted heralds" (l. 30). The real heralds of Henry's authority, in contrast to Marchmount and his companion in their emblazoned coats (IV.i.19 s.d.), are Hialas and Durham whose understanding of nobility is perfectly suggested by the "honour" of the politic marriage they negotiate for James (IV.iii.21).[11]

Nowhere perhaps is the incompatibility of the ideal and the real made more apparent than in the scenes involving Clifford and Sir William Stanley, which are so tellingly juxtaposed with three scenes of courtesy and high ceremony in Scotland. Henry, of course, parades his regret at the plight of Stanley, opposing the rigor of the law to "the softness of our nature" and the "chancery of pity in our bosom" (II.ii.9–12). The Perkin-like emotionalism of the speech may be partly genuine, but it is impossible not to notice how finely calculated it is to secure the very condemnation he professes to abhor; and once it is secured, he proceeds to a distinction between public and private selves worthy of the world of *Richard III:* "But I am charitable, lords; let justice / Proceed in execution, whiles I mourn / The loss of one whom I esteemed a friend"

---

11. Henry refers ironically to Hialas as "your own herald" (III.iii.34).

(II.ii.39–41). The posture simultaneously excuses him from confronting the human meaning of his decision and further enhances his reputation for honor and humanity: " 'Tis a King / Composed of gentleness," reflects Surrey in a muse of admiration (ll. 48–49); but the true meaning of his actions is not lost on the wily Fox ("every man is nearest to himself," l. 51). Nor is it lost on the audience, for the ensuing confrontation between Clifford and Stanley spells it out in the most brutally direct terms. Whatever Stanley has done, and whatever his motive, we are meant to accept that it leaves his sense of honor intact (ll. 98–102). Clifford, on the other hand, is the fatally dishonored denizen of a world where the canons of chivalry no longer have the power to command, as Stanley's hieratic gesture reminds us:

> I wet upon your cheeks a holy sign,
> The cross, the Christian's badge, the traitor's infamy.
> Wear, Clifford, to thy grave this painted emblem.
> Water shall never wash it off, all eyes
> That gaze upon thy face shall read there written
> A state-informer's character, more ugly
> Stamped on a noble name than on a base.
>
> (II.ii.85–91)

And Clifford, no simple traitor, but a state-informer, is part of the indispensable machinery of the new state with its ruthless ethic of necessity.[12] Remembering that Henry's chaplain, Urswick, and his politician-bishop have been Clifford's principal interrogators, there is a nice irony in the conjunction of Christian badge and traitor's emblem. Clifford's reward of banishment is the final twist of policy's knife: what honor should there be among Machiavels, however virtuous?

On the face of it one might expect the Scottish court, dominated by a monarch who likes to construct his life in imitation of the heroic legends of Bruce and Coeur-de-Lion (II.i.18–28) to be more sympathetic to the claims of traditional honor. War for James is less an extension of policy

---

12. Compare Bacon's remarks on Henry's use of spies and informers: Francis Bacon, *The History of the Reign of King Henry the Seventh,* ed. Roger Lockyer (London, 1971), pp. 231–232. Phillip Edwards, "The Royal Pretenders in Massinger and Ford," *Essays and Studies* (1974), 18–36, also stresses the Machiavellian aspect of Henry, arguing that the play asks us to choose between "two styles of life" represented by men whose claims to the throne are equally dubious.

than an opportunity for "high attempts of honour" (II.i.113), less a
testing of Perkin's effective "title" than a tournament for Katherine's
"honours" (III.ii.115–128). Even when the defeat of his campaign and
the Machiavellian persuasions of Fox and Hialas have brought him to a
more realistic understanding, he still contrives to couch his dismissal of
Perkin in a high style of chivalric compliment which distinguishes the
statist's necessity as "The dignity of state" (IV.iii.75). This seeming
idealism is matched by his courtiers' punctilious concern with honor.
Scotland has no equivalent to the new men of Henry's household; and
we are first introduced to its court in a scene between Huntley, Dalyell,
and Katherine which exhibits a nice sense of honor's rights and obligations, balancing Dalyell's "honourable ancestry" (I.ii.8, 115–116) and
personal prowess (ll. 9–11) against the Gordons' lofty title and estate
(ll. 14–18, 23–27). Paradoxically, it is precisely the "whoreson tale of
honour" which prevents Huntley's acceptance of Dalyell's honorable
suit. But if this reveals a latent tension within the conception of traditional honor itself, it is one which can still be contained inside a ceremonial tableau:

> Keep you on that hand of her; I on this:
> Thou stand'st between a father and a suitor,
> Both striving for an interest in thy heart.
> He courts thee for affection, I for duty;
> He as a servant pleads. . . .
>
> (I.ii.94–97)

The formal dressing of the stage and the archaic movement of Kydian
antithesis reduce conflict to a symmetrical order, resolving contradiction
in antinomy. Characteristically, the old man's grant of freedom to
Katherine ("Thou art thine own," l. 124) contrives to be at the same
time a reminder of "The lowest of obedience" (l. 128) implicit in the
knowledge of "whose thou art, and who: a princess" (l. 103). In this
world one's sense of self is to be determined not by personal inclination
(dismissed as "female wantonness" and "passion," ll. 112, 122), but by
social obligations defined in "The duty of a daughter" (l. 134) and the
"honour" of one's family (l. 123). By the end of the play, though it
remains her line of life, Katherine has come to a different understanding
of "duty," based on the recognition that, though the traditional scheme
of honor may define "who" a person is, it cannot show "what."

Huntley, too, is driven to question his own values, as a result of their betrayal by the king. For James's style of rule proves to be founded not on any coherent idea of feudal monarchy, but on a nostalgic romanticism reminiscent of that which inspired the Renaissance tournament. Moreover, his romanticism itself only masks a despotic willfulness which makes him the true kinsman of the duke in *Loves Sacrifice*. Like Caraffa, a passionate relativist, James makes value a function of individual will. In proclaiming his faith in Perkin, he seems to carry the chivalric notion of the indivisibility of honor to absurd lengths, arguing that royal language proves a king; but the parenthetic "be whate'er thou art" proves that this is no more than a gloss for the arbitrary indulgence of his will (II.i.103–107); and it is by a naked appeal to "will" and "Instinct of sovereignty" that he justifies the dishonorable match between Katherine and Perkin. For Huntley, such an action constitutes an assault on the very foundations of traditional order ("a' pulls down / What old desert hath builded," II.iii.56–57). In a world so stripped of honor, he can no longer identify himself in terms of title or hereditary nobility, and he becomes instead "Old Alexander Gordon, a plain subject, / Nor more nor less," (ll. 93–94). From this point in the play, Huntley ceases to be an effective spokesman for traditional honor as a coherent social ideal. Indeed, his impulse is actually to revolt altogether against the order on which his ideals depended (III.ii.52–55): but he falls back instead on a despairing assertion of divine right (ll. 57–59), and a stoical quietism:

> Tempests, when they begin to roar, put out
> The light of peace and cloud the sun's bright eye
> In darkness of despair; yet we are safe.
> . . . .
> Thou dost not know the flexible condition
> Of my apt nature. I can laugh, laugh heartily
> When the gout cramps my joints; let but the stone
> Stop in my bladder, I am straight a-singing;
> . . . .
> I love my wrongs; still thou'rt deceived in me.
>   (III.ii.26–44)

He does not actually go to the length of Tecnicus's withdrawal from the world; but his response at the beginning of the revels is symbolically appropriate:

> O, hark! we may be quiet,
> The King and all the others come . . .
> Dainty sport toward, Dalyell; sit; come, sit,
> Sit and be quiet.
>
> (ll. 81–111)

It is a note, frequently sounded in Ford, of simultaneous resignation and lament—a stoical recognition of defeat; and Huntley, though he maintains a conspicuous dignity to the end, can only confront the final tragedy in a posture of moral abdication (V.iii.209–211). Action, in Ford's philosophy, is the crown of virtue; but Huntley finds himself in a society which in effect denies the moral basis of political activity, and his response is to withdraw from all independent action. Ford's own conclusion, however, is that virtuous action is still possible in the public world, but only as a kind of acting, where honor is divorced from its social context and becomes a function simply of constancy to a chosen role.

II. "A Strange Truth"

A mannerist work of art can frequently be regarded, like Parmigianino's well-known self-portrait, as being a kind of Narcissus's mirror for the artist. Ford's display of *maniera* in *Perkin Warbeck,* in much the same way as Marvell's in the "Horatian Ode," invites admiration for the author as well as wonder at his protagonist. And Perkin, the player-king, can be seen as being, in a sense, the playwright's own shadow. In George Crymes's verses on the play, Ford's art is seen as having remade nature, so that the literal truths of Perkin's life, his dishonorable birth and degrading death, are transcended by a fiction in which Perkin is "crowned a king of new" (p. 9); in granting Perkin the eternity of fame, art has revived his "Title" to majesty in a way which makes mere legality an irrelevance. And in achieving this enterprise, John Brograve similarly maintains, Ford has produced "a story" which glorifies not only his hero, but himself, confounding his enemies, the "practic critics" (p. 10), as Perkin's art confounds his enemies, the practic politicians. The point is made even more directly by Ralph Eure in praising simultaneously

> The Glorious Perkin and thy poet's art,
> Equal with his, in playing the King's Part.
>
> (ll. 11–12)

Similarly for George Donne, *Perkin Warbeck* is as much a monument to Ford's "honour" as to that of its protagonist:

> Believe me, friend, the name of this and thee
> Will live, your story.

(ll. 5–6)

Ford himself cannot resist using a similar conceit in his epilogue—if Perkin's actions have finally vindicated his honor, disproving his alleged baseness and guaranteeing him the legitimate posterity of fame, then the play may do the same for its author:

> Who will please,
> Amongst such several sights, to censure these
> No births abortive, nor a bastard brood—
> Shame to a parentage or fosterhood—
> May warrant by their loves all just excuses.

(ll. 5–9)

The play itself is crowded with similar bravura flourishes, not only in its handling of the player-king theme, which has an obvious and familiar self-referential effect, but also in its treatment of the "chronicle" of the title. In the most literal sense (as when the prologue speaks of the play's story as "chronicled at home") a chronicle is a strict historical record of events in time, like the "chronicle" of Perkin's career recited by Henry in the opening scene (ll. 103–120). This chronicle is implicitly contrasted with the fiction it encloses, the pretender's performance on "The common stage of novelty" (l. 106). But, as well as recounting events in time, chronicle also has the function of preserving them for time; it is not only a narrative of acts, but a monument to their actors. Chronicle thus has a special significance as the final repository of the "honour" with which the characters are so much concerned: if honor is conventionally rooted in the past, it also seeks to preserve itself in the future, matching (as Huntley expresses it) "honourable ancestry" with "noble actions / For a brave mention to posterity" (I.ii.8–11)—chronicle will provide that "mention." Katherine, like her father, urges Dalyell's commitment to "worthy actions" which may

> guide ye
> Richly to wed an honourable name;
> So every virtuous praise in after-ages

> Shall be your heir, and I in your brave mention
> Be chronicled the Mother of that issue,
> That glorious issue.
>
> (I.ii.152–157)

Stanley, with the same concern for posterity, exhorts his brother to believe

> That I shall stand no blemish to his house
> In chronicles writ in another age.
>
> (II.ii.101–102)

Yet Ford, once he has made the decision so radically to reinterpret the histories of Gainsford and the politician Bacon, cannot be unaware of the extent to which chronicle itself may become the tool of the politician's "safety." In point of sober fact, it is Stanley's earlier epitaph of despair rather than any "chronicle of honour" which accurately designs his place in history, for in the world of pragmatic policy honor has no chronicles:

> I was as you are once—great, and stood hopeful
> Of many flourishing years; but fate and time
> Have wheeled about, to turn me into nothing.
>
> (II.ii.72–74)

Individual honor, like the fleeting honor of kindred sadly recognized by Dalyell, is:

> not ours when once the date
> Of many years have swallowed up the memory
> Of . . . [its] originals.
>
> (I.ii.34–36)

Time, for all that chronicle may do, will reduce the honor by which a man defines himself to "nothing" as surely as it reduces to nothing the body which defines his physical being.

Yet, in the closing stages of the play Perkin cheerfully commits his hard-won sense of indestructible being to the doubtful preservatives of memory, story, and chronicle. It is characteristic of this confidence that, where Katherine's reflection on their fate as "spectacles to time" (V.i.29) seems heavy with a melancholy sense of the destructive power of mutability, in Perkin's speech to Urswick and Simnel "spectacle" is invoked in a proud assertion of the power of his performance to compel time:

> But let the world, as all to whom I am
> This day a spectacle, to time deliver,
> And by tradition fix posterity,
> Without another chronicle than truth,
> How constantly my resolution suffered
> A martyrdom of majesty.
>
> (V.iii.70–75)

In the pages of chronicle his death is to be an immortal pageant-spectacle of constancy at which all time will gaze in wonder, impoverished "of its amazement" (V.iii.196). Katherine herself, whose "story" so outshines probability as to appear a "fable" (V.iii.97), is similarly granted "immortality . . . in the calendar of virtue" (ll. 128–131):

> Report and thy deserts, thou best of creatures,
> Might to eternity have stood a pattern
> For every virtuous wife, without this conquest.
> Thou hast outdone belief.
>
> (V.iii.92–95)

Of course, as Daubeney's comment reminds us, this Perkin is an impostor whose performance lies beyond the scope of conventional history —"No chronicle records his fellow" (V.iii.208–209). The "report" and "illustrious mention" on which Perkin relies to "blaze our names" (ll. 206–207) are not those of Bacon's and Gainsford's histories but the play itself. And it is upon the audience and readers of this strange chronicle that he calls to attest the meaning of his pageant:

> Read in my destiny the wrack of honour;
> Point out, in my contempt of death, to memory
> Some miserable happiness.
>
> (V.iii.123–125)

Likewise, the "truth" which is to be the sole "chronicle" of this triumph of artifice (V.iii.73) is not the bare truth of historical fact but the "strange truth" of art. Where the literal facts of Perkin's dishonor "lie buried in the story," the imaginative truth of his nobility is created, as George Crymes maintains, in the play:

> His fame
> Thou hast eternized; made a crown His game.
> His lofty spirit soars yet. Had He been
> Base in his enterprise, as was His sin

Conceived, His Title, doubtless proved unjust,
Had but for thee been silenced in his dust.

(ll. 5–10)

From a fiction of constancy poetry creates a moral and aesthetic Truth which transcends the petty truths of history. In this light (to adapt Sidney) the fabricators, the poet and his actor, are "paradoxically, but truly . . . of all [men] under the sun . . . the last liar[s]." [13]

The oxymoron of the play's subtitle, "A Strange Truth," draws attention to its paradoxical design: paradox indeed is the figure on which the "fancy" of *Perkin Warbeck* is founded.[14] For Puttenham, paradox was "the Wonderer," [15] and Perkin himself is a kind of living embodiment of this figure: first introduced in Oxford's sarcasms as a "wonder" and a "prodigy" (I.i.53–58), by the end of the play he has come to justify the appellation. Even Daubeney's description of him as "the Christian world's strange wonder" (V.ii.36) seems tinged with admiration, like his "imposter beyond precedent" (V.iii.208); while Huntley's tribute unequivocally acknowledges "the wonder of your frailty, / Which keeps so firm a station" (V.iii.173–174). Crawford responds to the strangeness of Perkin's fiction with a similarly reluctant admiration:

> 'Tis more than strange; my reason cannot answer
> Such argument of fine imposture, couched
> In witchcraft of persuasion, that it fashions
> Impossibilities, as if appearance
> Could cozen truth itself.

(II.iii.1–5)

Appearance, impossibility, things which are not, impose themselves upon the truth by the fine cunning of their artifice: "argument" and

13. Sir Philip Sidney, "An Apology for Poetry," in *English Critical Essays, XVI–XVIII Centuries,* ed. E. D. Jones (London, 1947), p. 43.

14. Paradox frequently reveals itself in oxymoron, like that of the subtitle: the "wonder" of Margaret's fruitful age and barren youth (I.i.53–54); Perkin's "miserable happiness" and "Even when I fell, I stood enthroned" (V.iii.125–126); or Katherine's "cruel mercy" (V.iii.121). The play is dotted with such devices—cf. Ure, p. lxv.

15. George Puttenham, *The Arte of English Poesie,* ed. G. D. Willcock and A. Walker (Cambridge, Eng., 1936), p. 226. Something of the paradoxical nature of Ford's *Perkin* is already hinted at in Gainsford's title, *The True and Wonderfull History of Perkin Warbeck* (London, 1618).

"persuasion," the magical arts of rhetoric, fashion not-being into the forms of being. The play itself may be compared to one of those paradoxical portraits of "Nobody" described by Rosalie Colie[16]—a Nobody who (to use the terminology of the prologue), though his history is indeed "forged," nevertheless makes himself worthy of a "chronicle."

In *Perkin* "truth" is bandied about with a freedom which should alert one to its ambiguous significance.[17] But while it is easy to accept that the deeper purpose of a comedy such as *A Midsummer Night's Dream* should be closely bound up with its extended quibbling on various senses of "truth" and "true" (especially since a sense of the author's controlling wit is so often an integral feature of comedy), it is perhaps harder to recognize that a historical tragedy like *Perkin* is constructed around a similar quibble. Yet nothing is more characteristic of the mannerist style in tragedy than that it should seek to approach the profound through the seemingly superficial. The subtitle's "Truth" is artfully toyed with in Ford's prologue where the audience, after being rebuked for their own "want of truth" as critics, are offered "a history . . . Famous, and true" which they are invited to judge by its handling of "Truth" and "State" —where "truth" stands at once for "historical truthfulness," a larger "verisimilitude," and for the transcendent "truth" of art.[18] The first and last of these are to be of particular concern in the play itself, where it is possible to distinguish two broadly different uses of the term. In the first and most literal sense it refers simply to verifiable facts, in the second to things whose "truth" is felt rather as a reflection of the ideal "Truth" in which all particular truths are included. The first use, naturally enough, tends to be associated with the hardheaded world of Henry Tudor; the second with the idealist world of Perkin. The first kind of truth is fundamentally amoral and pragmatic; the second, with its metaphysical reference, carries a strong moral charge; it includes such notions as "troth" (or constancy in love and allegiance) and the truth of art. The movement of the play gradually forces us to recognize a gap between

16. Colie, *Paradoxia*, p. 298.

17. The word, or variants of it ("troth," "true," "truely") occurs more than thirty times.

18. Compare the verses by George Donne and John Brograve, and Ford's dedication to Newcastle whose titles (with a neat glance at the play's treatment of honor) are said to be proved by "TRUTH."

these two concepts, and to see that what is pragmatically "false" may nevertheless correspond more nearly to moral and metaphysical "Truth" than what is literally "true."

To begin with, the practical indivisibility of truth is assumed by all parties in the play. When Henry denounces Perkin as a "false apparition" (I.i.2), he means both that Perkin's claim is literally fraudulent and that his kingship (not being based on "true" birth) lacks the sanction of Divine Truth. He is also, as a revolted subject, false to the "troth" he owes his king. Henry does not need to be conscious of these several meanings: at this point they are simply felt as one. The interrogation of Clifford, however, begins to open ambiguities: the informer hopes that the literal truth of his "paper" will restore the honor lost by his breach of troth to Henry (I.iii.21–34), but fidelity to one truth involves the dishonorable violation of another:

> O sir, here I must break
> A most unlawful oath to keep a just one.
>
> (ll. 73–74)

The uncomfortable paradox mirrors that which confronts Henry when he orders the execution of Stanley. On this act, as Durham reminds him, both the justice (truth) of the Yorkist claim and the troth of his peers will be seen to depend (II.ii.14–24), so that if Henry is true to his impulse to pardon one who has hitherto been true to him, he will thereby prove himself untrue. In the end the paradox has to be resolved with a kind of shrug (II.ii.26–27), since the "state's safety" is necessarily reliant on the dubious "truth" of the informer (l. 81), and the effective power of "six and twenty thousand" soldiers "loyal in their truths" (ll. 131–135). This is the lesson which James of Scotland has to learn; by denying his troth to Perkin for the sake of the "honest truth" of policy, he studies, in Henry's words, "to be wise betimes" (V.ii.18–19). His wisdom is precisely that of the politician Frion, a "wiseman" in the anti-stoic sense pointed out with gentle irony by Perkin, who knows "how to sooth / Adversity, not serve it" (IV.iii.136–137): for the politic-wise man, however "true," must always be "familiar with the Fox" (l. 147).

Not only by the standards of "state," but by all normal standards, Perkin's claim to "truth" is even less substantial than Henry's. For all his persistent appeals to "The truth of mine inheritance" (III.iv.60) and

"the truth / Of my dear mother's womb" (IV.ii.28–29), there is nothing
to suggest that the "true relation" (II.i.54) of his fortunes by which he
first establishes his claim to royalty is anything other than a finely contrived fiction. From the point of view of literal reason he is no more
than a "counterfeit," a coiner of false truth. In the language of Tudor
propaganda he even becomes the spokesman of the devil, the father of
lies, the embodied opposite of Divine Truth itself (V.iii.103–110). Yet
by the time we have indeed heard, in Perkin's own phrase, "A truth of
my sad ending" (III.ii.151), it so amply justifies his promise to die
worthy of his right "By falling like a King" (l. 154), that the fiction
seems transformed into a kind of truth. Appearance not only cozens
Truth, but appears to have become true, easily surviving Henry's re-
ductive explanation that a "familiar dialogue . . . learnt by heart, [is]
now received for truth" (V.ii.78–79). If Perkin is not quite "Truth in
her pure simplicity" (l. 80), he can at least with no hint of rodomontade
offer his performances to posterity "Without another chronicle than
truth" (V.iii.73). The mere events of Perkin's career may indeed belong
to the insubstantial realm of "dream" and "fancy," as Henry remarks
(V.ii.8–9), but his performance belongs to the lasting truth of chronicle.

What principally justifies Perkin's claim to truth is constancy—the
constancy which he himself displays, and the constant troth which he
commands from those nearest him. His determination to remain true to
the (false) role in which he has cast himself, to "prove as trusty in our
payments / As prodigal to nature in our debts" (V.iii.197–198), is best
expressed in the dizzying paradoxes of his rebuke to Frion:

> If, if I will appear!
> Appear a prince! Death throttle such deceits
> Even in their birth of utterance; cursed cozenage
> Of trust! Ye make me mad; 'twere best, it seems,
> That I should turn impostor to myself,
> Be mine own counterfeit, belie the truth. . . .
>
> (IV.ii.23–28)

In Ford's mannerist universe, as in Montaigne's, it is no light matter to
play but one man: to achieve that kind of consistency one has to become
the thing one has decided (however arbitrarily) to enact. For Perkin to
think in terms of the self-conscious manipulation of appearances would
be, in effect, to deny the reality of the persona he has elected to inhabit,

to substitute a willful deceit for a magically fabricated truth. He would become the counterfeiter of his own (invented) self and a falsifier of the (false) truth. The paradoxes on which Perkin's "truth" is founded are made to seem less outrageous by the simple truth of Katherine. Hers is also, in part at least, truth to a chosen role, but a role which is publicly determined rather than privately elected:

> Where my obedience is, my lord, a duty,
> Love owes true service.
>
> (II.iii.84–85)

Because the role is rooted in a sense of moral obligation, and because it supplies a definition of the self in terms of its relation to others, it helps to qualify the impression of narcissistic solipsism which the single-mindedness of Perkin's performance can create. Perkin himself senses that his own truth is validated and crowned by his monarchy "Of one chaste wife's troth pure and uncorrupted" (V.iii.127), her "true merit" (l. 130) serving as a warrant for his. In turn, Katherine's own fidelity to the initial "equal pledge of troths" (II.iii.88) is given warrant by the constant loyalty of her followers, above all Dalyell, whose "generous truth" wins a tribute even from Henry (V.ii.164). And the entire pageant of constancy (or truth) is finally endorsed by the unforced tributes of Huntley, himself hailed by Dalyell in their first scene together as "The living stock and root of truth and wisdom" (I.ii.125).

In the end Perkin, by his kingship of Katherine's heart and his kingship over death, does in some sense ascend "truth's old throne," the seat from which he imagined himself dispensing rule (IV.v.53). That conclusion may stretch paradox to its limits, but the wonder of the paradox affects even enemies like Daubeney. Henry, of course, maintains a judicious distinction between the wonderful and the true:

> We observe no wonder; I behold, 'tis true,
> An ornament of nature, fine and polished,
> A handsome youth indeed, but not admire him.
>
> (V.ii.37–39)

But Daubeney, as we have seen, is infected with reluctant admiration even in his final outraged "impostor beyond precedent" (V.iii.208). And in this remark there is lurking contradiction. For if there is indeed no precedent for such "imposture," it remains a question whether the word can properly be applied to Perkin at all, since it is in effect from precedent that words derive their meaning. It is as if the categories of ordinary language, for Daubeney as for Huntley, were somehow inadequate to cope with the "strange truth" of Perkin's imposition on reality. Before the triumphant paradox of a lie whose truth is proved by constancy, the resources of rational discourse fail; and Huntley's abnegation of judgment implies that there is an unbridgeable gulf between human reason and its social expression, law, on the one hand, and the world of art and imagination on the other:

> I have
> Not thoughts left; 'tis sufficient in such cases
> Just laws ought to proceed.
>
> (V.iii.209–211)

The sound political maxim which Henry attaches by way of motto to the spectacle of Perkin's execution is indeed "sufficient" for the pragmatic needs of "use"—

> public states,
> As our particular bodies, taste most good
> In health, when purgèd of corrupted blood.
>
> (V.iii.217–219)

But if the truths of Perkin's performance are irrelevant to the world of rational expediency, then the values which he represents are equally invulnerable to the judgments of political reason. In the public world, as Perkin himself points out, "Justice" (the instrument of Truth) simply amounts to what is required by the "safety" of king and commonwealth. In the private realm of the Cockpit, at least, Ford can allow his audience to glimpse the possibility of a world ordered by altogether different values.

III. Ontological Paradox: Perkin as "King of Hearts"

Kaufmann has spoken of Ford's interest in characters who chose to create themselves through certain arbitrarily selected roles,[19] and Perkin is perhaps the best example of such self-made heroes. But the phenomenon which he represents is not altogether a new one, for the paradox of

---

19. R. J. Kaufmann, "Ford's Tragic Perspective," *TSLL,* I (1960), 536.

pathopoeia—the process by which the rhetorician or actor creates a real emotion (and hence, implicitly, a personality) as it were *ex nihilo*—is a familiar constituent of mannerist drama from Hamlet's introspective agony to the naïve delusions of Massinger's Domitia in *The Roman Actor*. In *Perkin Warbeck*, Henry uses a crude version of this idea to account for what he takes to be the delusional madness of Perkin:

> The custom, sure, of being styled a king
> Hath fastened in his thought that he is such.
>
> (V.ii.132–133)

Ford does not so much reject this supposition as circumvent it. Since the "inner self" is something so inconstant, shifting, and obscure (even to ourselves) as to make any quest for it chimerical, we can only judge the man by the outward persona.[20] Thus Perkin is to be judged not by the literal truth or falsehood of his claims, nor by any readily attributable motive (madness, malice, or ambition), but simply by his ability, in Antony's words, to "hold this visible shape" (*Antony and Cleopatra*, IV.xiv.14). It is by this constancy to a role that the play defines the peculiar notion of "honour" or "nobility" which is its chief moral value. This "honour" is as far divorced from traditional honor of title and caste as is Tamburlaine's, but it is also quite unconnected with any claim to effective power: in the end it is purely a function of style, of *maniera*.

The problem of identity is one which asserts itself in several ways in the play. Sometimes it is implied by the contradictory demands of form and affection, of the public "person" and the private "self." Thus Huntley responds to Dalyell's courtship of his daughter with a para-doxical expression of self-division, "I would a' had my daughter so I knew't not" (I.ii.44), a self-division which his deceptively simple in-junction to Katherine ("Thou art thine own," l. 124) actually imposes on her too, and which is enacted in the ceremonial of choice he devises for her—"Keep you on that hand of her; I on this . . ." (ll. 94 ff.). In a similar way, Henry feels his identity threatened when the treason of Stanley, his other self, "The all of all I am!" (I.iii.109), forces a division between the demands of personal emotion and political safety; and his

20. Cf. Henry's own remark at II.ii. 829–830. For a discussion of *pathopoeia* see C. O. McDonald, *The Rhetoric of Tragedy* (Amherst, Mass., 1966), pp. 122–130.

response—"let me turn traitor / To mine own person"—is a threat to betray his royal "person" with the passion of his private self (ll. 110–112). Henry's sense of identity is shaken by Stanley's desertion, whereas Perkin's is confirmed by Katherine's constancy. A minor character like Jane can equally feel the reality of her "self" to be bound up with her allegiance to her mistress:

> I wait but as the shadow to the body;
> For, madam, without you let me be nothing.
>
> (IV.v.22–23)

Her speech echoes the imagery of Perkin's playacting in a tantalizing way, as do Dalyell's earlier tribute to Katherine and his compliment to Huntley:

> for, stood I in my first
> And native greatness, if my princely mistress
> Vouchsafed me not her servant, 'twere as good
> I were reduced to clownery, to nothing,
> As to a throne of wonder.
>
> (I.ii.38–42)

> How can you cast a mist upon your griefs?
> Which howsoe'er you shadow but present
> To any judging eye the perfect substance
> Of which mine are but counterfeits.
>
> (III.ii.19–22)

Perkin Warbeck presents a society where the language of Hamlet's philosophical perplexity has become part of the common currency of speech. In Ford's world it is taken for granted that the substantiality of being is always liable to mockery from the shadows of performance. In the very first speech of the play Henry feels his royal self so haunted by "false apparitions / Of pageant majesty" that the real and imaginary threaten to become interchangeable, the true king appearing as "a mockery-king in state" (I.i.1–4); so that "Ourself is scarce secure" (l. 14) —where the "self" concerned is both the enthroned public persona of the king and the personal self whose security depends on the maintenance of the public role. But as Henry knows (II.ii.51–52), and as James is later to discover, the secret of being a prince lies in the simple Machiavellian resolution to "live master of mine own" (IV.iii.82): one is king by virtue of what is one's own, what one possesses—royal identity is merely a function of effective power. For Perkin, on the other hand, the discovery of identity is a consequence of the stripping away of all claim to power, and of the stoical realization that only "our cause and courage are our own" (IV.iii.111)—that all one can truly "own" is private resolution.

In the early part of the play Perkin imagines the self in purely theatrical terms, recalling his childhood experience as a process of being "taught to unlearn myself" (II.i.69), as though personality were indeed a kind of actor's part. By the end of the play, however, such metaphors have become the property of Henrician propaganda (V.ii.67–69), while Perkin has become the thing he seemed to be; and if his cause fails in the pragmatic sense, it nevertheless succeeds in endowing him with royal "titles" which transcend those of mere political kingship. His achievement is a mannerist version of the Stoic paradox that kings are slaves and wise men kings.

A clue to the basic conceit by which Perkin's titles are established is provided in his reply to Henry's gibe at his "dialogue . . . learnt by heart (ll. 78–79)—"Truth in her pure simplicity wants art" (ll. 80 ff.). Perkin can appeal from art to truth, because an art which is learnt truly "by heart" becomes the truth. When, a few lines earlier, Henry urges him to "turn now thine eyes . . . upon thy self, and thy past actions," actions which he presents as the theatrical "revels" of a dancer in a masque (ll. 48–53), Perkin's appeal is similarly from art to the truth of the heart:

> But not my heart; my heart
> Will mount till every drop of blood be frozen
> By death's perpetual winter.
>
> (ll. 53–55)

It is characteristic of the play's paradoxical wit that the title "king of hearts" which becomes part of Perkin's blazon of triumph should be coined by one of his foolish councilors (IV.v.32), where it carries a strong charge of unintentional irony—the player as playing-card king. But it also echoes the imagery of love's monarchy introduced in Perkin's and Katherine's troth-plightings before and after their wedding:

> Acknowledge me but sovereign of this kingdom,
> Your heart, fair princess, and the hand of providence
> Shall crown you queen of me. . . .
>
> (II.iii.81–83)

You must be king of me, and my poor heart
Is all I can call mine.

(III.ii.168–169)

Perkin is to use the image again in a purely complimentary way during his farewell to James:

Two empires firmly
You're lord of—Scotland and duke Richard's heart.

(IV.iii.92–93)

But the title sounds with full power only in the last scene, in the splendid rhetoric of his tribute to Katherine's constancy:

Spite of tyranny,
We reign in our affections, blessed woman!

. . . .

since herein,
Even when I fell, I stood enthroned a monarch
Of one chaste wife's troth pure and uncorrupted.

(V.iii.121–127)

It echoes again in his legacy of "My heart, the rich remains of all my fortunes" (l. 143), and gives a special intensity to his simple leave-taking from Dalyell:

To you, Lord Dalyell—what? Accept a sigh,
'Tis hearty and in earnest.

(ll. 180–181)

In this context the final claim to the royal "style" of "Kings o'er Death" becomes not merely a reassertion of the old Stoic adage, but a fresh realization of the culminating paradox in *The Broken Heart* that "Love only reigns in death" (*Broken Heart,* IV.iii.43). In *Perkin Warbeck* art and heart combine to exercise a triumph over mortality and change, in a paradox that will "Impoverish time of its amazement" (l. 196).

IV. "A Mockery King in State": The Triumph of Ceremony

Ford's mannerist *dimostrazione* takes remarkable risks in the establishment of its fancy. The very theatrical metaphors that are ultimately used to declare Perkin's victory in defeat and to celebrate the triumph of

Ford's own art begin as images of fraudulence and insubstantiallty, supporting the judgment of historical orthodoxy exactly as they do in Bacon.[21] Having weighted the case so heavily against the Pretender in the first scene, Ford allows a complete act to elapse before Perkin himself is allowed an opportunity of redressing the balance. And even then the power of his rhetorical art is qualified by a remarkable stroke of dramatic artifice: Perkin's first three entrances are all set up as two-level scenes of the kind which Hoy relates to the mixed levels of mannerist painting.[22] This is particularly apparent in Act II, scene i, which is completely framed by the commentary of a stage "audience" composed of the Countess of Crawford, Katherine, and Jane "with other Ladies," who are placed, like many another stage audience, "above" where they may "observe . . . and be silent" (II.i.17). In the opening section they discuss the approaching spectacle of the "counterfeit" and his "goodly troop" of followers, "modest people" cast, in the best tradition of romance, as "disguised princes" (ll. 1–15). Within this framework, the ceremony of welcome is devised so as to draw further attention to its theatricality. The formal, masquelike entry described in the lengthy stage direction (ll. 39–40) is equipped by James with a suitably literary title, "majesty encounters majesty"; while Perkin in his opening address is himself made to image the fortunes of the House of York as a "tragedy" (l. 59),

> The vulgar story of a prince's ruin
>
> . . . .
>
> whose true relation draws
> Compassion, melted into weeping eyes
> And bleeding souls.
>
> (ll. 44–56)

The two subsequent scenes in which Perkin establishes himself at the Scottish court are both introduced by "audiences" who are more or less detached from the main action—Dalyell and Crawford in Act II, scene

21. See Ure, pp. xli–xlii, for comment on Ford's transformation of Bacon's acting metaphors.

22. Cyrus Hoy, "Jacobean Tragedy and the Mannerist Style," *ShS*, XXVI (1973), 63. Cf. Wylie Sypher, *Four Stages of Rennaissance Style* (New York, 1956), pp. 143–144, on the use of the *sprecher* in mannerism. Ure (p. lx) also notices the deliberate staginess of such episodes.

iii, and Huntley and Dalyell in Act III, scene ii. In the first of these the effect is emphasized by James's acting once again as a kind of presenter (ll. 73–76) and by the eagerness with which Perkin's antic followers display their enthusiasm for further "fashioning of shapes" in the projected court revels (l. 170).[23] These revels themselves in Act III, scene ii, reflect ironically on the histrionic nature of Perkin's performance, presenting in the wild antimasque of *"four* Scotch Antics . . . [and] *four wild* Irish *in trowses, long-haired, and accordingly habited"* (ll. 111–112 s.d.), a farcical image of the futile chivalric masquing in the coming invasion of England—later to be mocked by Henry as mere dancing "revels." [24]

Yet these very scenes, so mercilessly juxtaposed with others that reveal Henry's success in real action, impudently invite our admiration for the actor through the wonder he instills in his stage audiences. And in the last of them, after the masque has brought Perkin to his symbolic nadir, Ford begins the reversal through which heroism and histrionics are finally to become one. His vehicle is the moving farewell of the Pretender and his bride. It is the first time we have seen Perkin completely free from the ironic medium of a stage audience and also the only time we are to see him alone with Katherine, without a public at whom to pitch his performance. In consequence the scene must bear a good deal of emotional weight: but paradoxically its tone is not, at least to begin with, a conspicuously personal one. Instead of the expected revelation of Perkin's inner self, we get only an adjustment of the public mask, as he addresses Katherine in a style barely distinguishable from his public manner with its tendency to figurative abstraction and stylized emotionalism:

> Now, dearest, ere sweet sleep shall seal those eyes,
> Love's precious tapers, give me leave to use

23. Note also Heron's "Honour is honour, though cut out of any stuffs" (II.iii.111–112) and Skelton's "new suit of preferment" (l. 116), which cast an ironic light on Perkin's self-sufficient style of honor.

24. Cf. Perkin's unwittingly ironic description of war as "a sight of horror / For ladies' entertainment" (III.ii.149–150). Ure, p. lxix–lxx, discusses the ironic effect of the masque and suggests that it functions like an antimasque to "what may permissibly be called the main masque," the parting of Katherine and Warbeck. Barish (p. 170, n. 15), argues against this reading, but the irony is surely confirmed by the appearance of Perkin's followers in the uncomfortably suitable guise of barbarous "wild Irish."

A parting ceremony; for tomorrow
It would be sacrilege to intrude upon
The temple of thy peace.

(III.ii.139–143)

While elsewhere in Ford language of this kind may be deployed as a defense against intolerable feeling, here (in the absence of any context of passion) it strikes one simply as the projection of a self-image founded on the conventions of romance fiction:

thou withal
Shalt hear how I died worthy of my right
By falling like a King; and in the close
Which my last breath shall sound, thy name, thou fairest,
Shall sing a requiem to my soul, unwilling
Only of a greater glory 'cause divided
From such a heaven on earth as life with thee.

(III.ii.152–158)

And Perkin even completes the effect of studied artifice with a suitable motto—

For love and majesty are reconciled
And vow to crown thee empress of the West.

(ll. 161–162)

Katherine's reply is finely balanced between admiration and a still skeptical irony—the balance tipping upon the evenly weighted stresses on "noble" and "language," "right" and "me"; but the ambiguity disappears in the simple statement of duty and fidelity with which she concludes:

You have a noble language, sir; your right
In me is without question, and however
Events of time may shorten my deserts
In others' pity, yet it shall not stagger
Or constancy or duty in a wife.
You must be king of me, and my poor heart
Is all I can call mine.

(III.ii.163–169)

Katherine's restraint and plainness are doubly moving in contrast to Perkin's courtly eloquence, and the juxtaposition of opposing styles has an effect which is prophetic for the subsequent development of the play. Katherine contrives both to express, with a delicate indirection, her reservations about the rhetorical extravagance of Perkin's acted persona, and yet to acknowledge him as the sufficient object of her loyalty, at once to see the falsity of his role and yet grant it a kind of nobility. The moral decision involved, since it discounts the question of literal truth, may seem from one point of view as arbitrary as James's "instinct of sovereignty." But whereas events expose that "instinct" as mere caprice, springing from a fantastic opinion of his kingly role, Katherine's decision is a delicate exercise of the rational will, founded on the stoical recognition that

> What our destinies
> Have ruled out in their books we must not search,
> But kneel to.
>
> (III.ii.180–182)

It is important to notice also that this recognition constitutes not a passive resignation to fate but a commitment to that active cooperation with providence by which the neo-Stoic wise man made himself free. Katherine becomes "her own" by virtue of her constancy to that "duty in a wife" which fate has imposed on her, a constancy which is expressed in repeated moments of autonomous decision: when James dismisses Perkin from his court (IV.iii.101–103), when she finds herself in Cornwall forsaken and deprived of hope (V.i.19–33), when she is confronted by the courtly temptations of Henry (V.ii.155–162), and finally when she chooses to share Perkin's public dishonor in the stocks (V.iii.81–88, 112–120). The style in which these asseverations are made—spare, monosyllabic, stripped of all metaphor and artifice, except for the occasional decorous abstractions of moral allegory—is the verbal equivalent of the absolute, irreducible fact which she so stubbornly invokes:

> I am your wife;
> No human power can or shall divorce
> My faith from duty.
>
> (IV.iii.101–103)

> O sir, I have a husband.
>
> (V.ii.155)

> You abuse us:
> For when the holy churchman joined our hands,
> Our vows were real then; the ceremony

Was not in apparition, but in act.
But what these people term thee, I am certain
Thou art my husband, no divorce in heaven
Has been sued out between us; 'tis injustice
For any earthly power to divide us;
Or we will live or let us die together.

(V.iii.112–120)

This last speech, with its unflinching juxtaposition of "apparition" and "act," is both her boldest confrontation of Perkin's pretense and the final demonstration of its irrelevance. What knits up the distinction between apparition and reality, acting and act is "ceremony," a kind of performance which can confer its own reality through the magic of ritual. The rite of marriage is appealed to as the ceremony which invested Katherine and Perkin with the only titles which properly declare "what" they are, "wife" and "husband." It is Katherine's deep emotional commitment to the values of duty and decorum embodied in the ideal of ceremony as both the foundation and the expression of love which protects her from the destructive self-division of Penthea. Constructing her life by this severe moral aesthetic, and realizing her being in a consciously chosen and unflinchingly acted role, she supplies Perkin's own shadowy performance with the substance it otherwise lacks. Fittingly, therefore, it is through the conversion of Perkin's humiliation into a ceremony of love and duty that they are able to enact the final triumph of Truth over the accidents of Time.

As the play moves toward its close, the action tends to crystallize around moments of ceremonial calm. In Act IV, scene v, responding to Perkin's celebration of her as "Unequalled pattern of a matchless wife" (l. 11), Katherine composes a tableau of virtue in extremes, using the style of allegorized abstraction appropriate to such a "pattern":

I shall learn
Patience to hope, since Silence courts Affliction
For comforts, to this truly noble gentleman—
Rare unexampled pattern of a friend!—
And my beloved Jane, the willing follower
Of all Misfortunes.

(IV.v.14–19)[25]

25. I have slightly altered the capitalization of this and some of the following quotations in order to emphasize the allegorical aspect of the language.

Dalyell and Jane reply in stylized antiphons, sounding almost like allegorical embodiments of the two kinds of "service" (ll. 19–23). Again, at the beginning of Act V, when Katherine and Jane reappear conspicuously deprived of all the trappings of pomp, one is struck by the same tendency to reduce the personal situation to abstract, impersonal terms, which hold it at a distance like a formalized *exemplum:*

> KATHERINE
> It is decreed; and we must yield to Fate,
> Whose angry Justice, though it threaten ruin,
> Contempt, and poverty, is all but trial
> Of a weak woman's constancy in suffering.
>
> (V.i.1–4)

Genuine emotion is not so much excluded as transformed by this conscious stylization: they are "spectacles to Time and Pity" (l.29), figures of stoical Virtue in a pageant-tableau of Misery. A more elaborately artificial example of the same habit occurs in Act V, scene ii, where Perkin presents his enterprise as part of the archetypal struggle of right and wrong:

> Truth in her pure simplicity wants art
> To put a feignèd blush on. Scorn wears only
> Such fashion as commends to gazers' eyes
> Sad ulcerated novelty, far beneath
> The sphere of majesty. In such a court,
> Wisdom and Gravity are proper robes
> By which the sovereign is best distinguished
> From zanies to his greatness.
>
> (V.ii.80–87)[26]

For Henry, the figures in Perkin's speech belong to some ineptly moralized pageant—

> Sirrah, shift
> Your antic pageantry.
>
> (ll. 87–88)

But the continuation of Perkin's allegory neatly strips the rhetorical gilding from Henry's own performance—

26. Perkin's earlier speech at IV.v.47–64, though more extravagant, is built on a similar allegorical framework.

> I expect
> No less than what Severity calls justice,
> And politicians safety.
>
> (ll. 90–92)

As a result, Perkin's exit line becomes an acceptable motto for the whole scene: "Noble thoughts / Meet freedom in captivity (ll. 127–128). But the most splendid of these ceremonies of constancy occurs in the last scene of the play, where Perkin, humiliatingly displayed in the stocks and awaiting the dishonorable death of hanging, achieves his most celebrated tour de force. Appropriately, in a scene that concentrates and draws together the paradoxes of this "Strange Truth," it is at once the most lavishly theatrical and the most touchingly personal episode of the play, combining speeches in Perkin's most expansive grand manner with moments of extraordinary simplicity and directness of feeling. And Perkin himself is able to combine these opposites with an effortlessly graceful sense of decorum that contrasts sharply with his erratic changes of manner earlier in the play. In his confrontation with Urswick and Simnel, Perkin has already imagined his last memorable scene in highly theatrical terms (V.iii.70–75) as a "spectacle" which will prove a fitting subject for a "chronicle." The motto-title he gives it, "A Martyrdom of Majesty," could serve as an alternative subtitle for Ford's own "Chronicle History," and this piece of mannerist self-reference (the first of several in the scene) helps to emphasize its self-conscious theatricality.[27]

27. The scene can also be regarded, from the point of view of Henry's supporters, as a staged ritual of degradation, which Katherine upsets by crossing the appointed boundary between audience and performers—hence the anger of Oxford and Surrey (ll. 111–112, 133–137, 157–160). Henry's own attitude to ceremonial is well suggested by his remark to Hialas, "To fall on ceremony, would seem useless" (III.iii.22); though he knows well how to use it—witness the motto with which he confers ceremonial status on his greeting of Katherine: "Here lives Majesty / At league with Love" (V.ii.154–155). Another aspect of the scene's ritual which deserves notice is its manipulation of the temptation pattern from Morality drama, which Ford uses at several key points in the play. In Act III, scene iv, Perkin and Bishop Fox compete for the roles of Good and Bad Angel to James, while Crawford and Dalyell act as pious chorus (ll. 36–54). In Act IV, scene iii, when James enters with "Durham *and* Hialas *on either side,*" whispering their silky antiphon in either ear, he looks for all the world like Mankind beset by Vices, or Ford's own Raybright in the grip of Humor and Folly (*The Sun's Darling*)—except that these

Throughout the scene Perkin draws attention to the symbolic significance
of the action: by her sufferance in perseverance Katherine is transformed
from a "mere woman" (in Calantha's phrase) to a "Great miracle of constancy" (l. 89), "a pattern / For every virtuous wife" (ll. 93–94), a "Fair
angel of perfection" (l. 128), a "saint . . . in the calendar of virtue"
(l. 131); so that her performance is translated through "report" and
"story" (ll. 92, 97) out of the immediate moment into the "immortality" of
chronicle—into the realm of art. Like Ford's play itself, her story is a
strange truth which has so "outdone belief" that to future generations it
may even "appear a fable" (ll. 95–97). At the same time it has a transforming effect on Perkin's own actions, so that what was to have been
the "triumph" of Henry's fame (l. 102), becomes through Katherine's
faith, a triumph of Perkin's honor and royalty, a splendid realization of
the metaphors in which their love was first declared:

> Spite of tyranny
> We reign in our affections, blessed woman!
> Read in my destiny the wrack of honour;
> Point out, in my contempt of death, to memory
> Some miserable happiness: since herein,
> Even when I fell, I stood enthroned a monarch
> Of one chaste wife's troth pure and uncorrupted.
>   (V.iii.121–127)

This speech has a fine rhetorical breath which does ample justice to
Perkin's theatrical sense of occasion: it is spoken in full consciousness of
the "gaze so public" to which Oxford refers in his next speech (l. 135)[28]
—as the calculated wit of its oxymorons suggests; and it anticipates the

---

tempters, as befits the representatives of a purely politic "providence," use the
rhetoric of piety (ll. 14–19). But if the effect of using the Morality pattern in that
scene is simply to emphasize its irrelevance to the world of policy, when the device
is used a third time the effect is different: the threats and inducements of Urswick
and Simnel in their temptation of Perkin recall the hypocritical persuasions of Despair and Sloth, masked in piety (V.iii.10–80); and the Pretender's magnificent re-
sistance calls in question the decisiveness of political "providence," so that the old
form is invested with a new life and Perkin becomes the spiritual hero of a secular
morality.

    28. Oxford's line has the effect of further blurring the boundaries between acting
and reality by drawing the audience in a familiar way into the gallery of spectators at Perkin's end.

movement and manner of the last address to his followers fifty lines later. Yet it chimes beautifully, in its emotional restraint and the relative sparceness of its language with the private ceremony of duty enacted by Katherine. This begins with a new recitation of her marriage vows (ll. 116–120), and is completed in a kiss, which reenacts in a minor key Calantha's last ritual in *The Broken Heart:* [29]

KATHERINE

Sir,
Impute it not unto immodesty
That I presume to press you to a legacy
Before we part for ever.

WARBECK

Let it be, then,
My heart, the rich remains of all my fortunes.

KATHERINE

Confirm it with a kiss, pray.
. . . .
By this sweet pledge of both our souls, I swear
To die a faithful widow to thy bed—
Not to be forced or won. O, never, never!

(V.iii.139–153)

At this point Huntley enters, this time to pass the formal blessing on the marriage which he has so far withheld (ll. 160–174).

In its movements toward allegorical abstraction ("trials of a patience," "the wonder of your frailty, / Which keeps so firm a station"), Huntley's speech pays its surprisingly decorous tribute to the formal dignity of the pageant of constancy. But the main effect of his language is one of distilled simplicity quite different from the exaggerated Dekkerian bluntness with which he sometimes masks his feelings. Here all distinctions between manner and meaning are stripped away, the language is as unambiguous and unadorned as the truth it acknowledges. Where at their previous parting Katherine was "this sometime child of mine" (IV.iii.149), at best a mere image of his own misery ("This model of my

29. Like Calantha's ritual, it combines the paradoxes of Love-in-Death and Marriage-in-Funeral, as well as picking up the "will" conceit used by both Penthea and Calantha.

griefs," IV.iii.158), he is now able to accept the full meaning of the freedom he granted her in their first scene—a freedom paradoxically realized in the willed enjoyment of "duty to a husband." That this duty no longer seems incompatible with honor and "title to old Huntly's family" (IV.iii.152), is due to the transforming power of "constancy," "patience," and "sufferance." The ironic reservation of the earlier scene ("she *calls* you husband," IV.iii.158; italics added) is now gracefully replaced by the directness of "your husband— / For such you *are,* sir,"—(V.iii.168–169; italics added). Where so much emotion is invested in the slight change of verb, where so large a weight of moral judgment rests on the invocation of the bare terms of familial relationship, "wife," "daughter," and "husband," where the elaborate courtesies of speech are pared away, and only the ceremonial forms of action remain to supply the order of decorum, language hangs (as it so often does in Ford) on the brink of silence. And indeed Perkin's simple last exchange with Crawford and Dalyell ends with the failure of language in Dalyell's declaration of *veritas in silentio* and Katherine's breakdown into incoherent, wordless grief:

> DALYELL
>
> I want utterance:
> My silence is my farewell.
>
> KATHERINE
>
> Oh—Oh—
>
> JANE
>
> Sweet madam,
> What do you mean?—My lord, your hand.
>
> (V.iii.181–183)

Language and its refinements of meaning give way to a last hieratic gesture of fidelity.

But if language reaches the limits of its capacity to order and define in the realm of private relationships, it must still, by the paradoxical logic of the scene, have its final triumph in the public world. If the truth of personal constancy is most completely declared in silence, the strange truth of constancy-in-performance can only declare itself in a last flight of rhetoric. Rhetoric's "sounds" and "names of air" may in the end be validated only by silence, as the last bravura performance itself is validated by the silence of death; yet rhetoric and performance are in turn designed to encompass a victory over death and silence:

> illustrious mention
> Shall blaze our names, and style us Kings o'er Death
>
> (V.iii.206–207)

—a victory realized, as this last self-referential flourish reminds us, in the play itself which confers on Perkin the eternity of fame in a new "coronation" contrived by the arts of poetry and acting. Fittingly, Perkin's last speech makes commanding use of theatrical metaphor, picking up and toying with Oxford's implicit sneer at pageant majesty with the almost insolent ease of a true Courtier: at one moment he is the leading figure in a processional "triumph over tyranny" (l. 188); and at another (with a graceful self-depreciation quite new to him), merely the "Prologue" to "Innocent Warwick's . . . tragedy" (ll. 191–192). His and Warwick's executions seem to form the last part of a splendid historical pageant-show whose movement is imitated in the strong, ascendant rhythms of the verse:

> and then the glorious race
> Of fourteen kings, Plantagenets, determines
> In this last issue male.
>
> (V.iii.193–195)

Then, after a climactic appeal to the splendor of embodied paradox—

> Impoverish Time of its amazement, friends,
> And we will prove as trusty in our payments
> As prodigal to Nature in our debts
>
> (V.iii.196–198)

—the proud declamatory movement and confident sweep of the first part of the speech (the last and finest display of Perkin's royal manner), gives way without any sense of strain, to the curter style of Lipsian consolation. The rhythms here, abrupt, even staccato to begin with, nevertheless move toward their own superbly confident climax, evoking from Daubeney (of all people) a reluctant acknowledgment of the "wonder" he invited so mockingly in the previous scene (V.ii.36):

WARBECK

Death? pish, 'tis but a sound, a name of air,
A minute's storm, or not so much; to tumble
From bed to bed, be massacred alive
By some physicians for a month or two,
In hope of freedom from a fever's torments,
Might stagger manhood; here, the pain is passed
Ere sensibly 'tis felt. Be men of spirit,
Spurn coward passion! So illustrious mention
Shall blaze our names, and style us Kings o'er Death.

DAUBENEY

Away—imposter beyond precedent.
No chronicle records his fellow.

(V.iii.199–209)

Ecphrasis and Dramaturgy: Leonardo's Leda in Rucellai's Oreste

JOHN A. BERTOLINI

W HEN GIOVANNI RUCELLAI adapted Euripides' *Iphigenia in Tauris* as *Oreste* in the last decade of his life (1516–1525), he did not merely unearth a Greek corpse and costume it in Italian as did some other would-be revivers of Greek tragedy in the Renaissance; he chose instead to reconstruct it as a drama of self-discovery for an audience of sixteenth-century humanists. It bears the same relationship to its model as, say, Anouilh's *Antigone* does to the Sophoclean original; that is, the model is reshaped. His method was to invent details of plot and characterization and then transplant them into the body of Euripides' play in order to make it live again as something new. The action of Rucellai's play can be stated simply: Orestes survives the danger of becoming a human sacrifice at his sister's hands. But the soul of the play is interested in more than the question of physical survival; it is vitally concerned with the recognition of the brother by the sister as a form of self-discovery for the protagonist, as we shall see.

Yet the soul of a play only lives when it informs a body; and the legs upon which the body of this play stands are two separate expositions, one for Orestes and one for Iphigenia, both provided successively in the first

Leonardo da Vinci, *Leda and the Swan* (copy). Reproduced by courtesy of *Scala,* New York

act. Rucellai emphasizes the separateness of the two histories because he
means to focus his play on the climax of the two stories in the fourth act,
so that the play's structure, shaped by the intersection of the two story
lines, becomes symbolic of his meaning: recognition as rediscovery and
understanding of one's true identity. It is not merely that Orestes is unknown to Iphigenia and she unknown to him; Orestes does not know
himself. And he only attains self-knowledge when Iphigenia demands
that he prove his identity by describing a painting that hung in Agamemnon's bedroom. This ecphrasis by which Rucellai cunningly has
Orestes reveal himself to his sister is a detailed description of Leonardo
da Vinci's *Leda and the Swan,* which is also of course a kind of visual
family tree for Iphigenia and Orestes, showing their maternal ancestry.
Why Rucellai used a well-known and much copied contemporary painting as the device of recognition and what meaning he found in it can
only be understood through an analysis of his dramaturgy. Orestes' exposition in the first scene provides the initial direction toward understanding that meaning:

ORESTE

Se ben, Pilade, sai l'alto misterio
Che n'ha condotti in questa cruda terra,
Che'l pelago di Scitia attorno bagna,
Salvo ove si ristrigne, e'l sottil collo,
Quasi sporgendo in fra duo mari ondosi,
S'attiene al corpo de la madre antica,
Di cui l'empio Toante ha 'l freno in mano,
Barbar'uomo, e di barbari tiranno;
Non di men, se ti piace, a me fia grato,
A ciò che 'ntenda chiaramente il tutto,
Narrarti a parte a parte da principio
L'istoria con brevissime parole.

PILADE

Oreste, ancor ch'i più alti consigli,
Ch'ascondon le latebre del tuo petto,
Tralucan come vetro entro 'l mio core
Per la communion de l'amor nostro;
Pur, come di', per me'saperne il vero,
E perch'a me grat'è quant'a te piace,

Deh dilla dal principio insino al fine,
Ma non già con brevissime parole.[1]

(I.1–20)

ORESTES

Though you well know, Pylades, the profound mystery that has led us to
this cruel land, which the Scythian sea washes all around, except where it
narrows, and the slender neck as if jutting out between two rough seas
stretches itself to the body of the ancient mother, whose bridle the impious
Thoas keeps in hand—a barbarian himself and a king of barbarians; even
so, if it pleases you, so that you may understand everything clearly, I would
like to tell you step by step from the beginning the story in a few words.

PYLADES

Orestes, though the deepest deliberations which the depths of your bosom
conceal shine clearly (as through glass) into my heart because of the communion of love between us; yet as you say, so that I may know the truth
of it, and because whatever pleases you also pleases me, then tell it from the
beginning through to the end, but not just in a few words.

Though this opening is crude in technique, it is traditional and thorough in giving the audience essential information: we learn immediately
who the speakers are, that they are intimate friends, where they are and
who rules there, and generally why they have come—a profound mystery
("l'alto misterio") has brought them.[2] Their purpose is, as Orestes goes
on to explain, to take the statue of Diana from Tauris to Athens in order
that Orestes may be free of the Furies—that he may expiate the crime
of matricide and regain his lost self. But he can only erase his crime by

1. Giovanni Rucellai, *Opere,* ed. Guido Mazzoni (Bologna, 1887), pp. 109–110.
All quotations from the *Oreste* are from this edition.

2. The anonymous editor of the play in *Teatro Antico Italiano* (Milan, 1808–
1812), II, 12, complains that Orestes should have given Pylades all this information
while they were aboard ship, not at this dangerous moment of their arrival in
Tauris. And Pietro Napoli-Signorelli, in *Storia Critica dei Teatri Antichi e Moderni*
(Naples, 1813), v, 39, agrees with him. The anonymous editor further notes that
the only reason for these opening speeches is that the audience may know Orestes'
past. On the other hand he finds Iphigenia's exposition more natural because
Rucellai provides a reasonable motivation for it: Because she wants Olimpia to
help her send a letter to her brother, she must therefore explain her past.

bringing back to life the mother he has killed, by replacing her with a
substitute mother: gaining possession of Diana's statue is one way of
getting a second mother; recognizing Iphigenia his sister is another way;
remembering and describing a painting of his ancient mother Leda is
yet another, and the most important way as we will see. All three ways
are means to self-recognition for Orestes, to self-restoration, the healing of
his "spirito turbato insano" (I.67), the end of the wanderer's endless
wanderings:

ORESTE

Tu'l sai, ché non è monte o valle o piaggia,
Che stampata non sia da le mie strane
Furiose orme; e se l'aer serbasse
Le strida, saria pien de'miei lamenti:

(I.68–71)

ORESTES

You know it, because there is not a mountain, valley or shore unmarked by
my strange, madman's tracks; and if the air could store screams, it would
be filled with my cries.

Rucellai uses the conventional opening in part to convey necessary information, such as how Orestes avenged his father's murder, but also to
hint at other levels of meaning. That is why he makes Orestes describe
the topography of Tauris the way he does—the land narrows and
stretches itself, its slender neck, to reach the body of the ancient mother.
This is Orestes himself in search of the mother he has killed, the mother
who was dominated by the "infame e scelerato Egisto" (I.33)—infamous
and criminal Aegisthus—even as Iphigenia is trapped in Tauris, the bridle
of which is controlled by the impious Thoas, as Orestes himself tells us.
This is a relatively sophisticated use of exposition, considering that it is
only Rucellai's second play and only the third "regular" tragedy of the
Renaissance. Similarly, Rucellai turns the crude device of the confidant
to purposeful use. Pylades is a type, not an individual, because he is
Orestes' double. When Orestes tells Pylades his story, he is talking to
himself, to his mirror image: Orestes' most secret thoughts are as clear as
glass to Pylades—"come vetro entro'l mio core." They are not two but
one:

ORESTE

Da indi in qua, ch'io fui tuo, e tu mio,
Vive un'anima sola entr'a'due petti,
E vivrà sempre infino a l'ora estrema.

(I.56–58)

ORESTES

From then till now, when I became yours and you mine, lives one soul in two breasts, and will so live until the final hour.

Even that Orestes must tell his story to himself is significant: the set speech in which he narrates his crime is at once a verbal reenactment of that crime and a partial purgation of the guilt he feels because of it; it is also a work of art. So, too, his ultimate salvation lies in art, the acting out of the "profound mystery," possessing the statue of Diana, describing the painting of Leda and the Swan that was in Agamemnon's bedroom where he was conceived, the painting which shows his mother's mother, and which he must describe before he can recover his second mother, Iphigenia.

After this packed but static exposition, Rucellai animates the stage with movement. I say stage because, though there is no record of the play's having been performed until the eighteenth century,[3] it is clear that Rucellai imagines his play acted out in a theatrical space: the text is full of implicit stage directions, such as indications of setting, of movement from one part of the playing area to another, on and off stage, of the use of gesture and of properties. For example, Orestes and Pylades now cross from the shore to the temple, the inside of which they see through a nar-

3. Luigi Riccoboni, *An Historical and Critical Account of the Theatres in Europe* (London, 1741), p. 294: "I myself have, with Applause, played in 1712, in the *Sophonisba* of Trissino, and the *Oreste* of Rucellai." In his 1746 edition of the play Scipione Maffei indicates how it had been adapted for the stage in Venice. The main modification is in the deletion of all five of the choral odes and the substitution of an individual for the chorus where it takes part in the action. There are also indications for a temple and mountain to be seen in the background and a palace to be seen onstage, in place of the "forma dell'antica Scena, che facea veder più strade . . . parendo a noi in legendo gli antichi Drami, che uno faccia viaggio stando nell'istesso luogo"—the style of the old stage which showed several streets . . . which seems now to us sometimes while reading the old plays that one is traveling when standing still (*Teatro Italiano o sia Scelta di Tragedie per uso della Scena*, I, 165). Maffei's 1723 edition is the first printing of the play.

row window to be filled with gruesome evidence of the Taurians' barbarity, human heads dripping blood, human skins and piles of bones.
Such details are calculated to give the text a physical dimension that is
lacking in other sixteenth-century tragedies and to create a mood of
terror in which apprehension for the possible fate of the two strangers is
excited, a mood that Rucellai then extends into a suspenseful sequence.
One of the chorus of Taurian women enters, is overheard by Pylades
who, though he does not understand the language spoken, sees the danger
of discovery and persuades Orestes to flee.

Iphigenia enters after the chorus of virgins has lamented the barbarity
of human sacrifice; she dismisses them and narrates to her confidante
Olimpia the story of her life. The emphasis here, as it was with Orestes,
is on the revelation of the secret self: she has concealed her true identity
for fifteen years, but has now decided to reveal herself because she wants
to send a letter to Orestes and needs the help of Olimpia. She sees herself
mainly as the daughter of Agamemnon and descendant of Jupiter, and
because she has dreamed of the collapse of her father's palace, she is
anxious to communicate with her brother. In this way Rucellai contrives
to make the motivation for her exposition plausible.[4] Their discussion
is interrupted by one of the chorus, who explains at length how two
strangers were sighted and captured after much struggle. Iphigenia ad-
mires the reported willingness of each one to die for the other as she
prepares to enter the temple and pray there. The chorus ends the act with
an ode in praise of the strength and piety of the two strangers.

In the second act Rucellai continues the revelation of the past as Orestes
answers Iphigenia's questions on the fate of Agamemnon. The first step
bringing them together is Iphigenia's excitement at hearing her native
speech: language itself is seen as art and as emotional memory:

IFIGENIA

Ah lassa me, che suon di voce è quello,
Che mi ferisce per gli orecchi il core?
Oimè, che sent'io? quest'è favella
De la mia dolce patria dov'io nacqui:
Io la conosco, io la conosco, io sento
La sua bella pronunzia e i dolci accenti.

4. See above, note 2.

Quanti e quant'anni ha già rivolto il cielo,
Ch'io non udi'giamai sì bella voce?

(II.76–83)

IPHIGENIA

Alas what sound is this which pierces me through the ears to the heart? Ah
me what do I hear? This is that language of the land where I was fathered.
I know this language, I recognize it and I hear its beautiful sound, its
sweet notes. How many years, how many has heaven revolved since I last
heard that lovely sound?

Iphigenia is not the only one hearing her native language at this moment;
so is the audience hearing their native Italian. And though Iphigenia is
supposedly speaking Greek, there can be no doubt that Rucellai intends
his audience to become aware that they are hearing a tragedy in Italian.
There is nothing strange about this way of catching the audience's attention; it might almost be expected of a humanist to include praise of his
native language. But only a skilled playwright could make this self-
awareness on the part of the audience coincide with the pattern of recognition and self-discovery that makes the fabric of this play. Nor is this
the last time Rucellai will achieve a double perspective on the action of
his drama as a self-conscious work of art.

For the present he is content to project the audience's desire to see the
story enacted, or hear the story told, by a continuation of the telling of
events anterior to the action of the play proper. Iphigenia questions these
Greeks about the fates of the various actors in the Troy story. And the
first answer she gets defines these events as a mode of art, as subjects for
narration. Orestes is unwilling to tell what is well known: "Coteste istorie
son nel mondo sparse / Per molte lingue, e ne son pieni i libri" (II.179–
180: These stories are known well throughout the world in many languages; whole books are filled with them). Finally Iphigenia draws from
Orestes the story of Agamemnon's murder, in a fuller version than that
recounted to Pylades in the first act. Orestes sees the act of narration itself
as a reliving of the event: ". . . mentre ch'io narro il duro fato, / Quasi
mi sia una seconda morte" (II.289–290: while I tell of fate's harsh working, it will be for me almost a second death). The telling then is the
reliving; art is interchangeable with life; what the audience sees through
hearing is a kind of reality. As Orestes tells his story he is affected by it
in place of the audience:

ORESTE

Or ecco, oimè, ch'io tremo per l'orrore!
L'angusta voce da i sospir rinchiusa
Rimane in mezzo fra la lingua e'l petto.

(II.327–329)

ORESTES

Look now, ah me, how I tremble at the horror of it! My sighs suppress my words and they remain caught between my heart and my tongue.

Iphigenia reacts as a proper audience should by loosing her imagination to terror: "Ovunque io volga l'affannata mente, / Io veggio mille imagini di morte" (II.334–335: Wherever I turn my breathless thoughts, I see a thousand images of death). Again like a good audience she demands revenge and learns to her satisfaction that the murderers of Agamemnon were indeed killed and that their executioner was Orestes. He refuses to see his deed as the murder of a mother, though:

IFIGENIA

Oreste dunque Clitemnestra uccise?

ORESTE

Oreste è quel c'ha vendicato il padre.

(II.393–394)

IPHIGENIA

Then it was Orestes who killed Clytemnestra?

ORESTES

Orestes it was who avenged his father.

As he sees it, he no longer has a mother; he is in search of one, but he has not found her yet. And the result is a confusion within himself between his existence in fact and his existence in story. When Iphigenia asks the stranger about the fate of Orestes, he deliberately plays on his double identity:

ORESTE

E'non è morto, e non si può dir vivo.

(II.451)

.   .   .   .

Io lo lasciai in un periglio tale,
Che poco poco più era la morte.

(ll. 453–454)

> . . . .
>   Io credo,
>   Ch'abbia ad esser di lui quel ch'è di me.
>
>   (ll. 455–456)

ORESTES

He is not dead, nor can it be said he is alive.

. . . .

I left him in such danger, that death is not much worse.

. . . .

I believe that what is about to happen to me is the same for him.

The play is actually about the reintegration of these two halves of Orestes, his past and his present. As his present advances steadily toward death with the mounting danger of becoming a human sacrifice, the alternate revelations of anterior action by Orestes and Iphigenia to one another reach further into the past; as the play's action-proper advances, the successive reactions to the approach of death, the play's interior action, gradual self-discovery, moves back step by step into the past.

In the first part of Act III Rucellai is concerned with developing the line of present action. Thoas is introduced and expresses sentiments appropriate to a bloodthirsty tyrant.[5] Even so, Iphigenia is determined to ask mercy for the brave strangers. And with her exit Orestes and Pylades are left to discuss their readiness to die in the language of Neo-Platonism: in general they want to die because their souls will be happier when they return to God. But this is only their way of consoling themselves. Orestes has a more positive and specific motivation for desiring death; he does not like the part he has played in his own story:

ORESTE

>   Poi veder bramo il mio sí caro padre
>   Solo per cui soffrir potuto ho tanto,
>   Che divenuto son favola al mondo;
>
>   (III.108–110)

ORESTES

Then, I hunger for the sight of my father, for whose sake alone I have been able to endure so much, that I have become a story for the world.

---

5. Mario Apollonio sees Thoas mainly as a theatrical figure based on the traditional Herod of popular drama: *Storia del Teatro Italiano* (Florence, 1951), pp. 210–216.

He is distracted momentarily from his resolve to die as the place of
sacrifice is pointed out to him—"fra quelle due colonne"—and he discovers that the priestess who has gone to intercede for them is also the
priestess who is going to sacrifice them. He is horrified, first because he
cannot believe she is capable of performing the rite, and second, but more
importantly, because he is reminded of the sacrifice of Iphigenia at Aulis.
He goes on to describe this scene as he remembers it in a kind of vision-
tableau:

ORESTE

Quand'io rivolgo gli occhi in quella parte
A l'apparato orribil e funesto,
E guardo in mezzo lo solenne altare,
Veder sopra mi par ginocchion posta
Ifigenia con gli occhi gravi a terra,
Di smorta pallidezza ornata il volto.
A piè le forti Argolice falangi,
Per cui valor conversa è Troia in cenere,
Non use a versar lagrime, ma sangue,
Pianger e sospirare amaramente;
Tal che pel duol da le robuste mani
Cadder i pitti scudi a terra e l'aste:
Poi'l vecchio padre per vergogna e doglia
Con l'ammanto real coprirsi il viso,
Ammanto per ornar le regal membra
Fatto, e non per velar la regal faccia:
E ch'ei dica quell'ultime parole
Da fare a tigre intenerire il petto;
La cui memoria mi fa pianger sempre.
E se ben era allor picciol fanciullo,
Quella sembianza ne la mente infissa,
Sveglia sí lo pensier de la pietade,
Che la piaga mal salda in mezzo al core
Si rompe, e versa fuor, come tu vedi,
Amarissime lagrime per gli occhi . . .[6]

(III.187–211)

6. I suspect that the scene Orestes recalls here may be taken from a painting,
but I have been unable to locate any depiction of the sacrifice of Iphigenia from
Rucellai's time. Though Rucellai could have taken certain details of the tableau
from several places (for example, he could have found Agamemnon covering his
face with his cloak in Euripides' *Iphigenia in Aulis*, ll. 1546–1550), he probably had
in mind the following passage from Leon Battista Alberti's *Della Pittura*, 1436:

ORESTES

When I turn my eyes toward that place, toward that terrible, deathly structure, and look right at the middle of the solemn altar, I seem to see on high
Iphigenia kneeling there with her sad eyes cast down, her face adorned with
a deathly pallor. At its base the Greek forces, by whose strength Troy was
turned to ashes, used to shedding blood not tears, weeping and sighing so
bitterly for the pity of it that their painted shields and spears dropped from
their strong hands: Then the old father out of shame and grief covering his
face with his royal cloak, the cloak made to clothe the royal body and not to
hide the royal face; and his saying those last words which would have made
tender a tiger's heart; the remembrance of them always makes me cry. And
even if I was only a little boy then, that look of hers fixed in my mind
awakens so the memory of pity, that the wound poorly bandaged in my
heart breaks open and pours forth from my eyes, as you see, the bitterest of
tears . . .

Orestes' recollection of this tableau gives him the strength to endure
death: he wishes to be worthy of her example. Remembering Iphigenia's
gravity in the face of misfortune exorcizes for him the particular ghost
of her horrible end. It is these traumatic experiences that Orestes is
progressively ridding himself of—the murder of his father, the sacrifice
of Iphigenia, the latter further back in time than the former. But Orestes
has not yet gone back far enough. Reliving this particular experience by
remembering still leaves him preferring death to life. Orestes the actor
has found a role that suits him.

"Timantes of Cyprus in his panel, the Immolation of Iphigenia, with which he
conquered Kolotes. He painted Calchas sad, Ulysses more sad, and in Menelaos, then,
he would have exhausted his art in showing him greatly grief stricken. Not having
any way in which to show the grief of the father, he threw a drape over his head
and let his most bitter grief be imagined, even though it was not seen" (*On
Painting,* trans. John R. Spencer, rev. ed. [New Haven and London, 1966], p. 78).
The ensemble of the scene as action seems suited to painting insofar as it obeys
Lessing's dictum that a painting should show figures acting simultaneously in space,
not successively in time. Also, later in the play, when Iphigenia alludes to this scene,
she adds the following detail to the tableau:

> Ed io sopr'una nugoletta d'oro
> Con diversi color dipinta e varia,
> Miracolosamente fui portata.   (IV. 194–196)

And I upon a cloud of gold painted with many different colors was miraculously carried away.
If Rucellai did not have a specific painting in mind, he certainly saw the scene as
a painter would have.

At this point one of the chorus enters with a costume for him to wear in his new role, a "bruno ammanto," along with Thoas's decree that one of the two must die and therefore signify his choice by putting on the "brown cloak." Here is Rucellai particularizing his drama, concretizing its conflicts, theatricalizing the action: the cloak lies in front of the audience as a symbol of death. Orestes convinces Pylades that he must have the honor of dying in place of his friend,[7] for as he sees it his Sacrifice will be a rebirth into an eternal life—not through Neo-Platonic divine love, but into a new identity through art:

ORESTE

E si dirà dopo mill'anni forse:
Quanto fu'l cielo a quell'età cortese,
Che di vera amicizia illustrò il mondo!
E sarà mostra e detto da la gente:
Questa è la piaggia dove presi furo;
Qui l'un più volte l'altro col suo corpo
Coperse, e fegli con sue membra scudo;
Questa è la fonte dove ciascun bevve;
Ecco qua le bell'armi e i forti scudi,
Quelle di sangue barbaro ancor tinte,
Queste da dardi e freccie trapassati:
E questo santo altar fia mostro a dito;
E forse che fia sculta in bronzi e'n marmi
La nostra istoria; e poi da i chiari ingegni
Ne le scene e teatri celebrata,
Ed imitata da la gente umana
Tal sembianza di gloria e fortezza . . .

(III.382–398)

7. Lienhard Bergel, "The Rise of Cinquecento Tragedy," *RenD*, VIII (1965), 210: "*Oreste* is in essence one long drawn-out contest for the honor of dying a beautiful death." Though Rucellai certainly plays this theme, I do not think it is his essential concern. In choosing to emphasize this episode Rucellai may have been influenced by this passage from Cicero's *Laelius: On Friendship:* "For example, when my guest and friend Marcus Pacuvius produced his recent play, one incident earned loud applause from the entire audience. This was the scene in which the king was confronted by two men, and did not know which of them was Orestes. Pylades claimed that *he* was Orestes, in order that he should be the one to be put to death, in the place of his friend. The real Orestes, however, continued to insist on his own true identity. The entire crowd stood and cheered, although it was only a play" (in *On the Good Life,* trans. Michael Grant [London, 1971], pp. 189–190). Also, see below, pp. 164–165.

ORESTES

And they will say a thousand years from now perhaps, how kind was heaven to that age that it illuminated the world with such sincere friendship! And it will be pointed to and spoken of by people: this is the shore where they were taken; here one protected the other with his own body so many times and made a shield with his arms; this is the fountain where they both drank; there are the beautiful weapons still stained barbarously with blood and their mighty shields shot through with arrows and spears: and perhaps our story will be sculpted in bronze and in marble; and then celebrated on theater stages by great poets, and such an example of glory and prowess imitated by the human race . . .

The purpose of art, then, is to celebrate and imitate great and worthy deeds. In the fulfillment of that purpose Orestes sees the chance to obliterate the story identity he has acquired and to replace it with a new one. For the time being he has found his new identity to lie in the future, in the art that will celebrate him in such works as Rucellai's *Oreste*. The action of this play not only recedes into the past but looks forward to the future, the distant future of the play's performance, as it will later look back to the remote past of Leda. But it is not only for the sake of giving epic scope to his play that Rucellai makes it self-conscious in this way; it is also for the sake of achieving a double perspective on the action, the same double perspective he was aiming at with Iphigenia's recognition of her native language: making the audience aware of art as art. Shakespeare similarly plays on the idea of the performance as history and the representation of history in *Julius Caesar:*

CASSIUS

How many ages hence
Shall this our lofty scene be acted over
In states unborn and accents yet unknown!

BRUTUS

How many times shall Caesar bleed in sport
That now on Pompey's basis lies along
No worthier than the dust.

CASSIUS

So oft as that shall be,
So often shall the knot of us be called
The men that gave their country liberty.

(III.111–118)

The self-conscious moment in a play calls the audience to reflect on the purpose of art and its relation to life. It reminds them that they are looking in a mirror, that life itself is the subject matter of art, even if paradoxically, as in the case of Rucellai's *Oreste,* the work of art refers to itself. It may be that Rucellai had other works of art in mind besides his own (and those of the Greek dramatists whose works had recently been printed by the Aldine press);[8] works of sculpture perhaps "in bronze and in marble." For there were sarcophagi extant in Rucellai's time on which were depicted the adventures of Orestes, Iphigenia, and Pylades.[9] He may have known them directly, or at least have heard of them, and so counted on their being known to his Renaissance audience. In 1587, Marlowe is able to have Tamburlaine refer to "the love of Pylades and Orestes,/ Whose statues we adore in Scythia" (Part I, I.ii.243–244).[10] In the context Tamburlaine is comparing his friendship with Theridamas to that between Orestes and Pylades. Rucellai also uses them as exemplars of selfless brotherly love, but with a consciousness of the story of Castor and Pollux besides. They are the Dioscuri reborn, not only because each is willing to die for the other, but because they are to be the rescuers of Iphigenia as the Twins were the rescuers of their sister Helen. Castor and Pollux were also immortalized by Zeus as the twin stars; Orestes looks forward to the immortality that art can provide for himself and for Pylades.

Iphigenia has been offstage for most of this third act, but when she returns it is with a favorite dramatic device for precipitating the denouement—the letter. She asks Pylades to deliver it. He agrees (not knowing that it is addressed to Orestes) only on condition that he may bring his friend's ashes back with him to Greece where he may end his life and have their ashes mingled together. Pylades now reads aloud the letter in which Iphigenia explains what happened to her at Aulis, how Diana rescued her by substituting a hind on the altar and transporting her to Tauris. This is new information for Orestes and a continuation of his account of the sacrifice at Aulis in Act III. As a dramaturgical device, the

8. Marvin T. Herrick, *Italian Tragedy in the Renaissance* (Urbana, Ill., 1965), p. 43: "Aldus at Venice published the Greek text of Sophocles in 1502, all of Euripides save the *Electra* in 1503, all of Aeschylus save the *Choephoroe* in 1518."

9. See Carl Robert, *Die Antiken Sarkophagsreliefs,* vol. II (Berlin, 1890), fig. 167.

10. Christopher Marlowe, *Tamburlaine,* ed. John D. Jump (Lincoln, Neb., 1967), p. 24.

letter does two things: it makes more of the past a force in the action by correcting Orestes' knowledge of the events at Aulis, and at the same time it brings about his recognition of Iphigenia. As the interior action, the characters' knowledge of past events, reaches further back in time, the play's exterior action, the character's knowledge of the present situation, moves forward: the brother knows the sister. But the sister does not know the brother, yet. Iphigenia goes on to describe herself as a frightened, lonely woman in a hellish land:

PILADE

[*Reading aloud Iphigenia's letter*]
"E di questa mia dura ed aspra doglia,
Ne chiamo testimonio il curvo lito,
Il curvo lito e'tenebrosi orrori
Di quest'alpestri e solitarie selve,
Che piú volt'han risposto a'miei lamenti

(IV.216–220)

PYLADES

And of this my harsh and bitter pain I call as witness the curved shore, the curved shore and the dark terrors of these wild, deserted woods, that so many times have echoed my laments.

Here we may recall Orestes' description of himself as an exile vainly filling the air with his outcries of despair (see above, p. 155). Iphigenia's story is Orestes' story, and she considers him her second self: "Che tu mi venga a trar di quest'inferno, / E render te medesimo a te stesso" (IV. 280–281: May you come to take me from this hell and return your very self to yourself). In discovering Iphigenia, Orestes discovers himself; in learning her story, he relearns his own story. But he has not come to know himself wholly, and when he rapturously reveals himself as her lost brother, Iphigenia asks for proof of what he says. And once again Rucellai extends the line of anterior action further into the past, beyond the sacrifice of Iphigenia at Aulis to the ancestry of Orestes, the union of Leda and the swan. Before Orestes can be one with himself, can be recognized by Iphigenia, he must be reborn; he must define his parentage by remembering. Rucellai contrives the situation so that Iphigenia asks Orestes to describe the painting on Agamemnon's bedstead:

IFIGENIA

Ma dimmi: sopra il capezzal del letto
Ne la lettiera, che v'er'ei depinto?

ORESTE

Sopra un erboso rivo
Di corrente cristallo,
Un vago e bianco cigno
Porgea curvando il collo
Sopra'l candido grembo
D'una bella fanciulla,
Che tessea d'erbe e fiori
Fresche ghirlande:
Poi con gli schietti diti
Al petto, al collo, al fronte
De l'uccel le ponea,
Dipingendo di fiori
Di piú di color mille,
Come l'iride il Sole,
Le piumose ale.
Ed ei fiso mirando
Ne gli occhi di costei
Sospeso pende;
E poi l'aurato becco
Suavemente aprendo,
Parea dicesse: O donna,
Con visibil parlare,
Grazie vi rendo.
Né molto indi lontan sopr'un bel prato
Giacevan due grand'uova nate allora.
De l'un parean usciti quasi allora
Due gemini figliuoi: due freschi gigli
Diresti germinar fra i fiori e l'erba,
Ch'aveano i corpi a i corpi, e'l viso al viso
Congiunt'insieme, i bracci al collo stretti:
De l'altr uscian fuor due figliuoline,
Ch'a pena i pargoletti bracci e teste
Allor allor cavavan fuor del guscio.
Di queste l'una riluceva in guisa,
Che quasi lampeggiava fiamma pura;
L'altra era di color di vivo sangue.

(IV.394–431)

IPHIGENIA

Above the head of the bed in the bedstead, what was painted there?

ORESTES

Upon the grassy bank of a crystal stream, a fair white swan, bending his neck, leaned on the white breast of a beautiful young woman, who wove fresh garlands of flowers: then with slender fingers she placed them on the breast neck and forehead of the bird, painting the feathery wings with flowers of more than a thousand colors, as the rainbow does the sun. And he with his glance fixed in her eyes hangs suspended; and then suavely opening his golden beak, he seemed to say: Oh my lady (with visible speech) I give you thanks. Not far from there in the beautiful meadow lay two huge eggs hatched in that moment. From one two twin boys seemed to be coming out: two fresh lilies you would have called them budding among the flowers and the grass, who had their bodies and faces joined together and with arms around each other's necks. From the other came two little girls who just then barely pulled their arms and heads from the pod. Of these two one shone in such a way that she glowed almost like a pure flame; the other was colored red as blood.

This is an almost exact description of one of the many copies of Leonardo's lost *Leda and the Swan*. It matches most closely the so-called ex-spiridon version[11]—more so than it matches the Wilton House *Leda* which Kenneth Clark believes to be the copy closest to Leonardo's original.[12] That Rucellai based his description on the ex-spiridon version rather than on the Wilton House copy is certain because of the presence in the former of the "corrente cristallo" (crystal stream). Clark says that Cesare da Sesto, to whom the Wilton House *Leda* is attributed, "has made alterations in the landscape, which is characteristic of his style." [13] If Rucellai did in fact base his description on Leonardo's work rather than on one of the copies, then the ex-spiridon version would be the closest to Leonardo's original.

The evidence that Rucellai knew Leonardo's original is circumstantial. Certainly it was possible for him to have seen it, since it was probably painted sometime between 1504, when Raphael made a pen-and-ink drawing from Leonardo's study for the painting, and 1510, when Cesare

11. See the illustration on p. 152. A reproduction in color may be found in *The Life and Times of Leonardo da Vinci* (Philadelphia and New York, 1967), p. 29.

12. Kenneth Clark, *Leonardo da Vinci* (Baltimore, Md., 1939; rev. ed., 1967), p. 116.

13. *Ibid.*

da Sesto may have painted the Wilton House version.¹⁴ We know from Vasari in what regard Leonardo's works were held by the Florentines,¹⁵ and Rucellai may have wanted to add his personal tribute to the great painter by including a description of the *Leda* in his tragedy, or he may have wished simply to honor a fellow artist who had served the cause of theater in Italy.¹⁶ Rucellai wrote the *Oreste* between 1515 and 1520, and completed it in 1525.¹⁷ He therefore may have seen the painting in Italy, but he may also have seen it at Fontainebleau in France when he went there in 1520 on a diplomatic mission to Francis I. The painting itself is known to have been brought to France, but it is not known exactly when. Perhaps Leonardo brought it with him to France in 1516 along with the *Mona Lisa,* and after he died there in 1519 the *Leda* may have become a prized exhibition piece for visitors. If Rucellai had not already seen the painting in Italy, he may have gone to Fontainebleau to see it shortly after Leonardo's death, when his reputation would have been at its height and the opportunity to examine one of the few paintings Leonardo completed would have seemed irresistible. That the description of the *Leda* appears in the last fourth of the play suggests that Rucellai included it when he came to finish the play in 1525, after his visit to France. There is one other piece of evidence linking Rucellai to Leonardo, but again it is inconclusive and only tangential in regard to the painting: they had a mutual friend, a certain Tommaso Masini da Peretola, called Zoroastro, who once accompanied Leonardo to Milan and there practiced the profession of magic. He also lived for a time with Rucellai in Rome.¹⁸ But even if Leonardo and Rucellai did in fact know one another, that does not explain why Rucellai singled out the *Leda* for inclusion by means of

14. *Ibid.* The Wilton House *Leda* is reproduced as plate 40. A color reproduction may be found in Sidney, 16th Earl of Pembroke, *Paintings and Drawings at Wilton House* (London and New York, 1968), Plate 84.

15. Giorgio Vasari, *Lives of the Artists,* A selection translated by George Bull (Baltimore, Md., 1965), pp. 265–266.

16. See the following articles in *Le Lieu Théâtral a la Renaissance,* ed. Jacques Jacquot (Royaumont, 1964): Carlo Pedretti, "Dessins d'une scène, Exécutés par Leonardo da Vinci pour Charles d'Amboise," pp. 25–34; Kate T. Steinitz, "Le Dessin de Leonardo da Vinci pour la représentation de la Danae de Baldassare Taccone," pp. 35–40.

17. See Mazzoni's preface to his edition of the *Oreste,* p. li.

18. *Ibid.,* p. xiv.

ecphrasis in his play. What was it in the painting that made it so attractive to Rucellai?

In general, from the standpoint of the humanist, Rucellai may have looked upon Leonardo's work on the Leda theme as an effort in the plastic arts analogous to his own activity in the literary arts: the recovery of antique forms of art and their preservation in contemporary art through reinterpretation.[19] But Rucellai may have perceived more specific meanings in the painting with which he meant to enrich the action of his play. Edgar Wind believes the theme of the painting to be musical: the mystery of Leda implies "the union of Discord (Helen and Clytemnestra) and Concord (Castor and Pollux), as the Orphic-Neoplatonic principle of generation."[20] Relatedly, Kenneth Clark sees the *Leda* as an "image or allegory of generation,"[21] which he finds mirrored in the "continuous flow of the modeling," and in the "writhing intricate rhythms of growth [which] are carried through from the pose of her whole figure

19. John Shearman, *Mannerism* (Baltimore, Md., 1967), p. 49: "In the *Leda,* he (Leonardo) established a new canon of the female nude, which was a renewed classicism emulating but not imitating the formal qualities of the antique and far exceeding it in sensuousness." See also Sir Kenneth Clark, "Leonardo and the Antique," in *Leonardo's Legacy,* ed. C. D. O'Malley (Berkeley and Los Angeles, 1969), pp. 1–34: "the Kneeling Leda, the Standing Leda . . . all derive more or less from Graeco-Roman sarcophagi," (p. 12). It should also be noted that the Rucellai family collected works of art: see Arnold Hauser, *The Social History of Art,* (New York, 1951), II, 40.

20. Edgar Wind, *Pagan Mysteries of the Renaissance* (New York, 1968), pp. 167–168, n. 60. Wind also sees in the *Leda* an iconographic similarity to Filippino Lippi's *Allegory of Music,* reproduced in Erwin Panofsky, *Renaissance and Renascences in Western Art* (New York and Evanston, 1969), fig. 150, but Panofsky rejects the connection (p. 203, n. 3). Even so, I think there may be a musical dimension to the *Leda,* which we do not understand, but which the Renaissance and Rucellai may have understood clearly. Many portions of Rucellai's play are intensely lyrical, not only choruses but dialogues and short set speeches as well, occurring at heightened moments of the drama (for example, the duet between Orestes and Iphigenia after they have discovered one another's identity in Act IV, 468–483); he may have intended such passages to be sung to music, or chanted, or at least intoned, since the Renaissance understood Greek tragedy to have been musical. I believe that Rucellai's choice of Leonardo's *Leda* with its similarity to Lippi's *Allegory of Music* was more deliberate and meaningful than I am able to understand or competent to demonstrate.

21. Kenneth Clark, *The Nude* (Garden City, N.Y., 1956), p. 176.

to the plaits of her headdress and the grasses at her feet."[22] Clark also explains Leonardo's intent in the following:

He saw in it not the joy and beauty of sexual intercourse, but its mystery and its analogy with the creative processes of nature. His Leda symbolizes the female aspect of creation. . . . and at her feet, four human babies tumble out of the broken eggs.[23]

One could footnote these interpretations by pointing to the phallic nature of the white swan (a symbol of the poet—the flights of his imagination as well as the beauty and purity of his song), to the serpentine quality of its graceful, bending neck,[24] as a reinterpretation of the Garden of Eden myth, seen by Leonardo not as the introduction of original sin but as the simple beginning of human life, the union of the natural and the supernatural to produce the multiplicity of the world. The painting is a reconciliation of opposites: Jove becomes the swan; the serpent becomes the swan; Leda becomes Leonardo's Eve uniting in herself carnality and motherhood; the twins are antithetical but mirror images. The whole composition is an active harmony of nature understood and celebrated.

It is the remembrance and description of this second Eden that saves Orestes. His search for a mother has ended with this reach into the past for Leda, the mother of all life. Iphigenia, who incarnates Leda before him, replaces the evil mother Clytemnestra (till now Iphigenia was to have been his executioner), and also reconciles, like Leda, the opposites of woman as mother and woman as lover:

ORESTE

Non vi ricorda come la mattina
Tenendomi ristretto al vostro seno,
E talor cosí nudo com'io nacqui,
Mi mostravate e narravate a dito
Tutta l'istoria che dipinta v'era?

(IV.432–436)

22. *Ibid.*, p. 177.

23. Clark, *Leonardo*, p. 117.

24. The swan "curvando il collo," bending his neck to reach Leda and wind around her, recalls two images in the play: the "sottil collo" of the land of Tauris, which tries to reach its ancient mother, as Orestes sees it (above p. 153); and the "curvo lito," the curved shore which traps Iphigenia (above p. 166). In the image of Leda and the swan Orestes finds his ancient mother and Iphigenia finds a release from her despair because it enables her to know her brother.

ORESTES

Don't you remember how one morning holding me close to your breast, nude then as when I was born, you showed me and told me in detail the whole story that was painted there?

Orestes continues to remember how he somehow scratched out the figure of his mother from the painting (and as is fitting in this dreamlike memory he cannot remember exactly how or why), even as he is now erasing the memory of his crime with the protection of his second mother Iphigenia:

ORESTE

De le femine, quella che vibrava
Fiamma di foco, era la bella Elèna,
L'altra di sangue, l'empia Clitemnestra,
La qual'oimè, un giorno, non so come,
Graffiando la guastai con l'unghie mie:
E se voi non m'aveste allor nascoso
Dietr'a l'altar ch'è consacrato a Giove,
M'avria quel dí la mia madre battuto
Molt'aspramente per lo sdegno e l'ira.

(IV.441–449)

ORESTES

Of the two women the one who was vibrant as fire was the beautiful Helen, and the other woman blood-red was the impious Clytemnestra, whose image, alas, one day, I don't know how, I ruined by scratching it with my fingernails: and if you hadn't then hidden me behind the altar sacred to Jove, she, my mother, would have beaten me that day terribly in a rage of indignation.

The act of remembering has the force of reliving in this play, and the destruction of art here equals the destruction of reality; the erasure of the mother in the painting, in art, cancels his crime, absolves the matricide of guilt, but the act also destroys art, and art, Rucellai is concerned to show, is the salvation of man. Therefore the transformation of art into nothing by violence must be balanced by the transformation of violence into art: Iphigenia asks to see the birthmark on Orestes' arm, caused by Clytemnestra's evil food-craving during pregnancy,

il destro braccio ove tua madre
Col profondo desir de l'empia voglia
Dipinse quelle gocciole di sangue,

Che parean ch'una porpora marina
De la tridente fuscina ferita
L'avesse allor allor versate e sparse
Sopr'un bel bianco e rilucente avorio,
O rubin rossegiar fra l'Inde perle.

(IV.460–467)

that right arm where your mother with the deep desire of her impious craving
painted those three bloody marks, which seemed as though a murex wounded
by a fishing trident had just then poured them out and sprinkled them upon
fair white and shining ivory, or like a ruby glowing red among India pearls.

The transforming power of metaphor is here invoked by Iphigenia, the
real mother, to cancel the violence of the false mother, Clytemnestra:

ORESTE

Eccov', Ifigenia sorella, il braccio:
Ecco le vostre gocciole di sangue,
Cui baciavate mille volte il giorno
Con si gran tenerezza e tanto affetto.

(IV.468–471)

ORESTES

Here is the arm Iphigenia my sister, here are your droplets of blood which
you kissed a thousand times each day with so much love and affection.

The incestuous relationship between Aegisthus ("Quel che d'incesto e
per incesto nacque," II.336: He that was born of and for incest) and
Clytemnestra is here transformed into the approved mother-son, sister-
brother love between Orestes and Iphigenia. Rucellai has deliberately
made Iphigenia older than Orestes (he was only a "picciol fanciullo"
when she was supposedly sacrificed at Aulis), modeling her in this respect
on Sophocles' Electra.[25] As second mother, then, she replaces Clytemnestra, but in the play as reenactment of the past she represents Helen—
the raped woman who causes suffering to her kin in a foreign land
(Troy—Tauris), or in the parallel legend, the woman who is transported
by a divinity to a strange land, by Hermes to Egypt, and there is recognized and rescued by her husband. So, too, in the play as reenactment of

25. See Sophocles, *Electra,* ll. 1144–1148. It is also interesting to note that there
is another tradition which Rucellai may have found in Euripides and drawn upon,
that Leda raised Orestes: cf. Euripides, *Orestes,* ll. 463–466.

the painting Orestes and Pylades imitate the friendship of Castor and Pollux which in turn derives from the harmony between Leda and the swan:

PILADE

Donde noi ci abbracciammo insieme stretti,
E ci baciammo con pietoso affetto
Le verecunde e lagrimose guancie.
Allor *fiso mirando ne'nostri occhi,*
Non ancor sazii di guardar l'un l'altro

(III.335–339)

PYLADES

Then we embraced one another tightly, and we kissed with reverence and affection one another's blushing and tear-stained cheeks. Then with fixed glance in one another's eyes, not yet satiated with gazing,

This passage looks forward not only to the twin boys of the painting embracing tightly but also to the rapport between Leda and the swan, who looks into her eyes with the same "fixed glance" and seems to speak almost:

Ed ei *fiso mirando*
Ne gli occhi di costei
Sospeso pende;
E poi l'aurato becco
Suavemente aprendo,
Parea dicesse: O donna,
Con *visibil parlare,*
Grazie vi rendo.[26]

Rucellai has adapted the phrase "visibil parlare" from Canto X of Dante's *Purgatorio,* where the sculptures on the cornice of pride look so real that they seem to speak:

che non sembiava imagine che tace.
Giurato si sarìa ch'el dicesse "Ave!"
· · · · · · · · · · · ·

26. For translation, see above p. 168.

Colui che mai non vide cosa nova
produsse estu *visibile parlare,*
novello a noi perché qui non si trova.[27]

(X.39–40; 94–96)

she did not seem to be an unspeaking image. One could have sworn that he
said "Hail." . . . He for whom nothing seen is new created this visible
speech, new for us because we do not see it on earth.

Jean Hagstrum finds Dante's *visibile parlare* "in silent plastic art" to be
"a paradoxical comment which is at once a tribute to the verisimilitude
of the object and also a justification of the poet's addition of language."[28]
For Rucellai *visibil parlare* is a contribution to the theory of *ut pictura
poesis,* a reversal of the conceit of painting as mute poetry—a conceit that
Leonardo rightly considered an insult to painting.[29] By adapting Dante's
paradox to the context of Leonardo's *Leda,* he changed the conceit from
an insult into a tribute to the art of painting in the form of a reconciliation of opposites: if painting is visible poetry, then poetry is a speaking
picture.[30]

Rucellai's resolution of this aesthetic paradox reveals the pattern of the
play to be the harmony of mystery; how the present reenacts the past,
how life becomes art, and how mistaken identity becomes recognition
are the profound mystery that Orestes had identified as the cause of his
arrival in the land of the Taurians in the beginning of the first act.
Rucellai takes care to emphasize this meaning in the final chorus of the

---

27. There is an *Annunciation* by Simone Martini (1284?–1344) which pictures
the words, "Ave Gratia plena dominus tecum," coming from the mouth of the
angel. It may be that Rucellai had this literal representation in painting of *visibil
parlare* in mind, especially since it illustrates the passage in Dante, but also because
it portrays the fertilization of the Virgin Mary by the Holy Ghost as dove, and he
may have connected this image with the Leda theme. See also Ernest Jones, "The
Madonna's Conception through the Ear," *Essays in Applied Psycho-analysis* (London, 1951), II, 266–357.

28. Jean Hagstrum, *The Sister Arts* (Chicago and London, 1958), p. 53.

29. "If you call painting 'dumb poetry,' then the painter may say of the poet
that his art is 'blind painting.'" Leonardo da Vinci, *The Notebooks,* ed. Robert
Linscott, trans. Edward MacCurdy (New York, 1957), p. 35.

30. For the latest theories about Leonardo's *Leda* and its copies, see Carlo
Pedretti, *Leonardo* (Berkeley and Los Angeles, 1973), pp. 97–104.

last act: after Iphigenia (having tricked Thoas with a report of the gods' displeasure at the impurity of the strangers) has escaped with Orestes, Pylades, and the statue of Diana, the Taurian women tell the tyrant not to pursue the fugitives, since their escape is obviously by the will of the gods:

> Non si conviene a gli uomini mortali
> Voler saper di Dio gli *alti misterii,*
> Ne l'alto sen de la sua mente ascosi:
>
> (V.325–327)

It is best for mortals not to wish to know the profound mysteries of God hidden in the deep bosom of his mind.

Horace said in the *Art of Poetry* that in telling the story of the Trojan War the poet need not go as far back as the eggs of Leda (ll. 172–173), but Rucellai did not take his advice. In representing the story of Orestes and Iphigenia in the land of Tauris he found it necessary to construct a dramaturgy upon two lines of action: one advancing by stages from the threatened destruction of Orestes to his recognition by Iphigenia and their ultimate escape; the other reaching further and further into the remembrance of the past, a line of mental action that marks the stages of the first. Orestes and Iphigenia must each remember his and her own story as far back as their divine origin from Leda and the swan, and in that origin they must see the coincidence of their fates and reconcile their present with their past through self-recognition, an achievement that Rucellai symbolizes in his play by making their separate stories climax in the mirror of Leonardo's painting of *Leda and the Swan* in which all antinomies are resolved by art.

The Role of the Quem Quaeritis Dialogue in the History of Western Drama

TIMOTHY J. McGEE

UNTIL QUITE RECENTLY it had been assumed that the *Quem quaeritis* dialogue originated in the early tenth century as a trope of the Easter Mass Introit, to which dramatic actions were later added. Such assumptions had been based upon the heading *Tropos in Pasche* (or similar statements), which precedes the dialogue in some early manuscripts, and upon the appearance in some manuscripts of the Easter Mass Introit antiphon immediately following the dialogue itself. However, recent investigations by the present writer have brought to light a number of contradictory facts that make this "traditional" view untenable.[1] As a result the entire role played by the *Quem quaeritis* dialogue in the history of Western drama will need to be reexamined, and a more comprehensive theory of its origins advanced. This paper will attempt such a

1. Timothy J. McGee, "The Liturgical Origin and Early History of the *Quem Quaeritis* Dialogue," Diss., University of Pittsburgh, 1974. Much of the evidence is contained in a more condensed form in "The Liturgical Placements of the *Quem Quaeritis* Dialogue," *Journal of the American Musicological Society, XXIX:* (Spring, 1976), 1-29.

reevaluation, taking as its starting point some of the evidence unaccounted for by older theories of origin, and moving toward a fuller understanding of both the dialogue itself and its role in the history of early liturgical drama.

We might begin by noting that in six manuscripts from the tenth and eleventh centuries from the Abbey of St. Gall, the *Quem quaeritis* dialogue lines are *both* preceded *and* succeeded by procession antiphons, indicating that the dialogue probably was not an Introit trope at St. Gall but part of some pre-Mass processional ceremony.[2] The dialogue and antiphons from St. Gall MS. 339 will serve as an example:

Dominica sancta Pascae ad processionem[3]
[Processional] In die resurrectionis meae, dixit Dominus, alleluia congregabo gentes, et colligam regna, et effundam super vos aquam mandam, alleluia.
[Processional] Vidi aquam egredientem de templo a latere dextero alleluia, et omnes ad quos pervenit aqua ista salvi facti sunt et dicent alleluia, alleluia.
Interrogatio: Quem quaeritis in sepulchro, Christicolae?
Responsio: Jesum Nazarenum crucifixum, o celicolae. Non est hic, surrexit sicut praedixerat; ite, nuntiate quia surrexit de sepulchro.
[Processional] Surrexit enim sicut dixit Dominus: ecce precedet vos in Galileam alleluia; ibi eum videbitis, alleluia, alleluia, alleluia.
[Processional] Sedit angelus ad sepulchrum Domini stola claritatis coopertus videntes eum mulieres nimio terrore per territe astiterunt a longe. Tunc locutus est angelus et dixit eis: nolite metuere: dicto vobis quia illum quem quaeritis mortum iam vivit, et vita hominum cum eo surrexit, alleluia.
Versus: Recordamini quo modo predixit quia oportet filium hominis crucifigi et tercia die a morte suscitari.
Versus: Crucifixum Dominum laudate, et sepultum propter nos glorificate, resurgentemque a morte adorate, alleluia.[4]

A somewhat similar set of accompanying antiphons, but in a different order, can be found in a manuscript from Minden:

2. Karl Young, *The Drama of the Medieval Church,* 2d ed., 2 vols. (1933; repr. Oxford, 1967). Young labels this placement "The Easter Introit Trope in Transition" (chap. 8).
3. In this article all Latin abbreviations have been resolved and spelling standardized.
4. St. Gall, Stiftsbibl. MS. 339, p. 106.

In die sancto Pasche primo mane ad visitandum sepulchrum Domini
Interrogatio: Quem quaeritis in sepulchro, o Christicolae?
Responsio: Ihesum Nazarenum crucifixum, o celicolae. Non est hic, surrexit
    sicut praedixerat, ite, nuntiate quia surrexit de sepulchro.
Antiphona: Surrexit enim
Ad processionem: Salve festa
His versibus finitis hec antiphona canatur Introitum minoris a ecclesiae
Antiphona: Cum rex gloriae
In aspersione fontis Antiphona: Vidi aquam
Antiphona: In die resurrectionis
Antiphona unde supra: Sedit angelus
Antiphona: Crucifixum
Versus: Recordamini
Dominica sancto Pasche
Resurrexi[5]

Neither the St. Gall nor the Minden manuscripts use the word *trope,* but
in both there is reference to a sepulcher visitation. From the similarity of
the procession items in both manuscripts, it would seem that the pre-Mass
ceremony was much the same in both traditions. Therefore, to understand
better the ceremony indicated in these sources, it is necessary to look
further into the pre-Mass processional tradition.

A clear description of the pre-Mass procession ceremony can be found
in a document known as the *Pontificale Romano-Germanicum,*[6] a com-
posite of a number of manuscripts from the ninth, tenth, and eleventh
centuries. The *Pontificale* represents the liturgical tradition in the diocese
of Mainz, a prominent center during the centuries in question. Mainz
exerted a major influence on the liturgy of the late Middle Ages, and the
Pontificale can be regarded as representative of medieval liturgical practice. The following description of the ceremonies on Easter morning can
be found in the *Pontificale* immediately following the description of
Easter Vigil Mass:

Item ordo in die sancto paschae. Die sancto paschae, induti sollemnissimis
vestibus omnes clerici convenientes ad stationem ad sanctam Mariam majorem,
primitus canent tertiam. Qua finita, aespersi aqua sancta quae pridie collecta

5. Berlin, Staatsbibl. Theol. Lat 4° .15, fol. 120.
6. Cyrille Vogel and Elze Reinhard, eds., *Pontificale Romano Germanicum du
dixième siècle* (Vatican City, 1963).

est de fonte, tam ipsi quam et omnis populus procedunt cum omni decore, cum crucibus et thimiamateriis, praecedentibus etiam sanctis evangellis, cantantes antiphonas processionales: *In die resurrectionis*

Alia: *Vidi aquam*

alia: *Cum rex gloriae*

Item: versus in laudem sancti paschae:

Salve festa dies.

Quibus expletis, ingrediuntur ecclesiam cum antiphona:

Sedit angelus cum versibus suis:

Crucifixum in carne, Recordamini, Maria et Martha.

Et ita ingrediuntur ad missam. Ad introitum imponit cantor antiphonam: *Resurrexi et adhuc tecum sum.*[7]

Next the order on the holy day of Easter. On the holy day of Easter all the priests dressed in most solemn robes gathering together at the station for Saint Mary Major should first sing Terce. When this is finished, sprinkled with holy water which was collected from the spring on the previous day, both they themselves and all the people proceed with all decorum, with crosses and censers, and with the holy gospels going before them, sing the processional antiphons: *In die resurrectionis*

or else: *Vidi aquam*

or else: *Cum rex gloriae*

next: the verses in praise of holy Easter:

Salve festa dies.

When this is completed, they enter the church with the antiphon: *Sedit angelus* with its verses:

Cricifixum in carne, Recordamini, Maria et Martha. And thus they go in to Mass. For the Introit the Cantor gives the antiphon: *Resurrexi et adhuc tecum sum.*

The procession antiphons in the *Pontificale* include *Vidi aquam, Sedit angelus,* and *In die resurrectionis,* which are also found in the manuscripts from St. Gall and Minden, suggesting that the ceremony printed above probably took place before Easter Mass in both monasteries. The dialogue is not mentioned in the *Pontificale* because it was not a part of the official liturgy but an addition, a trope, which was not performed everywhere. However, the position of the *Quem quaeritis* dialogue in the pre-Mass ceremony at both monasteries can now be determined: at St. Gall it followed the first two processionals and preceded the second two.

7. *Ibid.*, pp. 113–114.

In terms of the sequence of material in the *Pontificale*, the dialogue at St. Gall could be placed either before or after the singing of the verses *Salve festa dies*. The example from Minden could indicate a slightly different placement of the dialogue, that is, before the remainder of the ceremony, or it may be evidence of a scribal practice of listing in one group all procession antiphons for a particular ceremony. In either case it is obvious that at St. Gall and Minden the dialogue was a part of the same pre-Mass ceremony indicated in the *Pontificale Romano-Germanicum*.

The ceremony described in the *Pontificale* is the *Collecta* ceremony which was a part of the stational church tradition in Rome from the early Middle Ages.[8] The service occurred before important liturgical ceremonies at a church known itself as a *Collecta* where the congregation and celebrants assembled for a short collect before processing to the stational church designated for the Mass of that feast, a tradition that was made possible by the proximity of so many churches in Rome. It would be difficult to overemphasize the popularity of the stational church tradition in Rome. The number of churches that took part reached the grand total of forty-two, sharing eighty-nine services on eighty-seven days.[9] In the eighth and ninth centuries, when the Roman liturgy was adopted as the model for Western Europe, this tradition of beginning important liturgical services with a *Collecta* ceremony was adopted as well. Evidence of the wide dissemination of the *Collecta* tradition can be seen in the rubrics of many manuscripts from all locations in Western Europe, and reference to the *Collecta* ceremony was found in the earliest Roman sacramentaries dispatched from the court of Charlemagne.[10]

It is clear from the above evidence that in its processional setting the *Quem quaeritis* dialogue was a part of the pre-Mass *Collecta* ceremony. A question arises immediately as to how widespread was the practice of presenting the dialogue in a processional, i.e., *Collecta* setting. A thorough search of the pre-thirteenth-century manuscripts produced heretofore unnoticed sections in three manuscripts from the monastery of St. Martial.

8. Richard Hierzegger, "Collecta und Statio," *Zeitschrift fur Katholische Theologie,* LX (1936), 511–554.

9. Robert Francis McNamara, "Stational Church," *New Catholic Encyclopedia,* XIII (New York, 1966), 662–664.

10. Hierzegger, p. 518.

Ten manuscripts survive from that tradition,[11] all containing the dialogue in a somewhat similar context:

Tropos in resurrectione Domini
Quem quaeritis in sepulchro, o Christicolae?
Responsio: Jesum Nazarenum crucifixum, o celicolae.
Responsio: Non est hic, surrexit sicut praedixerat; ite nunciate quia surrexit.
Responsio: Alleluia, ad sepulchrum . . .
En ecce completum . . .
Resurrexi[12]

There is no mention of a procession or of a *Collecta* ceremony on the pages where the *Quem quaeritis* dialogue appears, and therefore it would seem to be correct to assume that at St. Martial the dialogue was a trope of the Easter Mass Introit antiphon in agreement with the common theory of its original liturgical placement. However, three of the St. Martial manuscripts do contain procession antiphons for Easter, located not with the Mass trope material, but in a separate section devoted entirely to procession antiphons for various occasions. The relevant section from MS. P. 1121 is a good example:

f. 153[r] *Antiphona in Pascha processionales*
    Antiphona: Vidi aquam . . .
    Antiphona: In die resurrectionis . . .
    Antiphona: Lapidem quem . . .
    Antiphona: Vespere sabbati . . .
f. 153[v] *Antiphona:* Sedit angelus . . .
    Antiphona: Surgens Dominus . . .
f. 154[r] *Antiphona:* Surrexit enim sicut . . .
    Antiphona: Surrexit pastor bonum . . .
    Antiphona: Christus resurgens . . .
    Versus: Dicant nunc . . .
f. 154[v] *Antiphona:* Dum fabricator mundi . . .
    Antiphona: Oud mirabile precum . . .
f. 155[r] *Antiphona:* Cum rex gloriae . . .
    Antiphona: O crux ad mirabile . . .
f. 155[v] *Sci die pasche ad communicandum*[13]

11. The term *St. Martial School* refers to the several monasteries in the vicinity of the famous St. Martial which seemed to be influenced by its traditions.

12. Paris, Bibl. Nat. fonds Latin 779, fol. 36.

13. Paris, Bibl. Nat. fonds Latin 1121, fols. 153–155.

The rubrics give a clear indication of the placement of the procession antiphons. The first rubric identifies all of the following antiphons as processionals for Easter, while the last rubric printed above identifies the antiphons that follow it as communion processionals. The only precommunion procession possible at Easter Mass is the one preceding the Introit, and therefore, the antiphons cited above must be intended for this position. Further, the lists of processionals from the three St. Martial manuscripts include most of the antiphons mentioned in the *Pontificale Romano-Germanicum,* the St. Gall, and the Minden manuscripts.

The existence of these processionals to be sung at St. Martial before Easter Mass Introit indicates that a pre-Mass procession did indeed take place and suggests that a *Collecta* ceremony may also have been performed. The suspicion of a *Collecta* ceremony at St. Martial is confirmed by the rubric in another of the St. Martial manuscripts. The rubric before the dialogue in MS. P. 1118 states *In die sancto Pasche stacio ad sanctum Petrum item tropos in die.*[14] If the rubric is a mere copying of a Roman stational direction, the scribe has erred. St. Peter's was the Roman station for Easter Monday; the correct station for Easter Sunday is St. Mary Major. A further search through the manuscript yields six other stational directions, three at St. Peter's.[15] The prominence of St. Peter's and the absence of many other Roman stational directions suggests that, instead of erring, the scribe was reporting local custom: the pre-Mass ceremony for St. Martial on Easter Sunday began at the nearby monastery of St. Peter.[16]

Documentation of the pre-Mass *Collecta* ceremony at St. Martial and the probable performance of the *Quem quaeritis* dialogue within that ceremony casts serious doubt on the Introit-trope theory of origin, for the oldest extant manuscript containing the dialogue is P. 1240 from St. Martial. In addition, the separate section for procession antiphons in the St. Martial manuscripts suggests that processionals may be intended in other manuscripts in which, similar to the St. Martial documents, no indication is given on the pages containing the dialogue lines. The fact

14. Paris, Bibl. Nat. fonds Latin 1118, fol. 40.

15. Christmas, fol. 8; Epiphany, fol. 29; and Easter Monday, fol. 48.

16. The Abbey of St. Pierre was begun in the tenth century by Fulbert, Abbot of St. Martial. Details in L. Cottineau *Repertoire topo-bibliographique des abbeyes et prieures* (Macon, 1936), p. 621.

that the dialogue was presented within the pre-Mass *Collecta* ceremony at the important monastic centers of St. Gall, Minden, and St. Martial suggests that the custom may have been widespread.

A check of all fifty-six pre-thirteenth-century manuscripts in which the *Quem quaeritis* dialogue appears before Mass produces the following evidence: Procession antiphons are found with the dialogue lines in twenty-five manuscripts;[17] in eight others rubrics give strong indication of the *Collecta* placement,[18] for example the rubric *Versus ad Sepulchrum*[19] or a rubric following the dialogue such as *In Missam Introitum*,[20] which clearly separates the dialogue from the Introit material. In the St. Martial school, where the needed processional antiphons are found in a separate section of three manuscripts, all ten manuscripts can be said to give evidence of *Collecta* placement.[21]

Therefore, the total number of pre-thirteenth-century *Quem quaeritis* dialogues for which some evidence of *Collecta* placement can be found is forty-three, which is roughly eighty percent. In the face of this large percentage, which includes the most prominent monasteries of the time, it is difficult to believe that any other pre-Mass placement of the dialogue existed. In those manuscripts where the dialogue exists without any indication of procession antiphons, it may be assumed that the appropriate antiphons would be supplied from a liturgical book known as a *Processionale*.

If the dialogue did not originate as one of the many tropes of the Easter Introit, the entire theory of its source and presentation must be

17. Monza, Bibl. Capit. K 11; Bamberg, Staatsbibl. Misc. lit. 22; Metz, Bibl. Munic. 452; Oxford, Bodleian Lib. Selden Supra 27; Kassel, Landesbibl. Theol. 4° .25; St. Gall Stiftsbibl. 374, 376, 339, 387, 378, 391; Berlin Staatsbibl. Theol. Lat 4° .11, Lat 4° .15; Paris Bibl. Nat. Nouv. Acq. 1235; fonds Latin 10510, 9448, 9449; Cambrai, Bibl. Munic. 75; Cambridge, Corpus Christi Col. Lib. 473; Oxford, Bodleian Lib. 775; Paris, Bibl. de l'Arsénal Res. 1169; Munich, Staatsbibl. Lat. 14083, 14845; Turin, Bibl. Nat. F. 18; Rome, Bibl. Angelica 123.

18. Zurich, Zentralbibl. Rh. 97; Ivrea, Bibl. Capit. 60; Monza, Bibl. Capit. 14/77; Oxford, Bodleian Lib. Douce 222; Benevento, Bibl. Capit. VI 34; Piacenza, Bibl. Capit. 65; Verona, Bibl. Capit. 107, Rome, Vaticana 4770.

19. Ivrea, 60. p. 70.

20. Monza MS. 14/77, fol. 82.

21. Paris, Bibl. Nat. fonds Latin 1118, 887, 779, 909, 1121, 1119, 1120, 1240, 1084, and Nouv. Acq. 1871.

rethought. It is necessary to look again at the history of the Middle Ages to find circumstances under which the composition of a dialogue antiphon may have been encouraged.

There is no direct mention of the *Quem quaeritis* dialogue in sources dating prior to MS. P. 1240 (931–934), and therefore any discussion of the existence of the dialogue before the early tenth century must remain in the area of conjecture. Yet, in spite of the total lack of direct evidence, it is possible to speculate on the possible date and place of origin of the dialogue by examining certain events in the history of the ninth century, and various pieces of circumstantial evidence which lend some support to a possible ninth-century origin.

The earliest extant manuscripts containing the dialogue from the early tenth century are representative of a fairly wide geographical area, which suggests an origin earlier than the tenth-century manuscripts. This suggestion is supported by iconographic evidence described by Carol Heitz.[22] In a study of ninth- and tenth-century ivory plaques showing the visit of the three Marys to the tomb, Heitz observes that the Marys are dressed not like women but like monks, suggesting that they depict not the biblical story but a reenactment of the story at a monastery. Since the earliest of these plaques is from the Metz area, Heitz concludes that the *Quem quaeritis* dialogue may have been the result of the influence of Amalarius of Metz (ca. 775–850), who recommended representation within the liturgy for the education of the congregation.[23] Amalarius's proposal that even more ceremony should be added to the liturgy[24] coincides with the addition of much new material, including tropes and sequences, to the liturgy. A possible motive for this interest in ceremonial additions to the liturgy exists in the early-ninth-century Roman Imperial revival emanating from the court of Charlemagne.

No other situation or event suggests an atmosphere as conducive to the composition of the *Quem quaeritis* dialogue as does the Carolingian

22. Carol Heitz, *Recherches sur les rapports entre architecture et liturgie à l'époque carolingienne* (Paris, 1963), pp. 172–273.

23. Allen Cabaniss, *Amalarius of Metz* (Amsterdam, 1954), pp. 62–64; and Jean Hanssens, ed. *Amalarii episcopi opera liturgica omnia,* 2 vols. (Vatican City, 1948–1950), pp. 159–161.

24. Quoted extensively in O. B. Hardison. *Christian Rite and Christian Drama in the Middle Ages* (Baltimore, Md., 1965). pp. 37–79.

revival of the ninth century. Charlemagne inherited an empire which covered most of Europe after the death of his father Pepin in 768, and his brother Carloman in 771. Throughout his lifetime he added to that territory and carried out the intention of his father and grandfather Charles Martel to reestablish the Roman Empire which had been dissolved in the fifth century. The cornerstone of this revival program was the unification of all areas of the empire through a single liturgical observance. Steps were taken to suppress the local liturgical rites which had grown in the various areas and impose the rite observed in Rome. Charlemagne wished to reestablish the empire in what he believed to be the ideal Christian era, the fourth-century reign of Constantine.

Charlemagne attempted to construct a direct line from the era of Constantine to that of his own empire which would reverse the dependence of Rome on Byzantium and would establish himself as the next in the line of great Roman emperors. In his efforts to align himself with the past, Charlemagne claimed succession from the Jewish kings of the Old Testament (adopting in court the name David which was also given to Constantine), and descent from both an ancient Roman family (and thereby Roman citizenship),[25] and Theodosius (with implications of Byzantine legitimacy).[26] In this last connection a famous fresco at the Palace of Ingelheim depicts Charlemagne with his ancestors Charles Martel and Pepin adjacent to Constantine and Theodosius.

Charlemagne's effort to re-create the earlier era extended to the imitation of both pagan and Christian Roman Imperial art which carried symbolic meaning in its form, for instance the imitation of Church architecture found in Constantine's time.[27] Near Eastern-style churches which had been constructed throughout Europe before the Carolingian revival were replaced by ninth-century architectural copies of fourth-century Roman basilicas.[28] The evidence of Charlemagne's attempt to re-create

25. K. Heldman, *Das Kaisertum Karls d. Grossen* (Weimar, 1928), p. 247, cited in Peter Munz, *The Origin of the Carolingian Empire* (Leicester, 1960), p. 7, n. 39.

26. Heinrich Fichtenau, *The Carolingian Empire,* trans. Peter Munz (Oxford, 1957), p. 83.

27. Richard Krautheimer, "The Carolingian Revival of Early Christian Architecture," XXIV, *The Art Bulletin* (1942), 6–38.

28. *Ibid.,* p. 22.

the fourth-century empire of Constantine is sufficient to suggest that he would also have been interested in a revival of the drama which was an integral part of that culture.[29]

It is an old story how theater in the West flourished in the first four centuries A.D. but came increasingly under attack with the rise of Christianity. The clergy and the tenets of the Christian faith were a frequent topic for ridicule in the Roman comedies, and the Christian church replied with decrees condemning theater and forbidding Christians to attend. There is no record of drama from the fifth century to the mid-eighth century where, once again, the record is of Church condemnation.[30] Only mime seems to have survived.[31] In the late eighth and early ninth centuries the Church attacks against theater increased: in 813 the Synods of Tours, Chalons, and Mainz forbade clergy to attend performances of mimes,[32] and in 816 the Council at Aachen forbade the clergy to attend plays on stage or at marriages.[33]

Although it was forbidden to the clergy, drama obviously did exist in Aachen and the other centers of Western Europe, and it was probably presented on festive occasions at Charlemagne's palace. The secular drama at Charlemagne's court would not have been a model for the simple three-line dialogue in the liturgy, but the general attitude of a community where drama is a part of the culture is the right setting for the introduction of a dramatic dialogue into the liturgy. The Carolingian revival, which continued to flourish under Charlemagne's heirs for the remainder of the ninth century, certainly created an atmosphere conducive to the composition of the *Quem quaeritis* dialogue. The dramatic nature of much of the Roman service from as early as the sixth century has been well documented by O. B. Hardison,[34] and therefore the presence of

29. The fourth-century plays were mainly copies of Roman plays by Seneca, Plautus, and Terence. Young, I, 2–12.

30. J. D. A. Ogilvy, "Mimi, Scurrae, Histriones: Entertainers of the Early Middle Ages," *Speculum*, XXXVIII (1963), 606.

31. *Ibid.*, pp. 605–606.

32. *Ibid.*, pp. 609–610.

33. *Ibid.*, p. 610.

34. Hardison, *Christian Rite*, chaps. II, III, IV, and "Gregorian Easter Vespers and Early Liturgical Drama," *The Medieval Drama and Its Claudelian Revival* (Washington, D.C., 1970), pp. 27–40.

drama proper in the secular world must have lent additional impetus
toward the establishment of an actual dramatic scene. With the revival
of drama in Aachen in the early ninth century, the quasi-dramatic ceremonies within the liturgy, and the writings of Amalarius concerning the
addition of more ceremony to the liturgy, all that is missing is an actual
model of a dialogue in a liturgy. That model existed in the ceremonies
and embellishments within the liturgy of the Byzantine church.

There is little doubt that Charlemagne witnessed the Byzantine rite at
his home in Aachen. In the year 811, official representatives from
Byzantium were in Aachen for the purpose of negotiating a peace agreement between Charlemagne and the Byzantine emperor.[35] Charlemagne's
biographers record several visits to the palace in Aachen by bishops and
delegates from Greece and Persia.[36] Amalarius of Metz was also a visitor
to Charlemagne's court, where he was a teacher at the palace school from
809 to 813, and there is a strong possibility that the delegates to the court
performed the services of Byzantine rite before both Charlemagne and
Amalarius. The additions to the Roman liturgy of tropelike material and
ceremony may well have been suggested to Charlemagne on these occasions.[37] Considering that the writings of Amalarius began shortly after
he left the palace school in Aachen, and that the beginnings of liturgical
additions are from approximately the same time, it is reasonable to believe that the changes and additions to the liturgy came originally from
the palace of the Holy Roman Emperor.

The traditional theory concerning the presentation of the *Quem quaeritis* dialogue is that originally it was not dramatized but merely sung, as
were all other trope lines. If the dialogue were a trope line the conclusion
would probably be correct; it is doubtful that something as foreign to the
official liturgy as a dramatization could have been added without causing
a great deal of adverse reaction. In addition, there would have been the

35. Steward C. Easton and Helene Wieruszowski, *The Era of Charlemagne*
(Princeton, N.J., 1961), p. 130.

36. *Ibid.,* and Lewis Thorpe, *Two Lives of Charlemagne* (Harmondsworth,
1969), pp. 70, 142–146.

37. Egon Wellesz suggests that the origin of tropes was in the Byzantine liturgy:
Egon Wellesz, *Eastern Elements in Western Chant* (Oxford, 1947), pt. IV, chap.
I. He proves that a number of Roman chants are direct copies of Byzantine chants
(Part III).

obvious danger that the dramatized introduction, instead of merely introducing the Introit, would draw attention toward itself and away from the more liturgically important Introit antiphon. However, the *Collecta* ceremony was a recent addition to the northern monastic practices and was not itself an official part of the liturgy. The *Collecta* ceremony, performed at a separate location after terce and before Mass, was in fact paraliturgical, and a short dramatization could be added quite easily without disrupting tradition. The purpose of the *Collecta* service was to add more ceremony to important feasts. The secular drama, forbidden to the clerics, was meant to add ceremony to secular festive occasions. Thus it would follow quite reasonably for the Carolingian clerics to add a religious drama to heighten and enhance the pre-Mass *Collecta* ceremony on the most important feast in the liturgical year. In the light of Amalarius's suggestion that representations be made to educate the congregation, the logical next step is that the Church would adopt the secular dramatic form of presentation.

Since the *Quem quaeritis* dialogue did not grow from an introductory Introit trope but was added to the liturgy fully formed, there is little doubt that it was dramatized from the beginning. The very idea of presenting the lines in dialogue fashion with different singers performing the lines of the Marys and the angels invites dramatic reenactment. The purpose of adding the dialogue to the *Collecta* ceremony was to dramatize the occasion. It would have been the focal point of the *Collecta* ceremony and thus was intended to draw attention to itself.

If the above speculations are justified, the role of the *Quem quaeritis* dialogue in the history of medieval drama may be far more significant than has previously been believed. At the time of the origin of the dialogue, some time in the early ninth century, drama itself was in a peculiar and precarious position. It enjoyed a considerable popularity with the general public (and with much of the clergy as well, if one accepts the negative pronouncements of council and synod as evidence). Yet, theater was officially frowned upon by the Church, and all performances took place in opposition to official Church policy. In contrast to secular theater, the *Quem quaeritis* dialogue was not only officially approved but liturgically promoted, and it had a semiofficial position in the *Collecta* ceremony. In adopting drama via the *Quem quaeritis* dialogue the Church did not reverse its position on secular drama; the official pronouncements against secular theater continued throughout the ninth century and after. Only the three-line dialogue in the *Collecta* ceremony received Church approval.

Within a century of the death of Charlemagne the Carolingian revival gradually began to lose its thrust. Not all of Charlemagne's descendants had the same interest in culture, and soon after the end of the ninth century many of his artistic projects began to subside. Throughout the ninth century and into the tenth, eleventh, and twelfth centuries, the liturgical drama remained the only continuing evidence of the renewed interest in drama from the Carolingian revival. It survived the gradual demise of Charlemagne's artistic ideals because it alone was adopted by the Church and accepted as a legitimate liturgical as well as aesthetic expression.

At the end of the tenth century the placement of the dialogue was changed from the *Collecta* ceremony to the end of Matins for reasons quite possibly associated with the liturgical reforms begun at the Abbey of Cluny.[38] By the thirteenth century the dialogue was separated from the liturgy, and the original three lines were expanded to include several additional scenes and a number of additional characters. At this time also, the subject matter was extended to include additional biblical stories and religious legends.

No doubt the mimes continued in some fashion throughout those centuries, for the impulse to entertain is natural regardless of Church sanctions. But the new dramas of the thirteenth century, the secular plays of Adam de la Halle, and the fourteenth-century mystery cycles are descendants not of the mime but of the liturgical drama. They were accepted as "legitimate"—which means they were considered to be in the tradition of the only drama recognized by the Church: the liturgical drama. If it were not for the liturgical drama which sustained the tradition throughout the ninth through twelfth centuries, it is doubtful that the drama of the late Middle Ages could have developed. The authority of the Church was such that the traditional sanctions against theater would have prevented any official recognition had not the liturgical drama set a precedent. If the *Quem quaeritis* dialogue had not continued

38. McGee, "Origin and History of *Quem quaeritus* dialogue," chap. 4.

throughout the centuries, the development of legitimate theater in Western Europe may well have been delayed several hundred years until the lessening of the power of the Church and the rise of secular influence in the early years of the Renaissance. The role that the *Quem quaeritis* played in the history of medieval drama was to establish a legitimate, Church-recognized form of drama within the liturgy and thus carry to the late Middle Ages the dramatic ideal of Constantine's age as it was reestablished in Charlemagne's Carolingian revival.

Music as Dramatic Device in the Secular Theater of Marguerite de Navarre

LOUIS E. AULD

AMONG THE DIVERSE LITERARY PRODUCTION of Marguerite, Queen of Navarre, the seven dramatic poems grouped together as the *Théâtre profane* bear testimony to the flexibility and range of her spirit.[1] A learned lady in the best sense, she may also be considered the first modern French poet, the first—even before Ronsard—to entrust to her verses, however clumsily, her intimate personal sentiments, her fears, her sufferings, her rare joys, her devotion to those about her, and her intense, mystical love of God. The most personal of these plays is the *Comédie sur le trespas du roy*, written shortly after the death of her beloved brother François I in March 1547. It presents Marguerite and those close to her, thinly disguised as shepherds and shepherdesses, seeking solace for the loss of their king and companion, Pan. Although the denouement is in keeping with the princess's Evangelical mysticism, the play is neither

---

1. Marguerite de Navarre, *Théâtre profane*, ed. V. L. Saulnier, Textes Littéraires *Français* (1946; rev. ed., Geneva, 1963). (Hereafter cited as *TP*). See also Saulnier's "Etudes critiques sur les comédies profanes de Marguerite de Navarre," *BHR*, IX (1947), 36–77.

polemical nor didactic in essence, but an elegiac pastoral, "une déploration de Grande Rhétorique," in Saulnier's phrase (*TP*, p. 208). Having already poured out her grief in the *Chansons spirituelles,* generally considered some of the most admirable lyric poems of the century, in her melancholy epistles, and in the lengthy effusions of the *Navire,* the bereaved sister felt the need to couch it in yet another form, a form that could make meaningful to those close to her the terrible conflict she was enduring.[2] The shepherdess Amarissime, condemned to bitter tears, expresses her sorrow in a series of strophes of song interspersed throughout the dialogue; as the action progresses, the others join in until the arrival of the divine messenger Paraclesis, who informs them that the departed knows the joys of paradise; then all intone the praises of God. Two of the other plays, *L'Inquisiteur* and the *Comédie de Mont-de-Marsan,* also involve music extensively. In each case song is brought into the structure in such a way as to contribute to the dramatic effectiveness of the piece; and in each case music is used in an entirely different way. This paper proposes to examine the *Théâtre profane* from the point of view of Marguerite's skill in handling that association of the two sister arts.

Apart from the *Comédie sur le trespas du roy,* all the plays have polemical and didactic intention, and most employ the satirical manner common to farce. All but two defend, discuss, and illustrate the joyous and increasingly mystical Evangelical faith that sustained the erudite princess in the last, difficult years of her life. Secular only in contrast to her four mystery plays, whose subjects were drawn directly from the New Testament, they present their pious exempla sometimes in contemporary, sometimes in conventional bucolic settings. In the earliest, *Le Malade* (1535), a sick man is cured by faith. In the next, a cynical Inquisitor is converted to the religion of love by the songs of little children (*L'Inquisiteur,* 1536). All are strongly marked by a symbolic or frankly allegorical mode of thought. The most enigmatic is *Trop, Prou, Peu, Moins* (1544): two portly noblemen, Trop and Prou ("Beaucoup"), "parangons d'ambition impure et de mauvaise conscience" (*TP*, p. 127), are unable to hide the disgrace of their long ears (symbols of the Inquisition spy?), while

2. Abel Lefranc, ed., *Les Dernières poésies de Marguerite de Navarre* (Paris, 1896), p. xxviii.

their impoverished counterparts, Peu and Moins, rich only in spiritual goods, are protected from all harm by horns which "ne sont de chair, ne d'oz" (l. 368).

The *Comédie de Mont-de-Marsan,* the most fully elaborated of the plays (1015 lines), was performed in that city on Mardi Gras, 1547. Although set in the countryside, it has little of the pastoral about it, except in the use of songs.[3] Three women—La Mondainne, representing amoral materialism, La Supersticieuse, ascetic fanaticism, and La Sage, intelligent faith—debate the proper attitude to adopt toward life and faith, when a fourth arrives on the scene. She is La Ravie de l'Amour de Dieu, so full of joy in her complete and naïve love of her "ami" that she does not speak, but sings in answer to all their questions. The others are unable to share in or even comprehend her divinely inspired madness. Saulnier sees in this play a clear intention to answer Calvin's pamphlet *Contre les libertins* (*TP,* pp. 249 ff.). We will be more concerned with the way the shepherdess's snatches of song are made to serve the dramatic purpose.

Of the two plays which explore human love, the first does so in a realistic down-to-earth style, the second in a manner inspired by the author's study of Plato. Two maidens and two wives, representing a spectrum of attitudes and situations, seek out an aged woman for her advice—which all refuse to heed—on the proper conduct of their relationship with husband, lover, or suitor (*Comédie des quatre femmes,* 1542). "Pour la première fois au théâtre," comments Saulnier (*TP,* p. 82), "Marguerite accepte . . . de descendre sur le plan humain, sans préoccupation symbolique." Yet "descent to the human plane" does not automatically draw the artistic eye close enough to naturalistic detail to discover pimples and pockmarks. It remains at some distance from concrete reality; the allegorical mode—the habit of abstraction—is still operative, even here. The four figures in the Mont-de-Marsan comedy gave form to moral attitudes rather than to the more abstract moral qualities. Unlike the personifications of proverbial abstractions, Trop, Prou, et al., these women were designated as La Supersticieuse, not La Superstition; La Ravie, not L'Extase. The *quatre femmes,* if they illustrate real-life situations—one is jealous of her husband, another suspected by hers—as well

3. *Ibid.,* p. xxxii.

as moral postures, are still far from that world of dramatic reality in which a Pathelin or an Argan takes on the weight of flesh and blood. Called simply La Première Fille, La Seconde Fille, La Première Femme Mariée, etc., their activity consists entirely of discussion on a general level, as the opening lines attest:

> Tout le plaisir, et le contentement,
> Que peult avoir un gentil coeur honneste,
> C'est liberté de corps, d'entendement,
> Qui rend heureux tout homme, oyseau, ou beste.
>
> (ll. 1–4)

There are no doors or windows, no physical properties of any sort on the surface of these texts. The dramatic space is the mind and heart. Like Molière's *Bourgeois gentilhomme,* this playlet served as an elaborate prelude to a courtly dance spectacle and so has another kind of relation to music—but it is beyond the scope of this inquiry. The other truly secular, Platonic work, *Le Parfait Amant,* a trifle of 185 lines, written, in all probability, during the final year of Marguerite's life (1549), takes the form of a debate: Another wise old woman, this one more than a thousand years old, seeking to honor the perfect lover, considers three girls, but rejects each in turn as each sets limits to her love; she finally offers the crown to a man and a woman, each of whom insists that his partner and not himself is worthy of it.

Marguerite's literary production, whether in prose or in verse, is characterized as much by the sincerity of her emotions as by the constant and honest intellectual probing of her spirit, which Rabelais called "abstrait, ravy et exstatic." In all that she wrote she displayed greater concern for the matter she sought to express than for technique and form. Her preoccupations were moral, psychological, and spiritual rather than aesthetic. Thus, the plays present in dramatic form ideas, attitudes, beliefs, and feelings which she treated in other genres as well. Written for use among her entourage, they stand outside the scope of the professional theater of her time, that moribund medieval tradition. In fact, classification is difficult. In the embroiled terminology of the period, three are labeled *farce,* the rest, *comédie;* because of their abstract, allegorical character and nearly constant didactic intent, they could just as well be called *moralités.*

I

The foregoing summaries have meant to suggest—and to do no more than that at this point—the extent to which these plays depend on schematicization of their subjects, a conception far removed from that of modern theater. The constant simplification, the avoidance of concrete detail, the predilection for polarities and carefully calibrated intermediate degrees—all seem to bespeak a set of poems cast in dramatic form, but essentially devoid of necessary theatricality. Are they, unlike Musset's eminently playable "spectacles dans un fauteuil," fit only to be read? The reader, even one who enjoys that ability which Molière insisted upon as indispensable, "de voir dans ces indications tout le jeu des acteurs" ("Avertissement" to *L'Amour médecin*), finds little here to guide his visual imagination. In this Marguerite's plays are not unlike the other dramatic texts of her time. The realism was on the stage, in the gestures of the actors. Playwrights had not yet discovered the art of incorporating the telling gesture into the text itself. Indeed, they did not seek it. Professor Saulnier has testified, in a note to the revised edition (1963), that several productions undertaken since the first appearance of the entire set in 1945, revealed "que ces textes passaient la rampe" (p. xxv).

However disappointed we may be to find in the *Théâtre profane* so little of the density of the author's shorter poems, or the psychological realism of her *Heptaméron,* however frustrated by the resolutely general nature of the vocabulary, its relative colorlessness, we may still admire her skill at manipulating dramatic structures, creating poetic dialogue, handling a certain type of conventionalized dramatic rhythm, and finding varied ways to integrate song into the dramatic framework. In the highly personal dramatization of profound anguish that animates the *Comédie sur le trespas du roy,* as in *L'Inquisiteur* and the *Comédie de Mont-de-Marsan,* song serves both the development of the drama and the structural interplay of hidden meanings. This is a theater of the mind, intent on stimulating not so much the senses as the intellect. It draws its force from effective use of the rhetorical tradition. We tend to think of that ancient art either as a sterile collection of shopworn formulas or as a system of classification of tropes. But until relatively recently rhetorical learning concentrated more on forms, schemata, than on images. This play of forms—structures, in today's terminology—is what gives Marguerite's theater its dramatic power. The beauty of well-contrived schemes is intellectually perceived. This is not to say, of course, that these rhetorically based works have no affective power, that they touch only the mind and not the heart: rhetoric, after all, is the art of moving an audience. It is to suggest rather that the role played by music, as by the other constituent elements, employs that art's unquestioned affective power in a way specifically involving perception of forms.

Besides the variety of subjects and of levels of abstraction in this collection of essentially meditative chamber plays, the three that we are about to consider in detail furnish a note to the history of theater with music in France. Not only is the use of song a device clearly impossible in texts meant to be read, whether silently or aloud, but, since music has a very special effect in the theater, the way it is employed calls for study. Not the least of Marguerite's accomplishments is the distinctly different use of song in each case. In the first, *L'Inquisiteur,* she put into the mouths of children some of the most beautiful words of the Old Testament, those of Psalm 3; then, once the divinely inspired children have confounded and converted the worldly prelate to their "madness," the "Canticle of Simeon." In the second, the elegiac *Comédie sur le trespas du roy,* she set new lyrics to already existing, learned *chansons musicales,* using dialogue between strophes of song as less intense but still lyric episodes. And in the Mont-de-Marsan play she collected snatches of secular love songs, capitalizing on the ambiguous similarities in expression between sacred and profane love.

Music was not uncommon in plays of the early sixteenth century, but neither was it an indispensable element. In a thorough study of the repertoire from 1400–1550, Howard Mayer Brown found that "of the nearly 400 remaining plays . . . less than half mention any chanson specifically."[4] Marguerite's Mont-de-Marsan comedy is one of six plays which contain "ten or more chansons each, with at least a part of the text given. . . . The shepherdess . . . has twenty-nine sung lines and couplets, although some of them refer to different parts of the same chanson" (pp. 82–83). Marguerite's use of songs in the other two plays, while it

---

4. Howard Mayer Brown, *Music in the French Secular Theatre, 1400–1550,* (Cambridge, Mass., 1963), p. 82.

does not qualify them for mention among six out of four hundred, takes a form that Brown considers only "theoretically possible" in this period, the situation that arises when speech is "replaced by song, as in opera, where the audience must accept a convention it knows to be unrealistic" (p. 88). They do not, of course, truly anticipate operatic recitative; in fact, they draw their effect from that convention which denies ordinary mortals the right to sing on stage except in situations in which they might do so in real life.

Curiously, the earliest secular theatrical works known in France, the two plays by Adam de la Halle, not only contain examples of singing and dancing but offer a striking illustration of the two distinct ways in which song (and dance) can be used in nonoperatic theatre. In *Le Jeu de Robin et de Marion* (ca. 1283) Adam included pastoral songs and dances to help fix the action in that special realm which is peculiar to pastoral as a partially allegorized portrayal of human society.[5] The shepherds and shepherdesses of that play sing and dance as part of their normal everyday activities, but for ordinary communication they speak. Song and dance, which the audience may well appreciate as performance, are nonetheless presented primarily as amusement activities that the characters do among themselves. The tradition dates from antiquity; it would be revived in the later Renaissance through the influence of the Orphic myth, and in the device of the singing competition between rival shepherds.

The other play by Adam de la Halle, *Le Jeu de la feuillée* (1262), contains only one line of music, sung by fairies as they descend to earth.[6] This solitary line reinforces the miraculous effect in contrast to the otherwise realistic situation. It opens for the spectator, if only fleetingly, the door to another world, from which these supernatural beings come, a world in which the normal state is so different from that of ordinary mortals that its beings communicate in song. These two examples represent opposite poles of music's use in drama. (We are not concerned here with incidental music, preludes, horn calls, fanfares). On the one hand

5. *Le Jeu de Robin et de Marion,* ed. Ernest Langlois (Paris, 1896); or cf. the editions by K. Varty, mus. trans. Eric Hill (London, 1960); Friedrich Gennrich, (Frankfurt a.M., 1962).

6. *Le Jeu de la feuillée,* ed. Ernest Langlois (C.F.M.A.), 2d ed. rev. (1923; repr. Paris, 1964).

there is performance per se, whether presented as naïve amusement of the characters at play or as polished and accomplished artistry. This approach culminates in the play-within-a-play device, and sometimes, as a variant, in the ballet-within-a-play, as in Durval's *Agarite* (Paris, 1636). On the other hand there is song or dance as the natural mode of expression of the character: one who sings when others speak is immediately understood to be either "possessed" (by love or some other form of madness) or a being different from, and normally superior to, the other characters of the play.

II

It is the second approach which Marguerite adopted in the earliest of her plays to call for singing, as she dramatized the conversion of the evil Inquisitor, symbol of the spirit of persecution into which the established Church had fallen, brought by seven little children to recognize the true, joyous message of Christianity. As is often the case in these plays, the title character simply explains to the audience what he represents. In nine eight-line strophes he complains of the difficulty of dealing with "ce savoir neuf, qui le nostre surmonte," the new Evangelism whose adepts know the Bible better than he; he confesses himself venal and corrupt; then, with a casuistic argument which relates him to Tartuffe, he explains the efficacity of occasionally condemning an innocent man as an example for others, for one can always justify excessive cruelty by ascribing it to zeal:

> Le noir en blanc ainsi sçay convertir,
> Car ma fureur en zelle je desguyse.
>
> (ll. 55–56)

With that, he concludes that he is a "Rien-ne-vault."

The scene shifts briefly to the children, whose words suggest symbolically their nearness to God. A simultaneous shift to a five-syllable line expresses the carefree nature of their play. They are presented two at a time, each speaking a tercet, each pair of tercets following the rhyme scheme aab / aab. With the exception of the first set, in which the first child, Janot, has a sixain to himself between two of the exchanges, the three groups are perfectly uniform.

Shocked by their carefree play, the Inquisitor upbraids them for passing their time "ainsi en jeux et en chansons" rather than at their lessons. They answer each of his charges with riddles and enigmas of such infuriating wisdom and cleverness—

L'INQUISITEUR

Quel plaisir pouvez vous avoir
A jeu de si peu de valleur?

JACOT

Comment pouvez vous le jeu veoir,
Qui n'a ne forme ne coulleur?

L'INQUISITEUR

Je voy le jeu, où fourvoyez
Vous estes de faire tout bien.

THIERROT

Ha, vous dictes que vous voyez!
En bonne foy, je n'en croy rien.

(ll. 195–202)

—that he finally commands them to stop talking, whereupon they commence to sing, since they may no longer speak their faith. The Varlet takes up their defense and interprets their song for the incensed prelate, who needs an interpreter to comprehend the word of God. When the Inquisitor suspects that they are making fun of him, his servant reassures him:

Ce sont enfans, qui sans soulcy
S'accordent d'une voix ensemble:
Chacun est joyeulx comme ung roy.

(ll. 291–293)

Line 292, which at first glance seems doubly redundant, in fact suggests a contradiction, since *s'accorder* implies that they sing in harmony. The figurative meaning suggests that they praise God in complete accord, with the natural sweetness of innocence. It is not unlikely that the children sang a single melodic line in unison. But they may have adopted the learned, polyphonic style. Whatever the case, their song, so appropriate for the occasion (Marot's French translation of Psalm 3)—

O Seigneur, que de gens,
A nuyre dilligens,
Qui nous troublent et griefvent!
Mon Dieu, que d'ennemys,
Qui aux champs se sont mis
Et contre nous s'eslièvent!

(ll. 283–288)

—shows that without study or effort they naturally praise God in the worthiest of styles. Their untutored discourse, like that of Jesus in the temple, is shown by this device to be on a higher spiritual level than that of the churchman. As children they are still close to God. Thus, the step from speech to song is a short one for them, almost a return to a more natural means of expression.

Besides lifting the children above the base world of the Inquisitor—"Ilz [*sic*] sont hors de mérencolye" (l. 297)—their song also produces its wonted effect upon the soul. As the Varlet comments, again:

Escouttez leur chanson jolye,
De joye serez possesseur.

(ll. 301–302)

After the first sextet, sung in one section, every three lines of the psalm are punctuated by his increasingly ecstatic comments, comments that clearly delineate the stages of his conversion, as he comes to share in their accord. At the beginning of the scene he simply tries to defend the children from his master's wrath, arguing their youth and innocence. Just before the song the Inquisitor asks him if he means to take their side, and he quickly replies, "Non faiz." But as they continue to sing he remarks first on their joy and the beauty of their song, then on the unity of their singing, the absence of strife and discord in their wholly pure, Christian existence. This leads him to praise the lack of falseness in their hearts. When they begin to sing of nearness to God ("Poinct ne m'a repoulsé"), he decides to join them, to share in this communion which is a means of approaching God:

En liberté et sans contraincte
Jouans, chantans, tousjours joyeulx,
Passent le temps à chose maincte,
Mais tousjours ont au ciel les yeulx.
   Si congé me donnez, mon maistre,

Avecques eulx je demourray:
Car en pleur je ne veulx plus estre,
Mais avecques eulx je riray.

(ll. 323–330)

This affirmation of the joys and pleasures of life, which is one of the central currents of the rediscovery of pagan antiquity, takes on mystical significance in the revitalized Evangelistic Christianity of Marguerite's fellow-believers, who have indeed "become as little children," finding a source of joy in all the things of God's creation.

As the beauty of the children's song wins the Varlet to their side, as he begins to desire to live at one with them as they are in a sense at one with God, his thought begins to coincide with theirs in a striking verbal parallel:

LES ENFANS

Donq coucher m'en iray,
En seurté dormiray,
Sans craincte de mesgarde.

LE VARLET

L'oeil de Dieu tousjours les garde.

LES ENFANS

Puis me resveilleray:
Et sans peur veilleray,
Ayant Dieu pour ma garde.

LE VARLET

Je croy qu'à chacun d'eulx bien tarde
L'heure qu'en Paradis seront.

LES ENFANS

Cent mil hommes de front
Craindre ne me feront,
Encores qu'ilz emprinsent.

LE VARLET

Pleust à Dieu, sans tant sermonner,
Qu'avecques eulx ilz me retinsent.

LES ENFANS

Et que, pour m'estonner,
Clorre et environner
De tous coustez me vinsent.

LE VARLET

Et que leur chant si bien m'apprinsent
Que, comme eulx, vesquisse de foy.

(ll. 331–349)

Their faith takes root in him so solidly that he is ready to side with them,
as indicated in the words of their song, against a hundred thousand men
—even, and more immediately, against his master, the Inquisitor. Here
the poetess brings to bear her rhetorical skill by aligning the Varlet's
ruminations with the ideas contained in the children's song, so that, lost
in his own thoughts, he is at the same time carried along by the suggestions of the psalm until finally at the end of the passage his sentence
and that of the children dovetail syntactically ("Et que . . ." plus the
subjunctive verb), even though they started from syntactically as well as
morally different positions. Not only is this sort of device particularly well
suited to the schematic-symbolic style of the play, it is equally appropriate
for use with music, for it operates in the same way as musical forms. It
serves to set the servant and the children into a parallel relationship, to
establish a communion among them, even though the Varlet is not yet
filled with the divine madness that lifts their expression into song.

Moments later the learned cleric again questions the children. At first
the smallest among them answers in the most infantile way possible,
uttering great truths in double monosyllables, while the Varlet interprets:

L'INQUISITEUR

Mon filz, comme appellez vous Dieu?

LE PETIT ENFANT

Pappa.

LE VARLET

C'est tresbien respondu,
Père il est de tous en tout lieu,
Mais il n'est pas bien entendu.

L'INQUISITEUR

Qu'espérez vous trouver en luy?

L'ENFANT

Dodo.
. . . .

L'INQUISITEUR

Mais qui est ce Dieu là?

L'ENFANT

Bon, bon.

. . . .

L'INQUISITEUR

Des bonnes oeuvres, des mérittes,
Qu'est ce?

L'ENFANT

Cza.

(ll. 419–433)

Thus does even the smallest child confound the powerful, worldly prelate
with a verbal snap of the fingers ("Çà!"). Immediately, the children begin, in a series of nine quatrains, to propound the tenets of the Evangelical
faith.

Qui voyt Dieu partout en tout lieu
Et ne veoit plus ne soy ny homme,
Il est par grâce filz de Dieu,
Et Dieu, non plus homme, se nomme.

(ll. 448–451)

Having risen above the level of ordinary mortals in the eyes of their
interlocutors—and the audience—they can now return to the speech-level
of the play (i.e., poetry) for rational exposition of their position. The two
men are deeply moved by this demonstration:

L'INQUISITEUR

Ilz ne disent rien d'aventure:
J'ay tout dedans la Bible leu.
Et leur parolle est si trèspure
Que jamais tel sens je n'ay veu.

LE VARLET

Mais oyez le divin langaige
Que chacun de ces enfans tient.

(ll. 472–477)

The conversion of the Inquisitor is signaled as he bursts into a fast-
moving (pentasyllabic) odelike prayer which begins:

O puissant Esprit,
O doulx Jésuchrist.

(ll. 488–489)

His four twelve-line stanzas will be followed by four more spoken by the
Varlet, then by six half-stanzas as each of the children adds his voice to
the paean. Then all join hands in a visual indication of their spiritual
union as they sing the "Cantique de Siméon," newly translated by Bona-
venture des Périers:

> *Puis que de ta promesse*
> *L'entier accompliment*
> *Octroye à ma vieillesse*
> *Parfaict contantement:*
> *J'actendray sans soulcy*
> *De la mort la mercy.*

(ll. 624–629)

Marguerite's faith in the redemption of sinners is expressed in a dramatic
poetry largely devoid of imagery and concrete detail, a poetry of moral
preoccupation, built of the sort of structural blocks that rhetoric has in
common with music.[7] We need seek no realism here, material or psychological. What is portrayed is spiritual action. The Inquisitor's conversion,
like his inability to comprehend the children's transparent riddles, may
not be understood in realistic, temporal terms. They are abstract, or
symbolic, representations of events that might be observed in life in any
number of different specific forms. Similarly, if he is converted, suddenly
and without transition, to the pure, humanistic faith of the children,
that conversion is effected through essentially musical means, including
musiclike structures, which elevate the action of the play above the
constraints of realistic convention.

III

In the "mystical mascarade" performed at Mont-de-Marsan three
women discuss and finally agree upon the best way to live: neither to put
all one's faith in things terrestrial and material (La Mondainne), nor to
disdain the body in the attempt to elevate the soul (La Supersticieuse),

---

7. This observation and other assumptions made here concerning the union of
words and music are explained and illustrated, with specific reference to seventeenth-century practices, in my forthcoming book, *The Lyric Art of Pierre Perrin,
Founder of French Opera,* to be published by the Institute of Mediaeval Music.

but to accept the dualism of the human condition, and to gain peace through study of the Scriptures (the position urged by La Sage). A *coup de théâtre,* however, shows even this to be inferior to another approach to God, that of simple, complete love, as exemplified by La Ravie de l'Amour de Dieu, a shepherdess whose only occupation is loving her "berger" and expressing that love in song and dance. She hardly ever speaks, but responds in song to their every remark, with the exception of one short passage, where she condescends to reason with them. In the play just discussed the princess had incorporated into a dramatic context serious songs written, and probably set, by members of her entourage. In this case she simply drew bits of song from the standard repertoire. The trick, a not uncommon one in the later Middle Ages, consisted of placing the secular lyrics in a context where their nonspecific professions of profane love would be understood in a sacred sense:

> Jamais d'aymer mon cueur ne sera las,
> Car dieu l'a faict d'une telle nature
> Que vray amour luy sert de noriture:
> Amour luy est pour tout plaisir soulas.
>
> (ll. 603–606)

> J'ayme bien mon amy
> De bonne amour certaine,
> Car je sçay bien qu'il m'ayme
> Et aussi fay je luy.
>
> (ll. 628–631)

> Laisser parler, laissez dire,
> Laisser parler qui vouldra.
> Médire qui veult mesdire;
> J'aymeray qui m'aymera.
>
> (ll. 639–642)

Using lyrics in the familiar style of medieval popular songs, Marguerite profits from the prevalence of pastoral love songs to develop the conceit of the person who truly loves God as Shepherdess to the Great Shepherd of Psalm 23. None of this was new; Marguerite put it into a dramatic structure of her own creation.

She amused herself in a sort of tour de force that involved making these borrowed words to popular songs serve as answers to the comments of the three other women:

LA SUPERSTICIEUSE
Qui l'entretient en ceste amour aymée?

LA BERGERE *chante*
Doulce memoire en plaisir consommée.

LA SAGE
Voicy une nouvelle loy:
Comment venez vous si contente?

LA BERGERE *chante*
Seure et loial[e] en foy,
Jusqu'à la mort amante.

LA MONDAINNE
N'avez vous d'autre vie envie?

LA BERGERE *chante*
Chanter et rire est ma vie,
Quant mon amy est près de moy.

LA SUPERSTICIEUSE
J'oy d'elle ce que croire n'oze.

LA BERGERE *chante*
Helas! il n'est si doulce chose . . .

LA SAGE
En sa fasson ny chant je n'entend[z] rien.

LA BERGERE *chante*
Que ne m'entendz! assez je m'entend[z] bien.

(ll. 653–665)

The others will never know nor understand this state of ecstasy, and the end of the play leaves them uncertain as to whether "Elle est du tout ou folle ou beste, / Ou opiniastre ou glorieuse" (ll. 940–941).

La Supersticieuse and La Mondainne each sing a short passage at the opening of the play (ll. 41–46, 87–88). This is the same sort of music as that of La Ravie later on, but it has a very different purpose from hers.[8]

8. Some of the music to these plays has been identified by Lefranc, *Dernières poésies,* "Appendice sur les timbres des chansons," pp. 441 ff.; see also Brown, pp. 183 ff.; a complementary volume, *Theatrical Chansons of the Fifteenth and Early Sixteenth Centuries,* 1963, gives scores, sometimes several settings of a single poem or timbre.

The sextet and couplet sung by the first two set the pastoral atmosphere and foreshadow the climax, where the Bergere will give voice to thirty-four snatches of song, consisting of from one to six lines. Her song, which renders ordinary conversation impossible and thus disrupts normal social interaction, stands apart from theirs. A director would make sure that she had the sweetest voice of the three. La Supersticieuse, ancestor of Arsinoë, might have a harsh, dry sound, while her worldly companion could sport a torchy contralto, for instance. Then, if the Shepherdess had a clear, flexible soprano, the effect would be achieved without any necessity for other musical distinction.

In any case, the point is made dramatically. The satisfaction of the first two gives way easily before the sober arguments of the Wise Woman, while the complete and unreasoning abandon of La Ravie withstands the arguments of all three. Because the ineffable, mystical source of her joy lies beyond the expressive powers of human discourse, it is natural that she sing, just as it is effective dramatic convention that they, like the Inquisitor, not comprehend the true meaning of her statements when the audience does so with ease. In adapting these "chansons païennes" to pious intentions, the Queen of Navarre followed the recent example of the *Chrestienne Resjouyssance* by Eustorg de Beaulieu.[9] She devised her own way of putting them to use.

With that remarkable combination of erudition, charity, and mystical faith which caused Marot, who knew her well, to describe her as "corps féminin, coeur d'homme, et tête d'ange," the poetess cast in dramatic form with this play a forceful statement of a problem which haunted the Renaissance and which was to divide France in bloody strife later in the century: what place, in an increasingly secular society, should the true saint be accorded? The play offers no solution to the problem, other than the dramatically clumsy one of tolerance, as the three earthbound women decide to leave the young Shepherdess to her transports:

---

9. See the Addendum, *TP*, p. 323, with reference to the study by Harvitt, *Eustorg de Beaulieu* (Paris, 1918), pp. 114-139. Saulnier also notes three songs used by both authors. Confusion of secular and religious modes was a common practice, as amply demonstrated by D. W. Robertson, *A Preface to Chaucer* (Princeton, N.J., 1962), pp. 17, and *passim*.

Peult estre qu'un jour sera bonne;
Pensez que telle avez esté:
L'iver ne resemble à l'esté.
Retirons-nous, car il est tard.

(ll. 955–958)

They can see in her action nothing but madness. Saulnier has pointed out that the theme of the apparent folly which possesses those of true faith recurs constantly throughout this set of plays (*TP,* pp. 128, *passim*). That observation gives added support to the corrected reading he offers for the name of the heroine. Abel Lefranc, who first published the long-undiscovered manuscripts to these works, read her name as La *Reine* de l'Amour de Dieu.[10] *Ravie,* like those other "fous pour le monde," Peu and Moins, and the psalm-singing children, she is transported out of this world to a higher plane. (The same term, *ravi,* is used to describe the *trespas du roy;* he too has been carried away by perfect love, in a way not essentially different, but only more complete.) "Out of this world" may appear inaccurate unless we assume that the world of the play may be equated with that of basic human existence. This is true in the sense that, since reality is rich in multiple and often contradictory suggestion, no work of art can be other than selective. The qualities of the individual, as Aristotle knew, are infinite; every work of art must to some extent deal in species rather than individuals. Every play, from the most naturalistic drawing-room drama to the most allegorical morality, establishes a base level at some lesser or greater remove from undifferentiated, existential reality; that base level is then understood, within the framework, to stand for that reality. In the Mont-de-Marsan comedy, as in the Inquisitor farce, Marguerite presents a highly schematized view of life —existence on the level of moral perception. In order to present a character of a different stripe, one, as we might say, who has her head in the clouds, she has recourse to the device used by Adam de la Halle in the *Jeu de la feuillée,* the supraverbal power of song. On a different satirical level, Molière, for instance, allowed the two lovers in *Le Malade imaginaire,* to express their passion in improvised song before the girl's uncomprehending father. On yet another level, a popular farce of the

10. Lefranc himself revised his reading on this point; see Saulnier, "Etudes critiques," p. 47.

fifteenth century made sport of a man who refused to speak to his wife except in song.[11] Such deviant behavior is indeed folly in the down-to-earth world of farce. The traditional pastoral setting, reminiscent of *Robin et Marion,* which seems to be suggested at the outset of *Mont-de-Marsan* when each shepherdess absentmindedly sings a bit of a familiar tune, takes on an entirely different character with the appearance of La Ravie. Marguerite's playlet lifts well-known insignificant ditties out of their commonplace banality and, profiting from that ambiguity which is the special gift of musical expression, transforms them into vehicles of profound devotion.

IV

Yet another possible way of using existing songs is the frequent Renaissance device of parody, writing new words to old melodies. This Marguerite did in the *Comédie sur le trespas du roy,* in which courtly inhabitants of a pastoral society, Amarissime, her husband Securus, and their cherished friend Agapy, mourn the death of the chief Berger, Pan. She used a feminine form of Paraclesis, the messenger of comfort, who assures them that Pan has not died but risen to a new life in paradise. The transparently symbolic Greek names help to establish a humanistic infrastructure for the elaboration of a not quite typical medieval allegory. "Les personnages," noted Saulnier, "n'habillent pas ici, comme c'est si souvent le cas chez elle, un certain nombre d'attitudes differentes de l'âme" (*TP,* p. 212). If it is possible to identify the principals more or less convincingly as members of the author's family (Amarissime, Marguerite herself; Securus, her husband Henry d'Albret; Agapy, most likely her nephew, the future Henry II), the existence of such historical keys does not limit the meaning of the play by setting it in the realm of history, but adds yet a further level of significance. Marguerite mourns the loss of her brother, the King of France; on the stage a shepherdess bemoans the loss of her community's respected leader, Pan; his very name, however, shows him to be a demigod and sets the action on a level higher than that of the ordinary shepherd-play. For Paraclesis there can be no historical key.

---

11. *Le Savetier qui ne respont que chansons,* in *Recueil de farces françaises inédites du XVe siècle,* ed. G. Cohen (Cambridge, Mass., 1949), pp. 287–294.

Her arrival with words of Christian consolation not only raises the play
to the abstract conceptual level indicated in the other names, but firmly
anchors it within a context of Christian Evangelism, in an archetypal
situation patterned on that of the disciples overcome with grief at the loss
of their Messiah. The characters do not incarnate "a number of different
moral positions" in the sense that the work is not polemical, not a debate,
but eulogistic and elegiac. They share the same attitudes: what keeps
the subject from becoming unbearably static is a touch of psychological
realism that permits each to react in a somewhat different way.

Into this highly formalized rhetorical drama are introduced strophes of
song, with a regularity reminiscent of the slow drum beats of a funeral
procession. Each song is introduced with a notation indicating the most
familiar words of the melody used, the timbre (cf. "To be sung to the
tune of *God Save the Queen*"). Several stanzas or *couplets* of the same
song may appear, separated by dialogue, without further need for reference to the timbre; but when a new timbre begins, its first two lines
are given to identify it. These are *chansons musicales,* learned songs,
and most of the music has survived both in monophonic and homophonic
versions. Amarissime sings the first two couplets, to the timbre *"Jouyssance vous donneray."* [12] This would seem an incongruous vehicle for
such a doleful burden as "Las! tant malheureuse je suis," had not the
ability of a given piece of music to adapt to the most diverse textual meanings and moods so often been demonstrated. Besides, the emotional content of this sort of music was relatively indeterminate, with little or no
attempt made to convey a mood through the music alone. The second
chanson, a strophe of eight lines, uses the timbre *"Las! voulez-vous
qu'une personne chante / De qui le cueur ne faict que souspirer."*
Marguerite evidently followed the original text closely in this case, for

12. The original text (and perhaps the melody as well) is by Clément Marot; cf.
his *Oeuvres,* ed. Jannet, II, 177, and *Les Chansons de Clément Marot,* by Jean
Rollin (Paris, 1950). The music exists in several polyphonic versions, listed by
Brown, pp. 244–245. He also notes there that the Bergere in the Mont-de-Marsan
play sings two lines of this chanson, beginning with "Encores quant mortes seray."
And he points out an erroneous stage direction in the Saulnier edition (p. 221),
which would have Securus and Amarissime begin to sing to the new timbre: *Je
vous supplie, voyez comment / En amour je suis mal traicté,* whereas in fact they
merely intone a fourth stanza of the "jouyssance" chanson.

the first two lines of her chanson correspond structurally, and she even kept some of the original rhymes, with slight variations in the order.

In the other plays there is a clear distinction between the styles of the texts for music and those for spoken dialogue. In the *Trespas du roy* the two are virtually indistinguishable:

> O Pan, o Pan, mon maistre et mon amy,
> Puisque tu es de nos yeulx arraché,
> Et que ton corps en terre est endormy,
> Et avecq toy tout nostre bien caché,
> Que fera plus mon ceur triste et fâché
> Fors de pleurer, delaissant toutte joye?
> Pourquoy mon lut j'ay au saulle attaché
> Sans que jamais son armonie j'oye.
>
> (ll. 55–62)

> *Tant de larmes gettent mes yeulx,*
> *Qu'ilz ne voient terre ne cieulx,*
> *Telle est de leur pleur l'habondance.*
> *Ma bouche se plainct en tous lieux,*
> *De mon ceur ne peult saillir mieulx*
> *Que soupirs sans nulle allegence.*
>
> (ll. 63–68)

Of these two lamentations, the first is spoken by Securus, the second sung by Amarissime. Save for a few lines that serve to indicate and advance the stage action, all the speeches and songs until the appearance of the Paraclete mourn the death of Pan. The strongly rhetorical character of the entire text, which heightens the language of even the spoken passages in a way not observable in the other plays (where the poetic expression remains relatively unadorned), minimizes the distance between wailing lamentation and full-fledged song. Securus indeed takes his wife's song as an indication of her grief:

> Mais n'ay-je pas ouy la foible voix
> De la dolente et triste Amarissime,
> Devers laquelle à grand haste m'en vois?
> Car à l'oyr presque morte l'estime,
> Plaine de deuil du pied jusqu'à la cime.
> De desespoir j'ay son chant entendu:
> Elle a raison, soit en prose ou en rime,
> De lamenter, car elle a tout perdu.
>
> (ll. 69–76)

And if the inconsolable shepherdess consents to live for her husband's sake, she does so only that she may continue her dirge:

> Pour toy vivray en ceste vie amère.
> Mais chantons donc puisque ceste cymere
> Mort a de nous nostre joye ravie.
>
> (ll. 116–118)

All share the same overwhelming sense of loss, and thus transported out of themselves they communicate better in song than in speech. Whereas in the other plays song served to create distance between one group and another, now it brings all the characters into communion, it unites them in suffering. Agapy hears Amarissime's song as she approaches, and at first fails to understand its specific referent:

> Quel son, quel chant est-ce que j'oy de loing,
> Tant que je pers le sens et la parole?
>
> (ll. 153–154)

He nevertheless immediately perceives the mournful tone:

> C'est voix de femme et qui a grand besoing,
> A mon advis, que quelcun la consolle.
>
> (ll. 155–156)

She sings two more strophes, whereupon he exclaims that she is speaking directly to him:

> Ceste voix là me tire à soy,
> Car elle est semblable à la mienne:
> Et sens une douleur en moy
> Toute telle comme la sienne.
> Sa chansson me semble ancienne,
> Si sont les motz de neuf ouvraige;
> D'où que ce soit que la voix vienne,
> Ignorer n'en puis le langaige.
>
> (ll. 173–180)

That "language" is music, the most powerful mover of the passions. Almost as though it were a password to a secret society, that of mutual grief and suffering, Securus then sings a couplet: "Ma triste voix plus rien que dueil ne chante" (l. 201), to which Agapy responds with one of his own:

Ma douleur, [trop] grande au dedans
Du cueur ne peult sortir dehors.

(ll. 217–218)

Amarissime recognizes the community of spirit she feels with his mode of expression:

C'est Agapy: je congnois sa voix doulce.
Hélas, c'est luy, j'en ay bonne apparance.
Son chant piteux à lamenter me poulse,
Car, comme moy, il n'a que desplaisance.

(ll. 225–228)

The unanimity of their sorrow once established in this manner, they can speak their mutual pain until, rising to a new height of feeling, they join their voices as well as their hearts in the trio "Tant ay d'ennuy et tant de desconfort" (l. 351), which is interrupted by the messenger with words of reassurance and comfort. The play ends with a four-part Latin song in the tradition of the *Te Deum Laudamus* with which most medieval plays concluded.

V

Thus, in each of three *comédies profanes,* Marguerite made different and effective use of song: by putting poetic translations of biblical texts into the mouths of children; by transforming popular ditties into devotional lyrics; and by composing new, dramatically appropriate lyrics to preexistent music. Each device, far from being a facile adornment, makes a significant contribution to the dramatic effectiveness of the works. In all three cases she drew on the power that music has on the stage to set those who use it apart from other characters. Music, whose strangely affective structures are the only source of its meaning, often seems to reveal higher forms of existence; it is the Platonic art *par excellence*. It may place the singer above the others in the eyes of the audience, it may bring others up to the same spiritual level as the singer, or it may underline a common spiritual state. All three plays depend on the convention which decrees that ordinary mortals do not normally sing. In all three that refusal of norms produces perception of a higher, an ideal world.

There is no recitative here, no *cantar parlando* such as would be devised for the new genre of opera. Yet song in these plays does convey verbal along with supraverbal meanings. The device is not proto-operatic, but thoroughly and strictly dramatic. Professor Saulnier has suggested that the integration of song into these dramatic structures makes them "de vraies chantefables" (*TP*, p. xxi). Tempting though such comparison may be, it threatens to obscure the true character both of Marguerite's poems and of the curious medieval genre known to us through the familiar *Aucassin et Nicolette*.[13] That delightful thirteenth-century work alternates passages of prose with sections of chanted verse in a way that does indeed resemble the contrast of recited and sung passages in Marguerite's comedies. Yet, however slim the dividing line between narrative and dramatic material in an age when stories were normally recited, the *chantefable* remains a narrative, not a dramatic form. Its chanted sections contrast sharply with the prose narrative. They do not advance the action, but provide a lyric commentary on it through the lament, meditation, or rejoicing of one of the characters, or simply through remarks by the narrator on their psychological state. There is a distinct difference in style between the generally quite straightforward, bare-storytelling narrative passages and the lyric passages, full of descriptions, direct quotations, lamentations, etc. Since there are no actors, but only the narrator, the music need not be presented as a natural activity of certain sorts of characters. (There is only one passage of song as such, the lament of a guard sympathetic to the plight of the lovers: section 15.) Even the music is rooted in narrative tradition. Closely akin to the repetitive phrases of liturgical chant, it is intoned on a single repeated line of plainchant until the final line of each section, which gets a different melodic configuration to mark the ending. Marguerite's intentions and methods are essentially different.

Her playlets, written neither as popular entertainment nor for art's sake, as we think of art today, but in the service of her deep-seated re-

---

13. *Aucassin et Nicolette*, ed. F. W. Bourdillon (Manchester, 1919). Saulnier finds that "les chansons se mêlent agréablement aux textes (en trois des comédies) pour en faire de vraies chantefables" (*TP*, p. xxi). Grace Frank, in a chapter devoted to *Aucassin et Nicolette*, discussed the slim dividing line that existed between narrative and dramatic material, concluding that the *chantefable* was not essentially theatrical (*The Medieval French Drama* [Oxford, 1954], pp. 237–242).

ligious convictions, are among the first works to cast personal lyricism in a dramatic mold. In order to express her philosophically oriented thought, they take maximum advantage of the schematic tradition of rhetoric and music. Her dramatic technique, like her thought, deals in symbolic structures and high levels of abstraction. It is a constant of lyricism that musical setting wants simplification of verbal expression. It has the power, as it were, to fill in the spaces, created by the simplified expression of the text, with richer meanings of a supraverbal nature. By giving them the strongly affective force that abstract thought lacks, music plays a large part in making the schematized worlds of these plays dramatically viable.

The Musical Art of
Richard Brome's Comedies

R. W. INGRAM

CAROLINE AUDIENCES expected musical entertainment during their plays, but few of their playwrights were as adept as Brome at making the music serve any effective dramatic purpose. Playwrights too often relied upon a drably unimaginative use of convention: love scenes, whether romantic, gay, or melancholy, permitted, almost asked for, music to match their mood; pathetic singing of snatches of old songs was the regular embellishment of scenes of distress or madness; a tavern setting called for a lusty song, a brothel setting for a bawdy one; feasts and celebrations allowed for every kind of music. Brome subscribes to the same conventions, but handles them so expertly as to restore their vitality. He makes occasion demand music and not merely excuse it; he writes musical scenes rather than scenes with some music added to them. In his comedies music is a necessary delight.

Brome's musical art, like his dramaturgical art generally, is based on established forms and persisting conventions. His best critic, R. J. Kaufmann, has written of his consistent conservatism in basic thought and dramatic method, but that daunting word does not mean that he was

either timid or dull as a playwright.[1] For him, conservatism was a source
of strength, not a literary cripple's crutch. He was a traditionalist who
proved a principle enunciated by Bertrand Russell: "although direct
imitation is always to be deprecated, there is much to be gained by a
familiarity with good drama."[2] Brome's familiarity with good drama
came in a very direct way—he had once been Ben Jonson's servant, a
humble beginning his contemporaries did not allow him to forget. In
some prefatory verses to the 1647 folio of Beaumont and Fletcher's collected plays, he wrote:

> Y'have had your Jere: Sirs, no;
> But, in an humble manner, let you know
> Old serving-creatures oftentimes are fit
> T'informe young masters.

This was no idle brag, for he had as much to teach most young Caroline
masters as he himself had had to learn from Jonson. Not least, he could
inform in the sprightly and inventive use of musical conventions, especially in comedy.

Brome's natural medium was middle-class comedy and for his characters music is primarily a social pleasure; there is an engaging air of
practicality about it that nevertheless encompasses an element of satisfying emotional warmth. The musical range of the comedies is wide but
generally aims at rousing delight and excitement rather than passion or
intensity. Those qualities are more natural to the exotic world of
Fletcherian tragedy and tragicomedy. Brome traveled three times to that
world and demonstrates an able handling of its more overtly powerful
musical effects rather than a wholehearted exploration of them. The
strong and complex pressures exerted by such effects are as foreign to him
as to the nature of his comedy (whose musical effects, however, are no
less subtle and diverse). He is concerned with less exalted people in less

1. R. J. Kaufmann, *Richard Brome Caroline Playwright* (New York and London, 1961).

2. Bertrand Russell, "Portraits from Memory," quoted from *The Basic Writings
of Bertrand Russell 1903–1959,* ed. R. E. Egner and L. E. Dennon (London, 1961),
p. 65.

perilous situations. Both forms of drama, however, drew on the customs of seventeenth-century society for their musical usages.[3]

Music pervaded society at all levels to a surprising degree. It was the natural accompaniment of work and play. In many ways it bore no less a part in life then than it does today, save that our music has become more of a background noise—it is switched on or piped in and is incidental music in the saddest sense. Perhaps for this reason it is sometimes thought odd that the characters of seventeenth-century drama so casually and unembarrassedly break into song: music-making that for us has something of the air of a too deliberately contrived performance was, in Brome's day, accepted as natural and unexceptionable behavior. Brome took advantage of the opportunities offered by this given background for slighter decorations in his plays as well as for major motifs in their design. Everyday impulses to music are skillfully turned to dramatic ends.

Thus the conventions of the day allowed the creation of characters who were especially musical in some way without making them seem awkward excuses for the introduction of music. Their sincerity or insincerity only adds to their dramatic appeal. One such group of characters includes those who by necessity of their calling or the bent of their minds sing when others would talk. Crack, in *The City Wit,* depends upon his musical abilities for his livelihood and so brings music with him whenever he appears. Constance, *The Northern Lass,* on the other hand, is noted for her beautiful voice and a propensity to express her emotions by singing. Hearty and Tallboy Oldrents, in *The Jovial Crew,* tend at times to find singing more congenial than talking, and the Jovial Crew of Gipsies themselves continually express their corporate views of life in

---

3. Space prevents setting this sketch of Brome's musical usages in a detailed frame of reference to seventeenth-century musical beliefs and practices. Fortunately such details are readily available. "Ideas of Music in English Poetry 1500–1700" is the subtitle of John Hollander's *The Untuning of the Sky* (Princeton, N.J., 1961); also valuable on this topic is Nan C. Carpenter, *Music in the Medieval and Renaissance Universities* (Norman, Okla., 1958). J. S. Manifold, *The Music in English Drama From Shakespeare to Purcell* (London, 1956) is a convenient introduction to the musical resources of the theaters and the significance of the individual musical instruments. Two incisive and different books on general social background and music are E. D. Mackerness, *A Social History of English Music* (London, 1964), and Wilfrid Mellers, *Music and Society* (New York, 1950).

festival music. Enthusiastic amateurs make up another distinctive group. They range from rich gentlemen like Letoy (*The Antipodes*) who can afford their own musicians to humbler, less-gifted, but more incorrigible devotees, such as crowd the stage in *The Court Beggar,* all of them anxious to realize secret musical dreams, amateurs relentless in the pursuit of music. Ambitious climbers sedulously aped such manners, and their purses were therefore readily available to confidence tricksters who ran bogus academies to impart the necessary social graces. Brome anatomizes such an establishment in *The New Academy*. Set up by Strigood under the alias of Mr. Lightfoot, it kept "both men and women, as I am inform'd, after the French manner, That professe Musick, Dancing, Fashion, Complement" (III.i:2.55).[4] The timeless lure of anything French was irresistible to simple people like Hannah Camelion and tradesmen like Rafe. Strigood dazzles them with an easy flow of French and pseudo-French and even exhibits a likable boldness when, unabashed by the unexpected presence of some real Frenchmen, he cries out: "I feare no *French* flashes. Bear up *Cash*. If we cannot daunce them off o'their legs, our wenches can, I warrant thee. Musick be ready" (III.i:2.65).

The musical battles were not only between the dupes and the rogues; in *Covent Garden Weeded* the psalm tune strives with the pop tune. In that play Gabriel, sadly overflown with drink, begins to sing. Being of the narrow puritanical sort he chooses a psalm tune. Almost immediately he is interrupted by some tavern fiddlers outside, who are heard tuning their instruments. The psalm tune is momentarily put down as Gabriel pauses in his music-making to castigate the fiddlers: "Such cries as these went forth before the desolation of the great City." He is a prophet ignored and, as they stand "Fidling rude tunes" (doubtless popular ones well known to the audience), he rants on: "O prophane tinkling, the cymbals of Satan, that tickle the eare with vanity, to lift up the mind to lewdnesse. Mine ears shall be that of the Adder against the Song of the Serpent . . . I will roar out aloud to drown your Incantations. Yea I will set out a throat even as the beast that belloweth" (II.ii:2.32–34). The fiddling accompanies this outburst, and Gabriel's

---

4. All references are to the only edition of the plays, *The Dramatic Works of Richard Brome,* 3 vols. (London, 1873). I cite act and scene followed by volume and page.

efforts, first to shout it down, and then to raise his voice over it in some psalm or religious hymn, set up a gay musical situation that underscores his character and makes a neat commentary on the stricter puritan's aversion to popular music.

If genius were only the capacity for taking pains, Brome's status would be in no doubt. He is a careful craftsman, and not above remarking method to his audience: "Nay, mark, I pray you, as I would entreat and Auditorie, if I were now a Poet to mark the Plot, and several points of my play, that they might not say when 'tis done, they understood not this or that, or how such a part came in or went out, because they did not observe the passages" (*Covent Garden Weeded*, III.ii:2.50). This pleasure in taking pains is reflected in the tendency Brome shows to deal separately in his plays with particular aspects of theatrical music. A study of five plays will show this method in action as well as demonstrate the extent of Brome's achievement in musical comedy. *The Northern Lass* (1629)[5] focuses attention on the comedy of song. There is also singing in *The English Moor* (1637), but Brome is chiefly concerned here with the masque as a structural element in the play. *The Court Beggar* (1640) ends with a masque, and the latter part of the play is organized around the preparation for and performance of it; but all of this is only a part, albeit a major part, of a larger exploration of the comic potentialities of extravagant and grotesque musical comedy. In *The Antipodes* (1636/37), Brome had made some experiments in the same general area but along slightly different lines. In this play Brome does not insert the masque into the design and exploit its fanciful elements; rather he begins with the masque and, maintaining its world of fantasy intact, extends it by fusing into it elements of regular satiric comedy. Finally, in *The Jovial Crew* (1641), he leaves the masque world and its fantasy for the world of romantic comedy, where matters are more farcical than fantastic and in which the musical events exist in something of the manner of a subplot while at the same time setting the mood of the play as a whole.

The Northern Lass, an amusing comedy of no great pretensions, probably owed some of its popularity to the recipe Brome followed: no

5. Dates are those given in A. Harbage, *Annals of English Drama 975–1700*, rev. S. Schoenbaum (London, 1964).

comedy is more conventional in its ingredients: a pathetic heroine and her unpleasant guardian; a well-bred if somewhat obtuse hero; various vulgar, foolish, and idiotic suitors; a harsh-mouthed widow, witty servant, and other old reliables—all are shuttled briskly through the inevitable maze of misbegotten marriage and crossed love affairs to a happy ending. Recipes for popular success in the theater are not well-kept secrets, but there is more to writing a popular play than merely including ingredients that are known to be well liked. Beaumont, in *The Knight of the Burning Pestle,* and Fletcher, in *The Faithful Shepherdess,* wrote plays that contained a good deal of musical entertainment, but their audiences, ignoring the widely held assumption that music was sop thrown their way to assure success, disdained both plays. We may well say that the audience was at fault in rejecting those two plays, but the point is that mere inclusion of music is not enough to ensure popular success for a play.

Brome could not have chosen more well-worn musical material to demonstrate how far sympathetic skill in placing it can go toward rejuvenating it. Plaintive love songs, a prostitute's bawdy ditties, singing and dancing for a wedding and a party, instrumental music to ease pain are what he uses. The amount and variety obviously contribute to over-all liveliness and appeal, but mere amount will not do everything. There must be an order to the variety; each item must contribute its own effect. There is a planned order and each musical scene aims at a particular impression. This is nowhere better shown than in the songs. A distinctive trait of the heroine's character is that she "sings and speaks so prettily northerly." This promise is not made the excuse for a concert recital (such things were not unknown: Valerius, in Heywood's *The Rape of Lucrece,* had ten songs in the 1608 edition of the play, four were added in 1630, and five more in 1638; the Bard in Shirley's *St. Patrick for Ireland* [1639] was another relentless vocalizer; Cavendish inserted seven songs into one scene of *The Variety* [1639–1641]). Indeed, Constance sings only three songs, but two others are sung by a bawd who is mistaken for her. Thus the heroine's special vocal quality allows five songs but two singers. Brome further shows what dramatic context can do by making each of Constance's songs a plaintive love ditty, yet avoiding any sense of repetitiveness of effect as well as preventing his heroine from seeming too tearfully pathetic.

Constance's first song, "You say my love is but a man," pins its effect upon its very unassuming typicality. Constance's musing upon her un-requited love for Sir Philip is interrupted by the news of his arrival. Actually, it is the obnoxious Anvile masquerading as Sir Philip. Traine-well, the suspicious old nurse, goes to fetch help, and Constance is told to sing in order to keep Anvile placidly waiting.

Naturally enough Constance chooses a love song:

> You say my Love is but a Man,
>   But I can find more odds,
> 'Twixt him and others than I can,
>   Find between him and Gods.
>   He has in's eye
>   Such majesty.
> His shape is so divine
> That were I owner of the world,
>   He only should be mine.
>
> (II.iii:3.31)

It is an unexceptional lyric; the important thing is that the words are sufficiently vague to suit Constance's frame of mind as aptly as they do the quite contrary one of Anvile. For Constance the song sums up what she has just been saying about Sir Philip: for Anvile, who thinks he is in a bawdy house (he is confusing the Northern Lass with the cunning whore, as Sir Philip had done in rejecting the true Constance and causing her melancholy), this is just the kind of enticing song he expects to hear in such a place. He interprets it according to his lewd hopes and calls it a "sweet prologue to the interlude." In actual fact the song is the sweet interlude between the excitement caused by Anvile's arrival together with the discovery of his hoax and the violence of his ejection with Tride-well's boot behind him.

Constance's second song, "Nor Love, nor Fate dare I accuse" (II.vi:3.39–42) is very similar to the first, but its setting as part of the masque of willow presented before Sir Philip and his new wife, widow Fitchow, and its result give it a quite different impact. The masque is heralded by a regular flourish of cornets and an irregular one of Fitchow's tetchiness: "Some of your old Companions have brought you a fit of Mirth: But if they enter to make a Tavern of my House, I'le add a voice to their consort shall drown all their fidling." Notwithstanding, the masquers enter: "All in willow garlands, four men, four women. The first two pairs are Tridewell and Constance, Anvile and Trainewell. Before the Daunce Constance sings this song." It is a self-deprecatory song in which she blames herself for choosing a love so far above her in station. Its pathetic appeal, combined with the gentle melancholy of the willow dance, causes Sir Philip to question his early rejection of Constance and realize his hasty mistake in so doing. It brings home even more sharply the folly of his marrying Fitchow on the rebound as it were (eventually the marriage is found to be invalid, the officiating minister having been Sir Philip's servant, Pate, in disguise). The fact that the masque is allowed to go forward shows that Sir Philip has awakened to Fitchow's contrariness. Constance's singing effectively contrasts with Fitchow's sharp-temperedness and, in the progress of the plot, marks the first clear turn of events in Constance's favor.

It is too early, however, for matters to swing decisively Constance's way, and she suffers more, this time at the hands of her guardian, Sir Paul Squelch, who badgers her to marry the idiotic Widgine, brother of Fitchow. With her fortunes at their lowest ebb, Constance falls into a melancholia akin to that of the Jailor's daughter in *The Two Noble Kinsmen,* and when Nonsense, yet another foolish and obstreperous suitor, comes, thinking to humor her by pretending to be Sir Philip, she sings of the little bird she once had and of how it chirruped its name, Philip. The song is prettily adapted to her love's name. After it she chatters a little and leaves singing a sorry couplet from another old ballad. When she comes in again she is singing, in her northern dialect, another snatch asserting her refusal to go with any other man and her intent to be a maid to all but one. This is very reminiscent of other heroines melancholy for love and none the worse for that. The scene marks the nadir of Constance's fortunes and deliberately exploits her voice, her accent, and her situation. It confirms her character and within the larger musical pattern sounds the saddest notes, against which the music to follow will be heard with sharpened impact (III.ii:53–60).

The boldest contrast in the pattern follows on the heels of this mournful singing. It is the musical discomfiture of Fitchow, an apt business since her humiliation, as we have seen, began musically albeit quietly (III.iii:3.63–65). Her feeble brother Widgine, encouraged to take a stand against her, sings scornfully of the fate of the man married to a scold.

His friends rally to him splendidly. The stage direction reads: "They all take hands and dance round. Widgine in the midst sings this song. They all bear the burden, while she scolds and strives to be amongst 'hem. Tridewell holds her off." Eventually Fitchow breaks loose and flies at her persecutors, who exit in pandemonium, still singing. This boisterous finale to the act is virtually a parody of the willow masque and an instance of Brome's aptitude for balancing musical scenes against each other. The plaintive love song and gentle dance are replaced by a loud satirical song and a lusty masculine round dance, and instead of the lovelorn Constance there is the shrieking struggling Fitchow.

The two dance scenes are representative of what can be called musical action; in the last act the story of Constance and Sir Philip is happily concluded with music as background for action. A very simple example of this latter kind is found in *The Novella* (1632) when the titular heroine sings a trade song to attract customers: "Whilst she plays and sings above, Paulo waits below. Many gallants pass over the stage gazing at her" (I.ii:2.129). A much more subtle example is this earlier one. Pate, disguised this time as a doctor, persuades Constance to meet his master. Throughout their meeting "soft music" is heard. This is partly medicinal to help cure Constance's love-melancholy (her sad-mad singing when pestered by Squelch and Nonsense proves that her case is such as to need this traditional treatment), but its main function is to set the mood of tender reconciliation and love. When Squelch arrives to collect his ward, Pate tells him that she is in her room and that the music he can hear has been required to help her to sleep. The "Musick continues" and takes on a subtle satiric overtone as it now becomes the cover for the fleeing lovers, as well as for Pate who takes his chance to slip away while Squelch is kept in conversation by Constance's nurse, persuaded that so long as he hears the music his ward is safe (V.ii–iii:3.86–89). It provides, incidentally, a quiet interlude before the bustle of the denouement. The whole effect is typically Bromean in its simple means, its intricacy, and its deftness.

Two other songs are heard before this, in the fourth act, both sung by Constance Holdup, the whore (IV.iv:3.77–79). Widgine, duped into thinking she is the Northern Lass he covets, visits her pretending to be Sir Philip for whom, he has been assured, "Constance" has run mad. She enters singing a lullaby to a child which, it is intimated, is Sir Philip's.

This mockery of a lullaby over, Widgine humors her, exchanges snatches
of song with her and eventually wins her (it costs him £100 to break the
contract at the end of the play). Before he leaves she sings once more,
this time a true song of her profession, a smutty pastoral. The infatuated
Widgine is too blind to see reason and goes happily away. Both songs are
utterly unlike any the true Constance would sing, and they would take
in only a beguiled fool like Widgine. The singing in this scene depends
upon the establishment of the Northern Lass as a singer, the convention
that people made mad by love sing, as well as the fact that whores sing as
part of their profession. The lullaby drives home to Widgine the fact
that the girl has been made mad by love as well as confirming to his
feeble brain that she is the Constance he seeks. The insistence upon
impersonation in the scene—everyone seeming to take off Sir Philip at
one time or another while there is steady confusion in some minds as to
which Constance is which—sets up situations which the music underlines
and, indeed, helps to create. Songs of genuine love-melancholy are contrasted with forgeries: the simple song which Anvile took for a brothel
item is contrasted with a pair that are very unsubtle in their double
meanings. The blunt nature of Holdup's appeal causes the spectator to
wonder how Constance could have been mistaken for her. The second
song, "As I was gathering April's flowers," is something of an "extra,"
yet it is a legitimate part of what is an amusing scene of the gulling of
Widgine. The way in which other actions have been stressed musically
creates a pattern into which this scene, with its coarser songs, fits well.[6]

6. Brome's lively handling of the "Constance songs" contrasts interestingly with
Fletcher's equally lively handling of the song of the courtesan who is mistaken
for the heroine, Constantia, in *The Chances* (1625). Fletcher's courtesan sings a
seductive song quite unsuited to Constantia's character but put down, by those
anxiously searching for her, to "some strange melancholy she is laden with." The
quietness of the song and the nervous attention of the listening searchers is
amusingly shattered by an outbreak of fighting in the singer's room and the
discovery of a termagant instead of Constantia. This scene, and Fletcher's own
experiments in dealing extensively with a particular musical usage in a single
play, are discussed in my essay, "Patterns of Music and Action in Fletcherian
Drama," in *Music in English Renaissance Drama,* ed. John H. Long (Lexington,
Ky., 1968), pp. 75–95. Brome was obviously familiar with Fletcher's plays and is
the only Caroline playwright whose inventiveness and skill with musical conventions can compare with Fletcher's.

Brome's handling of music in *The Northern Lass,* early in his career, is confident and skillful, but it is not the best that he can do. In the four late plays, to which we now turn, Brome's mastery of musical conventions and his boldness in extending their inherent capacities as dramatic effects show to best advantage.

The plot of *The English Moor* or *The Mock Marriage* could stand as a display piece of Brome's ingenuity and control. Two large-scale musical scenes, each including a masque, are vital to the plot. Perhaps "masqued dance" is a better term than masque, for only in *The Antipodes* does Brome utilize the trappings of the court masque and present anything resembling a miniature court masque of the kind that Fletcher, for example, inserts in *The Maid's Tragedy.* Brome liked to use a theme for his dancers and have them dressed in some unusual and attractive costume, but otherwise he avoids the formality of the masque. When he does cleave more closely to the accepted structure of the masque in *The Antipodes,* he still contrives something quite different. However, the question of nicely distinguished nomenclature for such entertainments is not one to be straightforwardly settled. We are more anxious than the seventeenth-century playwrights to classify drama: Brome called his musical entertainments of this sort "masques," and in following him we must bear in mind the wide interpretation given names and titles in his day. It is a moot point whether their wide-ranging usage is any more convenient than the current tendency to sort everything out into countless subdivisions. The dance and masque had dramatic potentialities that many playwrights explored. Brome, as well as any, knew what a satisfying conclusion a dance made to a play. Geron and his country helpers have one ready at the close of *The Lovesick Court:* "some country sport" as Geron disarmingly calls it, adding:

> A dance I have projected for the Princess,
> Who ever marries her it shall serve.
>
> (V.iii:2.159)

Any remaining ill-feeling at the end of *The New Academy,* dealing as it does with dancing lessons for the socially ambitious, among other matters, is swept away with "One frisk, one fling now, one cariering dance" aptly called "in *English, Omnium Gatherum*" (V.ii:2.110). Seven of Brome's fifteen extant plays end with some form of dance or musical entertainment: *The English Moor,* though it makes ingenious and rich use of masque and music, does not. Usurer Quicksands' authority and plotting having twice been undermined by musical means in the first and fourth acts, the fifth act concludes his undoing without any music.

Millicent, having been forced to wed Quicksands, dampens his ardor on the wedding night by an outrageous display of wantonness largely created by singing snatches of crude songs (I.iii:2.13–16). This relies on the association of loose women with songs such as those that Brome had used for different ends in *The Northern Lass.* In the same predicament as Millicent, Florimel, Fletcher's *The Maid of the Mill* (1623), uses exactly the same technique. If Brome took the idea from Fletcher, he asserts his individuality by using it as the prologue to an even livelier musical scene. Quicksands is quite dashed by Millicent's performance:

> My edge is taken off: this impudence
> Of hers, has outfac'd my concupisence.
> Dasht all quite out o'Countenance!

But his trials have only just begun, "A sowgelder's horn blown" arouses fears that his manservant confirms:

> Vizarded people, Sir, and odly shap'd
> You'l see anon. Their tuning o'their pipes,
> And swear they'll gi'ye a willy nilly dance
> Before you go to bed, tho' you stole your Marriage.

Millicent delightedly simpers, "Some . . . to congratulate our honoured Marriage." There is another flourish and Mercury leaps in followed by "four Masquers with horns on their heads: a Stag, a Ram, a Goat, and an Ox followed by four persons, a Courtier, a Captain, a Schollar and a Butcher." Mercury makes sure the point of the masque is understood and, calling on the musicians to "strike aloud / The cuckold's joy, with merry pipe and crowd," the masquers "dance to musick of Cornets and Violins." The notion of a Horn Masque is very apt and brings Quicksands' marriage celebrations to a rousing conclusion. The whole sequence from the teasing songs and tormenting behavior of Millicent through to the stage full of leaping horn-decorated young roarers goading Quicksands to fury is splendidly carried out, and, although entirely dramatic as it stands, it strongly suggests, as other parts of the play will as well, its suitability for operatic treatment (I.iii:2.13–16).

The masque is quietly kept in the spectator's mind by a train of references to it during the play, culminating in its use by Quicksands as something that his Masque of Moors can answer. Brome methodically lets Quicksands explain the personnel:

> Yes I have borrowed other *Moors* of Merchants
> That trade in *Barbary*, whence I had mine own here,
> And you shall see their way and skill in dancing.
>
> (IV.iv:2.60)

Quicksands is hardly able to contain himself at this riposte to the young rakes:

> you shall see how I'le requite
> The masque they lent me on my wedding night.
> Twas but lent Gentlemen, your masque of horns,
> And all the private jears and publik scorns
> Y'have cast upon me since.
>
> (IV.v:2.65)

The complexities and double-crossings that spring from this second masque testify to Brome's mastery of plot construction. Quicksands has given out the news that Millicent has run away but intends to amaze his gloating enemies by producing her at the masque and feast. His enemies, of course, discover this and lay their own plans accordingly. Both sides are delighted with what they conceive to be astute plots. Further duplicities have been planned by ladies previously deceived by the young men who also plan to use the masque for their own ends. Thus all the conflicts are brought together, and the disguises of the masque (especially the blacked faces) enable a whole set of turns of fortune to be mounted one after the other with great panache. The variety of plots and counterplots is an addition to the different musical entertainments offered during the scene. The Moors in the masque "dance an Antique in which they use action of Mockery and derision to the three Gentlemen." Baneless, the leader of the young rakes, applauds the device and asks leave to dance: he is quite unusual in being specific about the music he wants:

> Musick, play a Galliard,
> You know what you promised me, *Bullis*.
>
> (IV.v:2.67)

If nothing else, Baneless had musical taste in using music by John Bull.[7]
Despite this carefully chosen music, Baneless "dances vilely," according
to the stage direction, and Quicksands is moved to raucous laughter at his
ineptitude. Deliberate or not, it makes a good contrast with the previous
dance. After Baneless has danced away with his partner—his ludicrous
performance was possibly meant to take attention away from this purpose
which he had—Buzard, a dismissed servant of Quicksands, enters pretending to be the idiot son whom Quicksands keeps hidden in the
country. Buzard sings crazily to maintain his disguise: "He sings and
dances and spins with a rock and spindle." The contrast between these
two turns is also explicitly marked in the stage directions: "Enter Arnold
like a Countrey man and Buz[ard] like a changeling, and as they enter,
exit NAT [Baneless] . . . the musick still playing." The music is Bull's.
The two fantastic dances taken together might almost be an antimasque
to the Masque of Moors.

Such is the fecundity of Brome's imagination that, as it were in passing,
he mentions another idea for a superb comic scene which, we must
assume, he felt the design of his play did not permit him to use. On the
morning after the horn masque, Baneless, leader of the rakes, comes in
and tells of another musical torment inflicted upon Quicksands.

> This morning, early, up we got again,
> And with our Fidlers made a fresh assault
> And battery 'gainst the bed-rid bride-grooms window.
> With an old song, a very wondrous old one,
> Of all the cares, vexations, fears and torments,
> That a decrepit, nasty, rotten Husband
> Meets in a youthful, beauteous, sprightly wife:
> So as the weak wretch will shortly be afraid,
> That his own feebler shadow makes him Cuckold.
> Our Masque 'er night begat a separation
> Betwixt'em before bed time: for we found
> Him at one window, coughing and spitting at us;
> She at another, laughing, and throwing money

7. John Bull (ca. 1562–1628), organist, member of the Chapel Royal, and one
of the most famous musicians of his day, a favorite of Queen Elizabeth. Which
galliard Baneless wanted is unsure: there are some by Bull, for example, in the
Fitzwilliam Virginal Book.

Down to the Fidlers, while her uncle *Testy,*
From a third Port-hole raves, denouncing Law,
And thundring statutes 'gainst their Minstralsie.

(II.i:2.23–24)

It is a sparkling scene that might have come from a Rossini comic opera.

Completely different from the rest of the loud gay music of the play is a little song that Lucy has a boy sing to cheer her up. She calls it a mournful song but her brother is angry at the singer, calling it a "wanton air." Lucy demurs:

I know not brother how you like the air,
But in my mind the words are sad, Pray read 'em.

(IV.iii:2.56)

He does so and agrees that "they are sad indeed." The song is more an interlude than most musical events in Brome; even so there is the suggestion that Brome makes something of it, for if both speakers are right it may be that sad words have been put to a well-known air used for a popular bawdy song or loose ballad, and an incongruous comic effect gained in this way.

Musical humor of this extravagant kind is the particular mark of *The Court Beggar.* Musical fantasticalness is made a basis of Sir Ferdinando's character. He has run mad for love, and whereas Constance in a similar state displayed quiet melancholy he displays the frantic side of the affliction. Such musical madness traces back to Ophelia and the Jailer's daughter in *The Two Noble Kinsmen.* Brome's twist is to try the effect in a man and, at the same time, extend the theatrical virtuosity of the dance. Twice Ferdinando exhibits his madness in what amount to vaudeville turns. First "he Dances a conceited Countrey Dance, first doing his honours, then as leading forth his Lasse. He danceth both man and womans actions, as if the Dance consisted of two or three couples, at last offering to Kisse his Lasse, hee fancies that they are all vanish'd" (IV.ii:1.241). Later he attempts to get out of an awkward situation by further musical madness: he "sings part of the old Song, and acts it madly" (IV.iii:1.247). The old song probably was "The Battle of

Musleborough Field," which had just been alluded to and would provide ample scope for a mad histrionic singer.[8]

This kind of humor is found even in the slighter musical parts of the play. Not all of it is very subtle: Sir Ferdinando's doctor undergoes a mock gelding that is accompanied by a sow-gelder's song intended as a crude anesthetic (IV.ii:1.243). Two catches are also heard: one offstage in the second act at Lady Stranglelove's that merely suggests the nature of the house but dramatically is hardly more than a tuneful connection between the two halves of the scene (II.ii:1.209); the other, a part of Ferdinando's antics before his first turn (IV.ii:1.241). To offset the casual nature of these entertainments Brome offers one of his best demonstrations of how to make a masque part of a play. In the second act Lady Stranglelove mentions a masque she intends, asserting that Court-Wit "shall performe the poeticall part, your servant Cit-Wit the Musicall . . . Dancers and speakers I have in store" (II.i:1.212). However, her optimism turns out to be founded upon intention rather than performance and, very late in the day, she admits to having done nothing more than invite the guests to watch the masque. With ostentatious modesty, Court-Wit, when she casually asks for a masque to be run up, murmurs: "I have cast the designe for't already Madam. My inventions are all flame and spirit. But you can expect no great matter to be done *extempore* or in six minutes" (V.ii:1.259). Swayne-Wit takes a more bucolic and placid view of the matter: "What matter ist so wee skip up and downe? our friend *Jack Dainty* here, Mr. Cut-purse dances daintily tho'." Happily, Dainty has the sparks of the born organizer in him. He swiftly takes charge and soon the others are stirred to action. He himself will be choreographer and "give you all the footing." The stage direction reads, "Practise footing": here, as so often in Brome when some special effect is intended, the directions are so full and carefully arranged that it is easy to realize his intentions. The doctor is hauled in to make up the numbers in the dance and seizes this chance to satisfy secret ambitions of com-

8. Sir Ferdinando is a satirical caricature of Sir John Suckling whose notorious cowardice at Berwick during the First Bishops' War of 1639 is very likely glanced at in the choice of material for this second musical display. Court-Wit takes off Davenant who had, at the time of the play (early 1640), won plaudits as a royal masque-writer which he was not very modest about. Kaufmann has an excellent discussion of this play in chap. 9 of his book.

posing music: "What think you of this tune sir for your dance?" he asks Dainty, and he begins to hum, "Tay, dee, dee, &c." Dainty is pleased: "I'll borrow a Violl and take it of you instantly."

The amateurs lose no time in abandoning themselves to their art, so that when Sir Raphael happens upon them in his search for Sir Andrew, the master of the house, he is sure he has wandered into some madhouse. No one has a moment to spare for his questions. Court-Wit is "creating," scribbling poetic fancies down, "sometimes scratching his head, as pumping his Muse." "Cit-wit Dances looking on his Feete," "The Doctor stretches his Throat in the Tune," while Swayne-Wit, in acceptable bucolic vein "whistels & Dances Sellingers round, or the like." [9] Dainty reappears with the viol, and Sir Raphael turns hopefully to him only to be dashed, for Dainty "fidls to him & the 4 Dancing and singing practise about him." Turning to Philomel, the chambermaid, he gets his first answer, but to no purpose as she only "speaks in a vile tone like a Player" and spouts fustian at him:

> O by no means, we must speake *Charon*
> Or Hee'l not waft us o're the *Stigian* Floud
> Then must we have a sop for *Cerberus*
> To stop his yawning Chaps; Let me alone
> To be your Convoy to *Elizium*.

She and the Boy rant wildly on, "Dainty playes softly & Doctor with him aside," and the absurd comical counterpoint goes on. The rehearsal is believable and so it is funny, because earnest amateurs such as these are the funnier the more seriously they pursue their elusive art. The entry of the disengaged Raphael provides a hub of normality round which the merry-go-round of fanciful comedy revolves with added zest. In some ways it is like a musical version of the last act of *Gammer Gurton's Needle,* where everyone argues violently about what they think has lately happened in the village while in their midst the sober figure of Baily stands trying to sort matters out. The scene is one of Brome's funniest pieces of "musical" comedy.

The masque is performed almost immediately, and the hasty

9. Sellinger's Round was an immensely popular cheerful dance tune of the period (originally probably a country maypole dance). It marks Swayne-Wit's musical taste as clearly as Baneless's calling for a galliard of Bull's marks his.

preparation and sparse rehearsal result in something that is akin to the Show of the Nine Worthies. Nonetheless it successfully concludes the play. The Boy, Cupid to Philomel's Venus, botches his lines. An ill-sorted group of representatives from the Pantheon enter and dance: "After they have Danc'd a while, Enter Projectors, breakes 'em off." They introduce a sort of antimasque crowned by the appearance of Sir Andrew himself "attir'd all in Patents; a Windmill on his head, and the other Projector." Sir Andrew, quite taken in by the Projectors, has notions as wild as Sir Politick Would-Be's. Dainty saves the day by having the music carry on: "They all Dance. In the Dance they pull off his Patents; And the Projectors Clokes, who appear all ragged. At the end of the Dance the Projectors thrust forth." Thus Sir Andrew is cured and all swiftly comes to a destined happy end. The dance is restarted by the indefatigable Dainty, and during it the last threads are unraveled and it turns into a traditional grand-dance finale to celebrate a wedding (V.ii:1.265–269).

In this last act Brome brings together a number of traditional devices and entertainments—the dance finale of comedy, the masque and anti-masque, the amusing clumsiness of amateurs in rehearsal and performance, the sudden and complete unveiling and expulsion of villains, the saving of good folk—and makes of them one hectic yet carefully controlled comic scene. *The Court Beggar* is a perfect union of dramatic and musical entertainment; none of the individual elements is new, but the manner of bringing them together and the emphasis given to the fantastic and extravagant in their handling is fresh and lively.

Fantasy is the mark of *The Antipodes,* an attractive play possessing that rare Caroline quality of distinctive individuality. There is much music in the play, but it is used more to illustrate the theme than as plot material in the manner we have seen in other plays. If elements of the grotesque usually associated with the antimasque might be said to have been a leading motif in the handling of music in *The Court Beggar,* then the general atmosphere of the masque as a whole, its exotic and unreal nature, permeates *The Antipodes,* and this applies not merely to the musical parts of the play. Whereas in plays such as Cartwright's and Strode's the static tableau effects of the masque tend to dominate, Brome manages a much more subtle infusion of masque and drama.

The action takes place in the home of the eccentric Letoy, whose many

servants can all act and play some musical instrument, he is entertained
by them nightly with plays and masques. Peregrine, the hero, suffers from
what might be called Mandeville-mania and dreams his life away in
quixotic fantasies of travel (incidentally neglecting his wife to such an
extent that she declines into melancholy). He is drugged and awakes at
Letoy's where the players are already performing a piece which has to
do with the Antipodes, the totally topsy-turvy world. Each act is introduced by flourishes, and toward the end of the play Peregrine is so
carried away by it that, like Don Quixote before Master Peter's Puppet
show, he takes part in the action and, after a rising in the tiring room,
proclaims himself King of the Antipodes. He is greeted with the shouts
of the people, "drums and trumpets," and the "loud harmony" of the
city waits on "hoboys." Upon the heels of this raucous noise comes the
"soft musick" and gentler song of welcome that the court brings to
Peregrine. The scene ends with the return of the loud music of the
"hoboys" (IV.x:3.313–315).[10]

In the masque that follows on the conclusion of Letoy's play (which
has effected a cure on Peregrine, and hence on his wife), contrasts are
worked out in terms of discord and concord. The plot is not advanced by
the masque, but the way in which it matches the mood of the play and
focuses sharply on the essential theme of the whole action makes it securely a part of Brome's design. There is an amusing and perhaps
tongue-in-cheek explanation of its presence. The play-within-the-play had
been broken off by Peregrine's entry into it. For completion it apparently
needed a musical finale:

> My lord gave order for't last night.
> It should ha'bin ith'play: But because that
> Was Broke off, he will ha't today.
>
> (V.iv:3.323)

Discussion accompanies the various parts of the concluding masque for
which Brome gives characteristically precise directions (V.viii–xi:3.335–338).

10. "Loud" music generally meant the reed instruments, brass and drums; "soft"
music was played by the strings, recorders, and flutes (the latter could be heard
in "loud" music also). "Loud" music might roughly be equated with outdoor,
public, festive music, "soft" music with indoor, domestic, more private occasions.
Manifold has some useful remarks on this matter.

"A solemne lesson upon the Recorders" brings on the actors. Peregrine "seemes somthing amazed," and only when all is ready does this preliminary music cease. Its sweet harmony is abruptly contrasted with "a most untunable florish" that announces the masque proper. There enter "Discord attended by Folly, Jealousie, Melancholy and madnesse." Discord, again "in untunable notes," sings a song, after which a dance (obviously a fantastic one according to their music and character) follows. "After a while they are broke off by a flourish, and the approach of Harmony followed by Mercury, Cupid, Bacchus and Appollo. Discord and her faction fall downe." Harmony's cutting across of the dance before it is finished stresses the opposition between the kinds of music. Harmony then performs her group's song. "After a straine or two, Discord cheares up her faction. They all rise, and mingle in the dance with Harmony and the rest. Daunce." Here, having made music the subject of some of his best comic scenes, it might be said that Brome makes it the subject of his masque. It stands in relation to his play much as a moral does to a fable.

The feeling remains that *The Antipodes* is an interim play, an experiment in a mode that might have been fruitfully developed had not the closing of the theaters ended Brome's career. *A Jovial Crew* also looks toward a later mode of drama but it is a more self-contained play. It is a mixture of romance and reality. Notwithstanding the jovial music of the crew (their music-making largely is their joviality), there is a certain ambivalence to the atmosphere of the play. It provokes smiles rather than laughter; a thread of nostalgia runs through it.

It is not a play with songs and music so much as a musical play. Behind it lies the tradition that any group generally considered to be rogues and vagabonds need only be singers in order to become thoroughly jolly fellows: thus Brome's crew join with Gay's beggars and Gilbert and Sullivan's pirates. The crew celebrate all their social events with music, and it is typical of Brome's method that he explains their notable gifts in this line by the presence of several runaway musicians among their number. They are usually heard singing offstage before being discovered to the audience. Their first song sets out their philosophy:

> From hunger and cold who lives more free,
> Or who more richly clad than wee?

> (I.i.3.365)

Even in the countryside they call to each other in imitated birdsong. They contribute a variety of musical entertainment. When Oldrents is saddened by his daughter's running away from home, his reactions are interestingly played against a background of the crew's offstage singing (II.i:3.386–392). They sing to cover the cries of one of their women in labor and then to welcome the birth of the child, while Oldrents talks sadly of his loss. Once discovered, they attempt to cheer up a well-loved patron with a cant song. Then drunken Autum-Mort sings "This is Bien Bowse," at the end of which she tumbles over and is carried out. The song is a straightforward entertainment, comic relief of a farcical kind contrasting with the prevailing romantic feeling, the songs of near nostalgia for the country and the cant song. The whole show, for such it is, concludes with a dance by the Clapper Dugeons and the walking Morts. The crew are heard no more until the fourth act when they make a great festive music at the wedding of two of their number. Three poems of praise are read aloud, and the invitation of the second of them to begin a dance is accepted. The festivity is abruptly ended by the entry of the watch to arrest the revelers, and this prevents the possibility that "If there were no worse, we might have a *Masque,* or a *Comedie*" (IV.ii:3.423–433). The crew does perform a play in the fifth act and the ending of their play-within-a-play is merged with that of the play proper in curious and lively fashion. Their performance is introduced by "A Flourish of Shalms" which one of the audience recognizes; "Heark!—the Beggars' Hoboys. Now they begin." There is, however, no musical finale to this last play of Brome. Possibly he thought that the closing display of bewildering revelations of long-lost relatives and friends and the mingling of his two plays was sufficient. As with the mock aubade in *The English Moor,* which is only described, he proved he was quite capable of resisting what might seem obvious occasions for music if he was in search of other dramatic effects.[11]

---

11. Jonson may have given him an example for this. *The New Inn* (1629) has reference to a drinking school of singers most dramatists would have been pleased to bring on the stage for a scene or two. In the epilogue, however, Jonson says:

> He could have hal'd in
> The drunkards, and the noyses of the Inne,

The crew belong to that band of specially musical people in drama that has already been mentioned. Accepting them in the play means accepting their music. Indeed, they form a subplot that is completely musical. The main plot is not without some music for Hearty, a kinsman of Beaumont's Merrythought, regularly sings but keeps to one topic, the virtues of sack and old songs. Eventually he persuades to his creed, Tallboy Oldrents, who loses himself in feeble melancholy for a while and even attempts on one occasion to sing a conventional love-melancholy song but breaks down. This is a cameo musical entertainment, the elderly man acting the part of the sad lover which is traditionally that of the young man: the scene is admirably rounded off by his abjuring such efforts and turning to drink and singing a riotous round, "The Singers are all Graybeards" (IV.i:3.419). Old men need not necessarily avoid either love or boisterous drinking songs, but Brome makes play with the cheerful incongruity possible in the idea.

Such a small instance, however, well illustrates Brome's skill in making comedy that is musical. His craft allowed him easily to extend his effects over long scenes, and even, as we have seen, allowed him to forgo the opportunity for them when he felt it right to do so. He is a playwright very hard-served by relegation to the study: his liveliness and clever handling of character and movement, and of musical sound, need the appreciation best offered by live performance. His faults are obvious: if it is a fault to set out to entertain rather than to teach, then this marks him: indeed the lack of intellectual stuff in his work is possibly reflected in the way one falls naturally to discussing his work in terms of craftsmanship, accepting playwriting as a "trade" for Brome. There is a certain sameness of situation and character in his work. He had nothing memorably poetic to say, though he had some delightful songs. However,

---

> In his last act; if he had thought it fit
> To vent you vapours in the place of wit.

Jonson, of course, was a notorious harper against what he considered improper dramatic entertainment, the more so at his career's close when he was less popular. In a transient mood of bitterness at the contemporaneous failure of *The New Inn* and the success of Brome's *The Lovesick Maid,* he had meanly written:

> Broomes sweeping doe as well
> Thear as his Masters Meale.

he knew his limits and was wise enough to keep within them. In choosing to stay in this naturalistic world rather than move into that rarefied one in which much Caroline drama in his own time was suffocating, Brome kept in the main line of English tradition. Caroline masque drama, as exemplified in such pieces as Cartwright's *The Royal Slave* or Strode's *The Floating Island,* might be said to incline toward opera seria and thence to grand opera, an art form that has always been alien to the English spirit. Brome's drama inclined more toward the opera buffa and light opera that stretches in rich line from the ballad opera to Gilbert and Sullivan and is the only operatic domain where the English spirit has comfortably settled. Operatic and musical analogies come quickly to mind when considering Brome. Baker remarked in the preface to his edition of *The Jovial Crew* that it was a "farce Gilbertian in its whimsicality," well planned and well sustained; he also noted its approach to ballad opera.[12]

It must not be thought, however, that such analogies and such suggestions about the direction of development mean that Brome had any notions of opera in his mind when he was writing, that he was consciously striving toward some such form. What needs to be emphasized is his conscious effort to make music an integral part of his plays' structure: he wanted his music to be essential, not merely incidental. He wanted something of the union that Letoy had in the musician-actors he kept in his home:

> Stage-playes, and Masques, are nightly my pastimes.
> And all within myselfe. My owne men are
> My Musique, and my Actors, I keepe not
> A man or boy but is of quality:
> The worst can sing or play his part o'th'Violls,
> And act his part too in a comedy.
>
> (I.v:3.245–246)

Brome attempted to make music act its part in his comedies: with vigor and liveliness he tried to make the action and music flow on together just as the musical notes followed one another. He sought the results that Letoy wanted when the latter was talking of words and action, meaning, by "action," dancing and music:

12. G. P. Baker in the prefatory essay to his edition of *The Jovial Crew* in *Representative English Comedies,* ed. C. M. Gayley (New York, 1937), III, 426.

> . . . words and action married so together,
> That shall strike harmony in the eares and eyes
> Of the severest, if judicious Criticks.

(II.ii:3.259)

The copious and careful direction for the large-scale musical scenes underlines Brome's intentions; he aimed always at the ears and the eyes; his effects are conceived absolutely in terms of stage performance. This consistent and careful aim gave him his success. In a time when most writers were content with a dazzling but uneasy and clumsy yoking together of action and words, Brome frequently succeeded in making a harmonious marriage of the two.

Shakespeare and Music: Unexplored Areas

NAN COOKE CARPENTER

A GLANCE at the elaborate bibliographies in recent books by Frederick Sternfeld, Peter Seng, and John Long[1] makes it abundantly clear how far investigation into the subject of music and Shakespeare has come since Edward W. Naylor published his pathbreaking *Shakespeare and Music* in 1896. But just as Shakespeare's own depth seems to elude all probing, so Shakespeare's use of music is apparently a limitless topic that still offers some attractive but lightly explored areas.

The largest unwritten book on Shakespeare and music, perhaps, is one long overdue—a thorough and definitive discussion of the poet's musical imagery and allusion. Possibly because the topic is so vast and the subject

---

This paper (slightly revised for publication) was originally read at the Second Annual Meeting of the Shakespeare Association of America in Pasadena, March 29, 1974.

1. John H. Long, *Shakespeare's Use of Music: A Study of the Music and Its Performance in the Original Production of Seven Comedies* (Gainesville, Fla., 1955); *Shakespeare's Use of Music: The Final Comedies* (Gainesville, Fla., 1961); *Shakespeare's Use of Music: The Histories and Tragedies* (Gainesville, Fla., 1972). Peter J. Seng, *The Vocal Songs in the Plays of Shakespeare* (Cambridge, Mass., 1967). F. W. Sternfeld, *Music in Shakespearean Tragedy* (London, 1963).

so formidable no one person has ever undertaken it. Many critics touch upon this aspect of the plays, but not in any organized way. And numerous separate articles have appeared discussing musical terminology in some particular play (especially *The Taming of the Shrew, Twelfth Night, The Tempest*).[2] A large work on musical imagery might be organized in several ways. The one that seems most workable would be division according to musical instruments, musical theory, musical ideas, the dance, secular song (and possibly sacred song, although there seems to be slight reference to this type of music in the plays). Conclusions drawn from such a study would surely illuminate many facets of the poet's style and artistic development. This sort of study would even be valuable for use as a touchstone in deciding who wrote what plays—for instance, when the old question of Marlowe versus Shakespeare, which apparently refuses to die, crops up. Anyone who has isolated and studied the few musical references in Marlowe's plays knows the almost complete polarity in musical usage of the two dramatists. John Stevens's essay, "Shakespeare and the Music of the Elizabethan Stage," in the book *Shakespeare in Music,* is a splendid beginning—in fact, Dr. Stevens is unusually well qualified to undertake the magnum opus on this subject.[3]

But while we await the appearance of this large work, there are other topics related to the subject that might be pursued rewardingly. How and where, for instance, did Shakespeare learn so much about music? His musical references and allusions are so numerous and varied that they seem to reflect all aspects of the musical knowledge of his day with one exception—that is, music as a discipline of higher learning, university studies based on Boethius, other ancient writers, and some later theorists. We are still not at all certain how much or what kind of musical instruction Shakespeare had at petty school or grammar school. In dealing with the latter[4] Professor Baldwin rarely mentions the word *music* and often elides quotations with musical references in order to get on to

2. See, e.g., the many items on separate plays listed in Seng's bibliography.

3. *Shakespeare in Music,* ed. Phyllis Hartnoll (London, 1964), pp. 3–48.

4. T. W. Baldwin, *Shakespeare's Small Latine and Less Greeke* (Urbana, Ill., 1944). For reference to music at Westminster and Shrewsbury, see I, 384 and 390. Whitelocke's observation about Mulcaster (from the *Liber famelicus*) appears in I, 420–421: "His care was also to encreas my skill in musique, in whiche I was brought up by dayly exercise in it, as in singing and playing upon instruments."

requirements for grammar and rhetoric, his own chief interests. Baldwin mentions music at Westminster and at Shrewsbury and cites Whitelocke's famous passage describing Richard Mulcaster's enthusiasm for and teaching of music at the Merchant Taylors' School (where Spenser was a pupil). But there is no discussion or even mention of music at Stratford.

Shakespeare's knowledge apparently covered the entire gamut of music, practical as well as theoretical, from the scale itself to the more sophisticated ideas on the subject (the music of the spheres, the power of music to sway man's soul, to heal, to affect the emotions). And we surely need no further proof of his understanding of the dramatic and lyrical effects of actual song, dance, and instrumental performance than is provided in the plays. Was Shakespeare schooled as a choirboy? Did he study music privately—in the manner beautifully described for us by Thomas Morley in his *Plaine and Easie Introduction to Musicke* of 1596? It has been suggested that Shakespeare might even have "picked up" most of his information about music from musical acquaintances, from hearing music played in taverns, bawdy houses, churches, and private homes.[5] Actually, this seems too easy an explanation for one with as much technical knowledge as Shakespeare displays. The difficulty here is that during the Renaissance the study of music was generally a private affair, depending upon individual talents and interests, and little documentation on the subject has come to light—unlike, for example, the situation in Germany where Reformation schools were organized under definite *Schulordnungen* which set the number of minutes a day to be devoted to music and even laid down what was to be taught.[6] A thorough investigation into this aspect of Shakespeare's background and training is needed to clear up the mystery.

To turn now to the verse itself: references to "the music of Shakespeare's poetry"—meaning matters of meter and rhythm, rhyme, assonance, and the like—tell a good deal, sometimes, about poetry but very little, usually, about music; for the two media, words and music,

5. See Louis Marder, "Shakespeare's Musical Background," *MLN*, LXV (1950), 501–503.

6. For easy reference to much documentation on this subject, see Nan C. Carpenter, *Music in the Medieval and Renaissance Universities* (Norman, Okla., 1958), pp. 362–367. See also Frederick W. Sternfeld, "Music in the Schools of the Reformation," *Musica Disciplina*, II (1948), 99–122.

are so entirely different that only vague analogies between them can be made. One finds puzzling, for example, a statement quoted by Professor Parker in his biography of Milton that in the irregular rhyming of *Lycidas,* Milton attempted "to give us, though secretly, a poetical image or draught of the mathematical structure of music."[7] This suggestion, says Parker, may be worth exploring. If anyone has ever solved this riddle, the solution has not been made public. What is its meaning? Could the same sort of observation be applied in any way to Shakespeare? A recently published attempt to analyze Paul Celan's well-known *Todesfuge* as a musical fugue is less than convincing to the reader, although the author is satisfied with his analysis.[8] One cannot construct a fugue in music without the essential element of simultaneity, and even though recall of literary lines may approach this—the author seems to equate the two—recall and simultaneous sound are by no means identical. (One can have recall in music, too, without simultaneous sound.) Actually, the closest a verse form might come to resembling a musical fugue would be in the down-and-across pattern, with words reading vertically as well as horizontally. In the same analysis of Celan's poem, the writer speaks of a first subject, and second, third, and fourth subjects, all different. Again, these cannot be equated with subjects in a fugue because a fugue (unless it is a double fugue which compounds all the complications) has the same subject entering at intervals in different voices and different keys (which we call imitation). What the writer here seems to have in mind is a sectional piece, with a new theme for each section. The analysis, in a word, is a brilliant interpretation of the poem but fails to prove the basic thesis—that the poem resembles a fugue in the musical sense. Perhaps the word's original meaning—"flight"—applies here better than fugue as a musical pattern.

Of late, however, new and more meaningful avenues of exploration along this line seem to be opening. To cite one example, Paula Johnson has demonstrated in a recent book[9] the importance of structural charac-

7. From Francis Peck, *New Memoirs* (London, 1740). See William Parker, *Milton, A Biography* (Oxford, 1968), II, 813–814.

8. See Karl S. Wesmar, "Paul Celan's 'Todesfuge': Translation and Interpretation," *PMLA*, LXXXIX (1974), 85–96.

9. *Form and Transformation in Music and Poetry of the English Renaissance* (New Haven, Conn., 1972).

teristics common to both music and poetry—for which she has invented a quite workable vocabulary—clarifying changes that take place in both arts, poetry as well as music, toward the end of the sixteenth century and that find their ultimate meaning in the listener's biological response. In describing what she calls serial form, Mrs. Johnson makes some interesting comparisons of analogues (by which she means structural units similar but not identical) in music and in poetry and shows how they operate in the over-all organization of a musical composition, a poem, or a play. She finds paired analogues corresponding to double plots in drama, as in *King Lear,* and subtotal analogues likewise effective as formal determinants contributing to one's over-all perception of a play—as the two quarrel scenes in *Richard II,* the emblematic scenes in *3 Henry VI* (where a son has killed his father and another father has killed his son). Similarly, Mrs. Johnson finds segmental patterns in music corresponding to what was once thought to be primitiveness in drama—e.g., the episodic structure of *Tamburlaine.* She notes that Elizabethan composers of variations began with the first variation, not with a statement of the theme to be varied (often a familiar tune). "This method of getting underway," she states (pp. 97–98), "operates psychologically much like the poet's device of asking, 'Shall I compare thee to a summer's day?' or of presenting a familiar fictional event to be elaborated"; and the increase in brilliance until the final variation—which is generally very complex in polyphonic interest, rhythm, rapid passages—corresponds to the new social harmony established in the last act of a Shakespearean comedy.

Through all of this Mrs. Johnson speaks of progressive and retrospective modes of thought and finds effective musical comparisons with various types of development, principles of alternation and return, as well as alternation and contrast. Mrs. Johnson devotes many pages to an examination of *The Merchant of Venice* in terms of serial form, finding its "mildly problematical structure" illumined by the musical comparisons, especially in the ending of the play. She analyzes Shakespeare's *Venus and Adonis* as an example of what she calls climactic progression in a work continuous rather than segmental, from the poem's abrupt beginning through various climactic techniques (rising, falling, delay, suspense) to its smooth ending, all of which (along with verbal dexterity, of course) make the poem uniquely sophisticated. Mrs. Johnson finds no other literary work showing the same perfection before 1600; she finds, however, a musical counterpart in the madrigals of Thomas Weelkes, one of which she proceeds to analyze in climactic progression. Mrs. Johnson's book is a brief one; but her approach could be elaborated indefinitely and successfully applied to other works of Shakespeare and his contemporaries.

Leaving poetry and returning to music, one notices a wealth of unexplored materials in the incidental or program music written for or based upon Shakespeare's plays by many of the nineteenth-century composers. Owing at least in part to the literary activities of the Schlegels and of Tieck in Germany, the English poet exerted a terrific fascination upon Romantic composers, whose list of compositions in his name is indeed staggering—operas, symphonic poems, overtures, ballets. Pioneer work in this area has been done by England's distinguished Handelian Winton Dean and by Roger Fiske; and their essays on Shakespeare and opera and Shakespeare in the concert hall appear in the book mentioned earlier, *Shakespeare in Music,* published during the 1964 centenary.[10] "Shakespearean opera," says Mr. Dean, "offers a history of the art in miniature," containing everything "from the *castrato* to serialism, from *bel canto* to *musique concrète*" (p. 98). *The Tempest* is bound to be the most popular of all the plays, having had at least thirty operas based upon it, and *Romeo and Juliet* is the most popular of the tragedies. In dealing with the symphonic poem, incidental music, the cinema, the ballet, Roger Fiske finds also that *Romeo and Juliet* has been perennially the strongest inspiration. Shakespeare's plays have inspired virtually no chamber music and only a few piano pieces (pp. 222-223). One wonders why. And how many know that Robert Schumann, while angling for a doctorate from Jena, contemplated writing a thesis on Shakespeare and music (p. 222)?

The essays by Dean and Fiske are, of course, surveys, filled with enchanting information that might easily be investigated in depth. For example, a musical composition may sometimes seem rather far-fetched when one tries to explain its programs in terms of the play it is based upon. Such a work is Berlioz's *Romeo and Juliet*—subtitled a "dramatic

10. Winton Dean, "Shakespeare and Opera," *Shakespeare in Music,* pp. 89-175; Roger Fiske, "Shakespeare in the Concert Hall," *ibid.,* pp. 177-241.

symphony" by the composer—for large orchestra, three choruses, and three soloists. (Incidentally, this is by no means the only work of Shake speare that inspired Berlioz.) Recently Professor Philip Friedheim has analyzed the work and come up with some startling conclusions.[11] The symphony, he tells us, contains some selections that are purely orchestral, others that are vocal in the style of a cantata or oratorio, and still others that are

theatrical in the manner of grand opera. Some parts of the story are omitted, while others are elaborated far beyond their position in the original drama. For example, Mercutio's Queen Mab monologue appears in two forms: first as an aria, and then as an orchestral scherzo. . . . Certain scenes crucial to the drama do not appear in the symphony at all, for example the deaths of Mercutio and Tybalt, and Romeo's subsequent banishment; at the same time the symphony occasionally presents musical portraits of scenes that do not exist in Shakespeare, for example a funeral procession for Juliet. Shakespeare's ending, the muted reconciliation of the warring families over the bodies of the lovers, is transformed in the symphony to a triumphant conclusion: a heroic chorus during which the two families swear eternal brotherhood.

The final line of the libretto, "Amis, amis pour toujours," seems far removed from Shakespeare's closing lines:

> A glooming peace this morning with it brings;
> The sun for sorrow will not show his head.

Why all this deviation—in addition to much more that I have not cited? Friedheim investigates and finds from Berlioz's *Memoirs* and other sources that, although he had read the play in French, the composer could not understand the English version he saw performed starring Harriet Smithson (whom, one recalls, he later married). But the stage performance he saw was a version by David Garrick, "With Alterations, and an additional Scene," printed in 1750.[12] Certain deviations in Berlioz's

11. In a lecture delivered in the School of Music, University of Georgia, November 29, 1973.

12. Fiske p. 192, had noted earlier: "The impossibility of relating [Berlioz's 'Romeo au tombeau des Capulets'] to Shakespeare's last scene led me to examine contemporary acting versions of the play. Garrick's appeared in 1750. . . . There

score, Friedheim notes, correspond exactly with stage business in the Garrick production. Friedheim poses the question: Why did Berlioz portray so many key episodes in the story without using voices, when he did use a chorus and soloists for other selections? Why make the lovers' scenes pure orchestral music? Friedheim's unique explanation is that "the initial impression the drama made on Berlioz was nonverbal, since he could not understand the language"—an explanation supported by the fact that "the purely orchestral passages most often parallel the Garrick version, the one he saw Miss Smithson performing." The prime impact of the main scenes, in a word, says Friedheim, "was transformed into orchestral music, not because Berlioz was writing a symphony, but because it was never the *language* of Shakespeare that moved him," as his *Memoirs* unequivocally prove.

There is much more to Friedheim's study—especially about Garrick's prolonged ending, the admiration for this that Berlioz expressed in his *Memoirs,* and correspondences (otherwise incomprehensible) in the music—all posed against the Romantic aesthetic with its emphasis upon the bizarre, the magical, the miraculous, the irrational. In conclusion, Friedheim finds *Romeo and Juliet* a mirror reflecting attitudes characteristic of the Romantic period—many of them directly related to the great vogue for Shakespeare. More studies in depth along these lines by musical people equipped with enough literary background to make such investigations meaningful would be especially welcome to both music historians and Shakespeare specialists.

We notice today a terrific, indeed often terrifying interest in extrasensory perception. Here again is fertile ground for Shakespeare exploration. Although Robert West has made a major contribution,[13] the realm of the mental, of magic, of the occult has never been thoroughly looked into. There is, for instance, no definitive book on Shakespeare and astrology—and the aspects were never more propitious for this than now. Music, of course, has always been thought to have powers of its own, and musical *ethea* (effects) have been touched upon by Sternfeld, Long,

---

can be no doubt that this was the version Charles Kemble took to Paris, and that Berlioz had it in mind when writing this symphony. All three of Garrick's major alterations are reflected in the music."

13. Robert H. West, *Shakespeare and the Outer Mystery* (Lexington, Ky., 1968).

and others. G. Wilson Knight long ago noted the connection of music
with love and miracles and mysteries in the final plays, and Hallett
Smith's recent book on the romances frequently alludes to this.[14] Everyone knows that musical magic pervades *The Tempest* and in fact orders
much of the action of the play. Ladies are revived or resurrected through
the supernatural powers of music in *Cymbeline, Pericles,* and *The
Winter's Tale;* and in *The Tempest* the distraught nobles have their
faculties restored by music, as did King Lear earlier. Shakespeare uses
the word *understanding* as being affected by music (cf. *Tempest,* I.i.79–
82). In one of his best-known passages on the power of music (*The
Merchant of Venice*), when describing "the man that hath no music in
himself," Shakespeare states that "the motions of his spirit are dull as
night." In the same play he speaks of Jessica's spirits being attentive, like
those of young animals all subject to music's powers:

> The reason is, your spirits are attentive.
> For do but note a wild and wanton herd,
> Or race of youthful and unhandled colts,
> Fetching mad bounds, bellowing, and neighing loud,
> Which is the hot condition of their blood.
> If they but hear perchance a trumpet sound,
> Or any air of music touch their ears,
> You shall perceive them make a mutual stand,
> Their savage eyes turned to a modest gaze
> By the sweet power of music. Therefore the poet
> Did feign that Orpheus drew trees, stones, and
>   floods,
> Since naught so stockish, hard, and full of rage
> But music for the time doth change his nature.
>
>   (V.i.70–82)

What theory lay behind all this? Where did Shakespeare get his information on the music of the spheres and its effects upon humans—
ideas that go back at least to Pythagoras? Ficino, we know, had works
on magic and music and had his own theory about music's strong effects
on man's *spiritus,* "a corporeal vapour centred in the brain and flowing

14. G. Wilson Knight, *The Crown of Life,* 2d ed. (London, 1948); Hallett Smith,
Shakespeare's Romances: A Study of Some Ways of the Imagination (San Marino,
Cal., 1972).

through the nervous system . . . the link between body and soul."[15] Later, Campanella too dealt with these subjects.[16] A rewarding study, surely, might be made of Shakespeare's ideas about musical therapeutics, *ethos,* and magical effects in general in the light of Neo-Platonic pneumatology.

In the opposite direction, what about expressions of mannerism in Shakespeare's musical references? No mannerist, apparently, quite agrees with any other mannerist, and indeed, not all are agreed that there is such a thing as mannerism, but some claim that Shakespeare's later plays are expressions of this distorted style.[17] If this is true, what about manneristic musical metaphor—that is, the *untuning* of the spheres, or *disharmony* in the cosmos, with its reflections in earthly affairs? (Ulysses refers to this, one recalls, in his speech on order in *Troilus and Cressida.*) And why is there no music at all in the witchery magic that pervades *Macbeth?* (I do not mean the elaborate spectacle laid on the play— witches dancing and singing—in Restoration times and later.)

At least as widespread today as interest in extrasensory perception is the vogue for eroticism in literature—never so prevalent since pre-Victorian times. If we need proof that the subject has been blessed with academic respectability, witness a recent two-day conference on sex and literature at the University of Louisville.[18] It has been said that Shakespeare is the most bawdy of all the Elizabethan poets;[19] he certainly is the most musical, and the two lines often meet. Yet his use of musical terminology for erotic purposes has had little investigation. In the music lessons that set up plot and characterization early in *The Taming of the Shrew,* much of the comic effect relies upon sex references, some of them fairly obvious, some never explained. It has never been pointed

15. D. P. Walker, *Spiritual and Demonic Magic from Ficino to Campanella* (London, 1958), p. 4. For a discussion of Ficino's works on music, astrology, and magic, see pp. 1–72; Ficino in the sixteenth century, pp. 75–185.

16. For a discussion of Campanella's works, see *ibid.,* pp. 203–236.

17. See, for example, Wylie Sypher, *Four Stages of Renaissance Style* (New York, 1955), *passim,* and Arnold Hauser, *Mannerism* (London, 1965), I, 339–352.

18. Second Annual Conference on 20th Century Literature: Love and Sex in Modern Literature, University of Louisville, Louisville, Ky., February 28, March 1–2, 1974.

19. A. L. Rowse, *Shakespeare the Man* (London, 1973), p. 46.

out, for example, that the high point in this episode has definite erotic overtones—breaking the lute over the music master's head. *Romeo and Juliet* is filled with musical wordplay of a most erotic nature, some of it puzzling to its editors and most of it unglossed but all of it perfectly plain in the light of the vocabulary of the day. When Juliet's pseudo-death is discovered and mourned over, Shakespeare introduces comic relief with the musicians who joke with Peter and the Nurse. This becomes more meaningful, however, when one realizes that the musical jokes are all erotic—although they are not so glossed in most editions of the play (including the old variorum). The accumulation of sex imagery based on musical wordplay obviously does much to build up the erotic undercurrent that is so much a part of the tragedy.

And so, doubtless, in other parts of the canon. But where—and why? Surely a study of musical eroticism would illuminate Shakespeare's changing attitudes on the subject, variously commented upon by critics —from his youthful interest in the Dark Lady to the later time when (in the words of one critic) he was "obsessively disgusted" with sex.[20] It might also help explain "the intense sexuality that is one of the enigmatic features of Shakespeare's last plays."[21]

During the past few decades, much interest has centered upon the actual music for the plays, and by now a large part of this has been identified and made available to the public by John Cutts,[22] Frederick Sternfeld, and Peter Seng. When authentic music is not available, John Long has suggested contemporary tunes to fit a given text or scene, certainly a convenience for modern performers. None of these studies and editions, however, is completely impeccable, according to the learned and detailed reviews in *Shakespeare Studies* and elsewhere; all show some sins of omission or commission. And some music continues to defy discovery—for example, the country songs associated with the role of Autolycus in *The Winter's Tale*. Whether "The Amazonian Masque" (BM Add. 10444) was actually the music for the masque in *Timon of Athens* has not been definitely settled either; there are contenders for

20. *Ibid.,* p. 212.

21. Clifford Leech, *The John Fletcher Plays* (Cambridge, Mass., 1962), p. 165.

22. *Musique de scène de la troupe de Shakespeare,* ed. J. P. Cutts (Paris, 1959) contains music in all plays acted by the King's Men, 1603–1625.

and against. Obviously, research into the actual music performed in the
plays will be continued by those equipped in knowledge and sources until
the last song or dance is found, the last problem of transcription and
performance solved.

Similarly, in writing about musical instruments Sternfeld notes (apro-
pos the latest edition of Canon Galpin's *Old English Instruments of
Music*) that we still lack a correct explanation of lute tuning contemporary with Shakespeare.[23] And continuing research into the use of such
wind instruments as cornets and trumpets along the lines started by
W. J. Lawrence in 1928 will throw light upon Blackfriars performances
and the dating of some plays.[24]

We are still largely in the dark, too, about musical people (possibly)
associated with Shakespeare. High on the list is Thomas Morley. What
was the relationship between poet and musician? Did they collaborate
on the songs (two of the most beautiful in all the plays—"It was a Lover
and His Lass" and "O Mistress Mine"), or were both tunes and poems
popular before being taken up by Shakespeare and Morley? The controversy that has raged for decades about all this (neatly summed up in
Peter Seng's book, pp. 96–100) is still unsettled. Then there are Shakespeare's clowns, especially Robert Armin. Musician and poet himself,
Armin is thought by some to have written the song he sings in *Twelfth
Night*. What does the song mean? And how does it fit in *King Lear,*
where Armin (if indeed he played Lear's fool as well as Feste in *Twelfth
Night*) sings one quatrain? Opinions vary and much ink has been spilt
without finding any definite answer to the questions (Seng, pp. 123–128).
Several other musical people may have known and influenced Shakespeare—John Bull (composer, virtuoso keyboard performer, and reader
in music at London's Gresham College), Giles Farnaby (composer of
madrigals), John Daniel (Samuel's musical brother), royal lutanist John
Dowland, and even Henry Lawes (member of the royal chapel of
Charles I, friend of Milton, and composer of the music for *Comus*), who
set one of the sonnets. All these and more have been suggested as at least

23. See F. W. Sternfeld's review of Francis W. Galpin, *Old English Instruments
of Music,* 4th ed. (London, 1965), in *ShS,* II (1966), 333.

24. W. J. Lawrence, "A New Shakespearian Test," *Shakespeare Workshop* (Oxford, 1928), pp. 48–74.

acquaintances of Shakespeare. A definite investigation of the entire subject—relationships and influence—if sources manifest themselves, would
illumine a very confused chapter of Shakespeare studies.

One must not forget to include here, of course, a last musical mystery,
the noblest mistress of them all, the "she" who parallels in a way Beetho-
ven's "immortal beloved," a lady likewise never satisfactorily identified—
the Dark Lady of the Sonnets.[25]

In bringing this discussion to a harmonious close, I should like to
refer to George Steiner's recent assertion (*In Bluebeard's Castle*) that
the dominance of the word is ending, that literature (because of mass
media and other influences) is passing into the keeping of the specialist.[26]
What is to take its place? One answer, says Steiner, is music—recorded
music, that is—with which we are surrounded from morning to night.
We live in a decibel culture; we are encapsulated in sound. Our lapse
from ceremony and ritual has left a vacuum, now filled with music. And
so an ancient circle is closing. Steiner quotes the statement of Lévi-Strauss
that melody holds the key to the *mystère suprême de l'homme*. "Grasp
the riddle of melodic invention, of our apparently imprinted sense of
harmonic accord, and you will touch on the roots of human consciousness" (p. 94). Only music, says Lévi-Strauss, "is a primal universal language, at once comprehensible to all and untranslatable into any other
idiom."

Shakespeare knew all this, intuitively or consciously. Our continuing
effort to pluck out the heart of the musical mystery simply reflects our
desire to see Shakespeare as his contemporaries did and to understand
him with their understanding. We shall perhaps never get at the ultimate
mystère, but our continuing explorations, with music as touchstone, will
inevitably lead us closer to the essence of Shakespeare.

25. Professor Muriel Bradbrook has a very likely candidate for this position,
but since Miss Bradbrook has not proposed the lady's name publicly, I shall not
disclose it at this time.

26. George Steiner, "Tomorrow," *In Bluebeard's Castle: Some Notes Towards
the Redefinition of Culture* (London, 1971), pp. 77–107. See especially pp. 82–95.

The Imperialist Arts of Inigo Jones
Review Article

LEONARD BARKAN

S ELDOM DO WE HAVE the chance to experience the work of a Renaissance artist as though we had never seen it before. It does not undervalue the contribution of editors Stephen Orgel and Roy Strong in *Inigo Jones: The Theatre of the Stuart Court*[1] to acknowledge that this book is primarily the work of a genius whose efforts are at this date beyond review. With that limitation in mind, let us proceed rather to describe what the book contains, to discuss the ways it can be used, and then finally, and most importantly, to offer some beginning sense of what students of Renaissance drama can learn from it.

The book's principal mission is to reproduce all the known drawings executed by Inigo Jones (or, in a few cases, by an assistant) for the court theater of James I and Charles I. They number nearly five hundred, ranging from a few pencil scrawls to large and magnificently detailed drawings that include all the numerous elements of a masque setting: wings, borders, shutters, machines, proscenium arch, and even (alas, rarely) lighting effects and the position of actors on the stage. In each

---

1. (London, Berkeley and Los Angeles, 1973).

case, the editors provide a discussion of the precise medium in which the drawing was done, the size in both inches and centimeters, and the subject, whether it is certain or conjectural. Also included are transcriptions of any words written on the drawings, provenance when they are not from the giant Duke of Devonshire collection that forms the basis of this compilation, and references to any printed discussions or data on exhibition.

Since many of the drawings are in some fundamental way enigmatic, the editors provide various identifications and analyses in addition to the vital statistics. These analytic captions, often lengthy and revealing, may discuss the controversies surrounding the assignment of the drawing to a particular masque, its aesthetic or iconographic qualities, its precise relation to the text of the masque, or significant analogues between this design and other Renaissance graphic or theatrical examples. To aid in our understanding of these analogues, the editors provide reproductions of art works that may represent Jones's sources. Comparison between the putative source and the Jones drawing is partly treated in analytic discussion and partly left to the reader. All these interpretive aids are highly useful, indeed virtually indispensable to an understanding of the drawings as anything more than attractive English Mannerist sketches. In addition to these drawings, a considerable number of diagrams, ground plans, and elevations come to us directly from the original productions of the masques. To supplement these fascinating (but so elusive) original diagrams, the editors often provide their own conjectural ones. All these indications are as indispensable as the captions to a full perception of the art.

The visual arts are the principal but not the only focus of these volumes. The editors have endeavored to provide as complete a record as is possible of all theatrical events presented at the court and at ceremonial occasions elsewhere—at least when Inigo Jones is known to have had a hand in the design. They consequently publish the texts of all twenty-eight masques for which even putative Jones designs survive. This would represent a major achievement in publication even without the visual materials, for it offers us a virtually complete record of a literary and dramatic genre in its great English flowering. Besides the reprinted masques, five plays are represented. These are too long to reprint, but we are given sufficient description or plot summary to make the Jones drawings meaningful. In a number of cases, the editors include entries for other forms of entertainment in which Jones's designs played a part, e.g., tilts and barriers. In addition, there are numerous unidentified masques that can be located by contemporary allusions; while no text has survived, the editors can putatively assign drawings on the basis of subject or style.

As a further attempt to present a complete record of court spectacles, the editors include a substantial entry for each dramatic event, whether or not the text can be reprinted or identified. This entry lists the date, occasion, and location of the performance, as well as the names of the artists involved, including (when possible) poet, composer, and choreographer. Of particular interest here are the precise terms in which the individuals are credited for their accomplishments. Two illustrative examples reveal a great deal about Jones himself: the text of the first masque, a collaboration with Jonson, tells us that *"the bodily part . . . was of Master Inigo Jones his design and art"* (*The Queen's Masques: the First, of Blackness,* ll. 78–79), while the last, a collaboration with Davenant, informs us that *"The invention, ornament, scenes, and apparitions, with their descriptions, were made by Inigo Jones, Surveyor General of his Majesty's Works. What was spoken or sung, by William Davenant, her majesty's servant. The subject was set down by them both"* (*Salmacida Spolia,* ll. 489–494). We need look no further to observe the increasing primacy of Jones over all the elements of these spectacles. Other entries in this historical catalogue inform us of the names of the participants, when they are known; and each entry closes with a listing of important secondary-source materials on the individual masque.

All of these are decidedly helpful, but the two most revealing entries detail the cost of the masques and the contemporary opinion of them as recorded in print, in diaries, or in letters. Not only is the question of cost interesting in studying the economic priorities of the Stuart court, but the extensive reprinting of financial records, often for the first time, can also afford important insights into the masques themselves because these records occasionally take the form of detailed lists of properties or of payments to artisans for specifically described services. The survey of contemporary opinion, also set out for the first time, has the same double usefulness. It gives an important glimpse into the historical milieu, raising and perhaps answering questions about the nonroyal audience of

the masques and about the relations between the English art form and
the expectations of visitors from the Continent. But more importantly,
these reprinted contemporary opinions occasionally include detailed and
lengthy descriptions of what took place both onstage and in the audience.[2]

These hundreds of pages of drawings, texts, and explanatory materials
—modestly referred to by the editors as "the Catalogue"—are comple-
mented by a far-ranging introduction that amounts to a book-length
study of Jones and his theater. This general essay on Stuart court
spectacle is not always closely tied to the materials presented in the bulk
of the volumes, but it is a highly interesting statement nonetheless. The
first chapter, "The Poetics of Spectacle," discusses the nature of Renaissance spectacle, both as an idea and as a practical work of art. The
famous quarrel between Jones and Jonson is used as a means of understanding the relative place of the word and the image in spectacular
theater, and similar distinctions are drawn by discussing the gulf that
seventeenth-century audiences would have observed between plays and
masques. Masque, Professor Orgel demonstrates, is a very particular kind
of spectacle, which acts through the enthusiastic use of perspective and
technology to celebrate the king. It transforms the masquer and spectator
in part by crossing over the line between stage and audience: this flow
suggests that the ideal world inside the masque can come to include the
real world of the court and thence, by extension, of the kingdom.

The second chapter, "The Mechanics of Platonism," concentrates upon
the technology of the masque, emphasizing its development in the reign
of King James. There is some description here of the *machina versatilis,*
the *scena ductilis,* and the scene of relieve, though the reader is assumed
to have already understood the basic nature of the wing-and-border
theater that has persisted well into the twentieth century. Where this
chapter is most revealing, however, is in the analysis of the relation between machine and meaning. Fancy technology is placed in the service
of Platonic idealization of the monarch and of the approved virtues. The

---

2. See, for instance, *Pleasure Reconciled to Virtue, Pan's Anniversary, or the
Shepherd's Holiday,* and *Coelum Britannicum:* in each of these cases there is a
lengthy inventory of goods and services. These lists offer considerable insight not
only into the materials that appeared on stage but also in the system of artisanship
that made the execution of Jones's work possible.

heavenly glories of the good could be made real by means of breath taking discoveries and gravity-defying mid-air displays, while the in-substantial nature of evil could be proven through the use of quaint devices like shutters and traps that produced quick disappearance. Indeed all the masque's technology is in the service of making the ideal real; and that transformation is a principle at the heart of the texts themselves.

Dr. Strong is responsible for the third chapter, "The Arts of Design," which considers the drawings in terms of Renaissance (largely non-theatrical) art history. He makes important points about the chronologi-cal development of Jones's art. In the early years Jones was an indifferent draughtsman, but he taught himself to draw by reference to the works of Continental artists represented in England and to the engravings of the Italian Mannerists, especially such figures as Parmigianino and the Carraccis. The inevitable Italian journey (in 1613–1614) intensified these influences and contributed to a steadily increasing fluency in Jones's draughtsmanship. But as Jones's art of drawing grows in maturity, the author suggests, his originality decreases, so that by the late 1630's the range of subjects has become predictable and is restricted to rocks, Ar-cadian landscapes, sea and harbor scenes, and topographical views. These value judgments do not always seem altogether justified, but it is certainly true, as the introduction suggests, that by the end of the Jonson era (*Albion's Triumph,* the last Jonson masque, was produced in 1632), Jones was becoming more an artist of ideas than of actualities.

The final chapter, "Platonic Politics," shows the authors at their very best. The most interesting and convincing of those arguments that under-lie this whole project is the assertion of a close tie between the masque and the political ideologies of the Stuart court, and this chapter concen-trates upon that connection. It is clear from the introduction, as well as from the texts and designs, that at Charles's court the masque became a medium for official expression of the monarch's will and what we might call the royal image. Messrs. Orgel and Strong point out very convincingly that in Charles's case this official line was a mixture of Platonism and Machiavellianism, the merging of love and power. As if in response to the increasing turbulence of parliamentarianism, the masque became more imperialist, and the king's absolutism in the masque reflected an attempt to be absolute in the realm. The masques in the middle years of Charles's reign become more patriotic, more single-minded, more abstract; and in addition, they seek to engulf and control more realms, notably including the cosmic, the mythological, and the extraterrestrial. By the very end—and here I extrapolate from introduction and text—it seems as though the troubles of the kingdom caused Jones and his associates to turn their backs upon the real world and concentrate exclusively upon those remoter, but safer, realms.

In all respects these volumes represent a massive scholarly achievement. At the very least, they make available the complete Jones drawings for the theater in catalogue form, so that they will serve as the basis for any future references to these works, far superceding the half-century-old Simpson and Bell edition of *Designs by Inigo Jones for Masques and Plays at Court*.[3] They are indeed handsome volumes attaining a high standard of reproduction, and the publishers have been generous with the size of pages, of margins, and of the reproduced artworks themselves. But the editors have sought to accomplish more than simple compilation; and here they have succeeded in some interesting ways. On the purely historical side, the book will probably be most remembered for the immense achievement of attributing drawings to particular dramatic works and occasions. This is, of course, a vital scholarly issue, since if we intend to draw interpretive parallels between particular texts and drawings, we must be reasonably certain of basing conclusions on correct attributions. Many of the drawings, especially in the first half of Jones's career, are open to at least some question of attribution. While Simpson and Bell did the pioneering work in this field, the present edition seeks to identify a larger number of the drawings and makes a good many important changes in the earlier identifications. Undoubtedly there will be disputes over the more controversial attributions. One man's cloud is another man's mountain, and the editors use so many systems of identification that different explanations often lean on each other a bit unconvincingly. All the same, this is the work that future scholars will argue from.

Besides the historical work of assigning drawings to texts, the most important achievement here consists of a number of polemical assertions, some explicit, some implicit. The underlying polemical message is stated

3. *The Twelfth Volume of the Walpole Society* (1923–1924).

in the first sentence of the preface: "Inigo Jones is the most important single figure in the arts in seventeenth-century England" (p. xiv). Both the primary and secondary materials go a long way toward proving this claim. A more complex kind of assertion about Jones conveyed on every page of these volumes is the coherent progression of his development as an artist. Orgel and Strong discern distinct periods in his style of drawing, and from these they frequently draw conclusions about the attribution of designs—hence occasionally causing one hypothesis to depend on another for proof. The development has more serious ramifications, though, in Jones's changing conceptions of the nature of the theatrical spectacle. Another convincingly proved assertion, as we have already seen, is the close tie between theater and politics. Finally, the very existence of these volumes asserts that the masque of the Stuart court cannot be understood without a consideration of all the arts that were brought to bear in it.

This last assertion is decidedly implicit. Orgel and Strong bring together a great variety of materials, but they remain curiously aloof from a holistic conception of the masque. In some ways the book almost defeats any attempt on the part of the reader to realize this conception. Generous as the explanatory captions are, they rarely help us to visualize in three dimensions what is presented perforce in two. Texts are kept completely separate from drawings, so that the reader must repeatedly flip large-sized pages back and forth if he is to correlate a design with a moment in the text, and drawings are only rarely cross-referenced to line numbers in the text. Even the captions are often several pages away from the drawing they describe—on one occasion, nearly fifty pages away. These limitations are mentioned not so much to quibble—though it would be splendid if they were corrected—as to establish clearly that this is no coffee-table book. It is a gold mine, but it does not give up its riches easily.

The riches that can be coaxed from the book could constitute a book themselves, and the present article can scarcely do more than list some of the areas of speculation that the Inigo Jones material inspires. Perhaps it would be worthwhile to begin by negation. Reading *The Theatre of the Stuart Court* is astonishingly unlike the experience of reading the masques themselves. When one peruses Professor Orgel's Yale edition of the Jonson masques or T.J.B. Spencer's *Book of Masques in Honour of*

Allardyce Nicoll,[4] one is likely to get the impression that these works are, at most, spoken poems. They are indeed great structures of words with that combination of imagery, allegory, verbal iconography, mythology, learned allusion, and abstraction which reminds one of the decidedly nondramatic poet Edmund Spenser. To be sure, this is a true impression, even if it does not represent the whole truth: scrutiny of the Jones designs, however intense, need not deprive the masques of their poetic concentration or ever transform them into dramas for the public theater. They are not that kind of theater, but they are three-dimensional works intended for public performance. Far from being the least theatrical of public presentations, they are revealed by these volumes to be the most theatrical, if we understand that term to concentrate upon the gulf between the mere printed text and the complete experience that the creators envisaged.

Understanding the masques as theater liberates them in many ways from antiquarianism. For all that they perfectly reflect their time and political milieu, they do not always benefit from being subordinated to chronological considerations. Once presented in this fuller form, they reveal their kinship with the spectacular and nonmimetic drama of all ages, from Roman triumphs and circuses through to popular spectaculars of our own time. These comparisons are not frivolous. The texts (especially but not exclusively Jonson's) read as elitist and recherché, with their lengthy speeches, learned references, and laborious allegory. Now we are reminded, however, that the text was a very small part of the totality. The other parts—some of which the Orgel and Strong volumes make more nearly available—may have their subtle and learned aspects, but the visual experience and the technological marvels (to say nothing of the music and dance) were breathtakingly beautiful, sensuous, and, above all, accessible.

To appreciate these drawings fully, it is probably best to be steeped in the visual idioms of the theater. The style of the sketches, for instance, is uniquely theatrical because these works are intended not directly for a viewer but for another artist, who will execute them. Thus they tend to

---

4. Ben Jonson, *The Complete Masques,* ed. Stephen Orgel (New Haven, Conn., 1969); T.J.B. Spencer, *Book of Masques, in Honour of Allardyce Nicoll* (Cambridge, Eng., 1967).

have a combination of meticulousness and impressionism. The best of the costume sketches, for instance, give the impression of hasty composition, as though drawing a line is the visual equivalent of thinking aloud. A natural emphasis falls upon the most striking or original elements of the costume, while the greater parts of the space may scarcely be filled in. These informal sketches are completely unself-conscious: since the artist does not think of them as a finished product, he is free to cross out, revise, write messages on them, even doodle irrelevantly.

When we turn to the scenic sketches, we can observe another kind of theatrical medium: the illusionistic stage, including a large number of wings, borders, and drops. The central principle is the creation of complex and profound three-dimensionality through a multitude of two-dimensional surfaces placed at significant distances from each other. It is partly "realistic" because real space is created in the mind's eye, but it never allows the viewer to forget that he is the willing victim of an illusion since each element in the design is obviously nothing more than a painted surface. The progressive revelation of more depths—frequently the scenario of Jones's stagecraft—keeps renewing the play of reality and illusion and keeps making it more delightful. Stationary three-dimensional elements, which were not uncommon, tease the viewer further. Mobile three-dimensional elements, which could be chariots, ships, clouds, or, most significantly, human beings, take on immense importance. They quite literally create the dimensional space because without them a perfectly executed perspective set is largely indistinguishable from a one-piece, continuous two-dimensional drawing. So the wing-and-border theater, in 1600 or 1900, combines illusionism with a striking emphasis upon the human form.

The illusionistic stage was Jones's medium but only an unconscious part of his message. Yet as we approach an understanding of that message, we must still concentrate for a bit on the medium of theater. Anyone who loves the theater must recognize in joy and sorrow two of its major attributes: it is a multigeneric medium, and it is hopelessly impermanent. These are the two great coordinates of Jones's theater. The masque used multimedia elements to their fullest possible extent as bulwarks against the impermanence of the theater and indeed of all human endeavor. The significance of nonverbal aspects cannot be overestimated. Ground plans of some of the early productions like *Lord Hay's Masque* (1607) and

Prince Henry's Barriers (1610) reveal the shallowness of the stage compared to the area where the dancing or tilting took place; and even in the late masques seating was arranged around the edges and not in the middle of the hall. The prime space was occupied by dancing, which could be viewed with equal pleasure from any angle. What went on behind the proscenium was highly directional (that is, visually meaningless to spectators on the sides) and may well have been seen, quite literally, as a backdrop for the main business of dancing.[5]

We must not of course conclude that Jones was at the mercy of some Philistine public taste for meaningless spectacle. The multiple elements of the masque maintain not an adversary relationship but rather a creative one. The triumph of Jones's vision was the celebration and integration of all the media. In fact, consideration of the volumes under review here brings the masque into focus as a conscious piece of theatrical imperialism—an art form that seeks to engulf all other art forms and goes beyond them to forms of culture, society, and history, and ultimately to the workings of the cosmos. If the "Great Theatre of the World" ever flourished in England, it was under the direction of Inigo Jones at the Stuart court. What remains to be considered here are some examples of that imperialism: the theatrical conquest of the graphic arts, architecture, technology, and the workings of the cosmos itself.

Jones's aggressive attitude toward the graphic arts is particularly apparent as we observe his desire to conquer the real and transform it into the ideal. Hence his complex attitude toward iconography. There is no more persistent tension in Jones's art than that between representations that convey a visual meaning and those that are intended to idealize beauty. When we read the texts of the masques, particularly those of Ben

5. Even from the king's perfect vantage point—and Orgel and Strong are surely right in emphasizing the special significance of that position—the glories of perspective lose something when they occur in a space that is remote and quite shallow relative to the space between the perceiver and the perspective setting. As to the primacy of dancing, there are numerous indications in the more lengthy contemporary opinions reprinted that the observers were particularly struck by the dances. In addition, of course, there is the famous comment of King James as he watched *Pleasure Reconciled to Virtue* wear on through the evening: "Why don't they dance? What did you make me come here for? Devil take all of you, dance!" (Orgel and Strong, p. 283).

Jonson, we get the impression that the visual component was weighted decidedly toward the cognitive and away from what the poet may have considered the frivolity of mere decoration. But when the designs are placed next to the descriptions, we begin to observe that, while Jonson may have yearned for meaningful picture-reading, Jones tended to concentrate on graceful aesthetic satisfactions.

That the two approaches could be in conflict must have been abundantly clear to both men, because their very first collaboration, *The Masque of Blackness,* seems to have foundered on this very tension. The conceit of the masque, along with its companion piece *The Masque of Beauty,* is that the black-faced daughters of the River Niger will serve the shining goddess Aethiopia and thence become white. In the service of this allegory (which the queen herself had suggested), all the ladies of the court wore blackface. The meaning was clear enough, but the aesthetic experience left much to be desired if all the masquers had to be disfigured. Dudley Carlton wrote to Ralph Winwood: "Instead of Vizzards, their Faces, and Arms up to the Elbows, were painted black, which was Disguise sufficient, for they were hard to be known; *but it became them nothing so well as their red and white, and you cannot image a more ugly sight, then a troop of lean-cheek'd Moors*" (Orgel and Strong, p. 89). Nor was this the only *outré* touch intended to identify pictures and meanings:

Oceanus presented in a human form, the colour of his flesh blue, and shadowed with a robe of sea-green; his head grey and horned, as he is described by the ancients; his beard of the like mixed colour. He was garlanded with algae, or sea-grass, and in his hand a trident.

(ll. 40–43)

Alas, there is no surviving drawing to indicate whether Jones actually carried out this grotesquerie. Very likely he did, and the results made future practice clear: the message of the masque and the iconographic identification of the participants must never (at least in the main masque) compromise beauty.

Throughout the early years Jones became increasingly adept at introducing iconographic touches in the costuming that enhanced, rather than detracted from, the beauty of the masquers and the performance. In *Tethys's Festival* (1610), the costume sketches for Tethys, a Naiad, Zephyrus, and an Escort to the Duke of York (who presented Zephyrus) include seaweed, coral, shells for the maritime theme, and flowers for the vernal theme. But these are always kept very much within the bounds of contemporary fashion. If the seaweed hangs a bit luxuriantly off the Escort's shoulders (#58), it merely provides an arresting touch that unites his costume with the concerns of the masque. The cockleshell motif, on the other hand, is not at all permitted to interfere with Tethys's perfect coiffure. By the time of *Chloridia* (1613), a masque with very similar mythology, the iconographic touch of leaves in Chloris's costume has been relegated to an even less prominent position. The tension remains throughout Jones's career: figures from remote times are frequently costumed in contemporary dress with mere touches of antiquarianism; and on a number of occasions when Jonson's descriptions differ from Jones's sketches, the issue on which they differ is the extent to which characters are arrayed in distinctively iconographic fashion. At his best, the designer succeeds in conveying both grace and specificity at once.

The dangers of disfiguring iconography apply almost exclusively to the ladies and gentlemen of the court, and we must not forget that the dramatis personae included innumerable figures with whose design iconography could run riot. In the first place, the masque texts include many actors who are half-personified abstractions. For these figures Jones pillaged the emblematic tradition stemming from Cesare Ripa's *Iconologia*. Entheus, in *The Lord's Masque,* and Jealousy, Disdain, Fear, and Dissimulation, in *Chloridia,* are copied closely from emblematic engravings by Ripa and Enea Vico. But even in these cases the artist's penchant for gracefulness wins out: the costumes are normalized and made more nearly contemporary, while the imitation of the emblem concentrates on physiognomy and body position.

The antimasque, of course, must have offered the most spectacular opportunities for striking graphic effects united with deliberately ungraceful iconography. From its first real appearance in Jonson's *Masque of Queens,* the antimasque is a direct counterexample to the glorified individuals and abstractions in the main masque. The antimasque is perfectly suited to Jonson's particular genius: what, after all, are plays like *Every Man in His Humour, Volpone,* and *Bartholomew Fair* but great sequences of counterexamples? Within the texts of the masques, these sections not infrequently seem to outshine the passages of fervent idealization. But Jones proves to be another sort of artist, one whose greatest achievements are the dramatization of perfection. Again and again he seems to mitigate the extremity of Jonson's iconographic excess. Sometimes he attains magnificent heights of the Mannerist grotesque.[6] For the most part, however, Jones's vision of the antimasque is not of a grotesque transformation of the human. He gravitates rather toward the literary type of the *caractère* and its dramatic relative—commedia dell' arte. The great series of antimasque sketches, such as in *Love's Triumph through Callipolis* (1631) and *Britannia Triumphans* (1638), are simply of character types. The costumes may be a bit old-fashioned or derivative from some of the stranger types of *Pantalones;* but the drawings leave no doubt that these individuals are representatives and not grotesques. Even the style of these drawings partakes of this self-consciously representative quality. They are not so much costume sketches as emblems themselves. The fact that they tend to have captions perfectly suits their generic nature.

The representative nature of the antimasque characters reminds us of that ambition discernible in so much of Jones's work: total inclusion in the scope of the masque. Jones may have an uneasy relationship with iconography, but he is a much more wholehearted participant in other graphic traditions. Orgel and Strong give us ample opportunity to observe how often Jones directly copies contemporary engravings, usually from Italian or French sources. He wants to construct a representative and all-inclusive art, one that is modern and in touch with the great graphic works of his time. Among the graphic works that Jones copies there is a striking incidence of spectacular and grandiose representations: giant pageants, architectural renderings of the most magnificent classical buildings, great vistas of heaven and earth. Jones seeks out spectacular sources on which to base the grandeur of his own creation, but more than that, he chooses to express monumental ambition by daring to translate great ideas into great three-dimensional realities.

If Jones seeks to represent the familiar works of art in his theater, he

6. There is, for instance, in *The Temple of Love* (1635) an antimasque of spirits that includes some spectacular sketches for the costuming of fiery, airy, watery, and earthy figures. The best of them, the Watery Spirit (#304, 305), is virtually engulfed in his element, so that the human form is almost lost in the costume, which turns normal dress into scales and seaweed, while the headdress turns the human head into that of a fish.

also has a strong penchant for unfamiliar works of nature. Jones's ambition extends very strikingly to the New World, and his drawings are peppered with examples of exotic people, plants, animals, and settings. When dealing with these subjects, he departs from his usual practice of turning exceptional things into a kind of graceful generality. Rather he exploits the exotic for its capacity to produce wonder and to act as a foil for the representations of more familiar kinds of beauty. A striking sketch of an Indian Torchbearer in The *Middle Temple and Lincoln's Inn Masque* (#84) offers a good example. The figure is decidedly exotic, scarcely half-dressed and wearing almost nothing but feathers, which form the basis of his headdress, boots, and skirt, with a more conventional cloak hanging a bit skimpily from his back. If Orgel and Strong are correct in their assertion that Jones's source is the drawing of an African Indian in Cesare Vecellio's *Habiti antichi et moderni di tutto il mondo*,[7] then our artist has reversed his usual procedure and has produced a figure considerably more recherché than his source, for Vecellio's figure is an unmistakably Old World warrior with a few exotic touches of feathers and armadillolike armor. The concentration of Jones's design enables him to convey remoteness at the same time as the exotically dressed figures can form a feathery background for the more familiar beauties of the masquers. So Jones is at once realizing the remote New World on his stage and also domesticating it through the coherence of his design and through a technique of staging that enables the exotic figures to become part of the background (even part of the set) once they have established themselves as exotic. Chapman's description of the torchbearers' appearance illustrates this process whereby the exotic is given a brief moment in the limelight and then tamed as part of the background for the masquers:

The torchbearers' habits were of the Indian garb, but more stravagant than those of the masquers, all showfully garnished with several-hued feathers. The humble variety whereof stuck off the more amply the masquers' high beauties, shining in the habits of themselves; and reflected in their kind a new and delightfully-varied radiance on the beholders.

(ll. 51–56)

7. (Venice, 1598). Vecellio is depicting the *Indo Africano*.

The torchbearers are extraordinary in their exoticism but humble in the simplicity of their design. The aesthetic is one of sequential reflection: the masquers gain radiance from the exotic torchbearers, and the beholders gain radiance from the exotic masquers. Foreign and remote elements must retain their strangeness but at the same time must be closely integrated into the plan of the masque, which always leads back to the re-experiencing of the familiar.

If Jones hastens to appropriate styles and subjects that will identify his art as contemporary, his most insistent appropriation is the use of that peculiarly Renaissance graphic obsession—perspective. Without a complex and creative understanding of perspective as it operates in both two and three dimensions, Jones could not possibly have created his set designs. Messrs. Orgel and Strong treat the subject of perspective incisively and at length in their introduction. They demonstrate, among other things, how influential Jones was in introducing the reading of perspective to English audiences, what a great change he wrought from the Elizabethan graphic conventions whereby a picture was its own world rather than an extension of the viewer's world; and they make clear the potential of perspective for political statement:

Through the use of perspective the monarch, always the ethical centre of court productions, became in a physical and emblematic way the centre as well. Jones's theatre transformed its audience into a living and visible emblem of the aristocratic hierarchy: the closer one sat to the King, the 'better' one's place was, and only the King's seat was perfect. It is no accident that perspective stages flourished at court and only at court, and that their appearance there coincided with the reappearance in England of the Divine Right of Kings as a serious political philosophy.

(p. 7)

No assertion could better corroborate the imperialist ambitions of the masque: Jones takes perspective, a technique of realist representation, and makes it over into his own instrument. He then turns it into a basic principle of visual reality and thence into a medium of social, political, and cosmic organization.

Throughout his production Jones uses perspective with a vengeance: there is rarely anything subtle about the narrowing of the central space toward the vanishing point or about the decreasing height of the wing structures as one moves upstage. Indeed comparisons with the Italian originals nearly always reveal that Jones has either exaggerated the geometric effect or else has eliminated decorative details that tend to work against it. This self-conscious stress on perspective is no accident. The artist's strategy is simultaneously to create the illusion that perspective design fosters and also to keep the viewer aware that he is witnessing an illusion.[8]

Because in the theater perspective becomes three-dimensional, it accounts for a great deal more than a purely visual message. By the middle (at least) of Jones's career he was very conscious not only of the differences between two- and three-dimensional perspective but also of the stage's capacity for mingling the two types. In his Roman Atrium for *Albion's Triumph* (1632; #191), for instance, he includes downstage three pairs of monumental pillared wings at a relatively subtle angle and with only a moderate diminution of height; but the upstage shutter is itself a perspective drawing at greatly diminished height. The mixture of two and three dimensions represents a daring attempt to induce us to read the shutter as more three-dimensional perspective and, in addition, to see it as considerably more distant from us than it really is.

The three dimensions become meaningful, of course, when they are used and perceived. Jones further enlivens his three-dimensional perspectives through the movement of the stage, the movement of the actors, and the strategic arrangement of the audience's perceptions. His most distinctive achievement in perspective may well be the versatility of his theatrical manipulation. He frequently uses moving stage pieces to drama-

---

8. Jones's artistic self-consciousness achieves an identification with the latest news from the Continent at the same time as he modifies the Continental practices. In a relatively early perspective drawing, from *The Vision of Delight* (1617; #89), Jones deliberately borrows architectural elements from two stage representations in Sebastiano Serlio's *Tutte le' Opere d' Architettura,* one of "The Tragic Scene," the other of "The Comic Scene." By alluding to the two, Jones communicates the deliberately mixed style of his own theater. Yet his design is very different from Serlio's: where the Italian design, particularly for "The Comic Scene," involves a three-dimensional world in which perspective is a subtle tool, the English drawing drops almost all the detail so that the perspective line toward the far-upstage archway is the crucial thrust. Jones thus alludes to a tradition but drives it toward singleness and away from the diversity with which it was originally adorned.

tize and give meaning to the effects of perspective. The most splendid example, and one that can stand as among Jones's greatest moments, is the Vale of Tempe in *Tempe Restored* (1632; #216). This is the first scene discovered in the masque (*"a delicious place by nature and art,"* says Townshend in the text), and it is a curious combination of a classical, almost urban, perspective setting including three pairs of pillared and balustraded side wings with a decidedly nonurban background of Tempe's steep mountains (just barely visible in the drawing) that do not seem to take part in the perspective. Nature surrounds and impresses itself upon the perspectivist art. Clearly this setting suggests the best of both worlds, an almost deliberately Spenserian Bower of Bliss, with the same combination of attractiveness and danger.

Once the beauty of the scene has established itself, a young man, newly escaped from Circe's thralldom, appears and begins to revise into negative terms our estimate of the moral meaning of the space we have been observing. The rocks of the Vale of Tempe open to reveal the palace of Circe: *"a sumptuous palace with an open terrace before it and a great stair or return descending into the lower grounds, the upper part environed with walls of marble alongst which were planted cypress trees"* (ll. 100–103). With this discovery (for which we have, alas, no drawing) the perspective lines of the wings are, presumably, continued and find their vanishing point in Circe's palace itself. The manipulation of perspective has given an entirely new moral significance to the scene we so admired at first: it may be the glorious Vale of Tempe, or it may be a scene of luxury with license at its center. After the grotesque antimasque of Circe's victims, the shutter closes again: this is the true restoration of Tempe.

Even though Jones clearly delighted in stage effects for their own sake, his use of perspective is nearly always coordinated with striking possibilities for the human figure in the midst of the perspective. An example from *Prince Henry's Barriers* (1610; #37), called by Orgel and Strong "the earliest surviving design for a perspective stage-set in England" (p. 164), makes it clear that even in Jones's first works of perspective his intention was to set off the actors. This design consists of side wings in a potpourri of architectural styles and with a rather gentle perspective, while upstage center is occupied by St. George's Portico, an elaborate archway with behind it what appears to be a deep corridor whose lines

move very strikingly toward the vanishing point. All the lines in the
design move toward that corridor and its upstage end; they thus exag-
gerate the depth of the corridor and place inordinate emphasis upon it
as a point of entrance. In the action of the masque each of the knights
entered through this corridor and moved straight downstage, off of the
set itself and into the middle of the Banqueting House space, where the
Barriers themselves took place. The stage setting must certainly have
conveyed the feeling of *multum in parvo:* from out of the vividly defined
vanishing point appeared fifty-six knights with their trains, and each
proceeded through the great (apparent) depth from that point to the
center of the room, the perspective perfectly emphasizing the grandeur of
the flower of British knighthood.[9]

Near the other end of Jones's career, in *Britannia Triumphans* (1638;
#339), he uses the same technique of perspective. But the terms of the
actor-audience relationship have reversed themselves from James's reign
to Charles's. In this setting, for the Palace of Fame, there are three pairs
of side wings in perspective and upstage the palace itself with a magnificent central door covering the vanishing point. Now the king is not the
chief observer but rather the chief participant, and he alone entered
through that door. By this time Jones the stage director has become more
sophisticated: not only the setting but the actors themselves are deployed
in a perspective pattern, with allegorical personages representing Arms
and Science as well as the masquers placed symmetrically along the
perspective lines. The stage direction is very revealing: *"The masquers
came forth of the peristylium and stood on each side, and at that instant
the gate of the palace opened and Britanocles appeared"* (ll. 531–532). At
the same time as the actors and masquers were forming their positions
the palace itself was being raised from a trap. It seems clear, then, that the
perspective of both people and objects was being created right before the audience's eyes; and at the moment when the perspective had

9. A comment by Edmund Howes on this moment seems particularly apposite:
"Against these Gallant Challengers came six and fiftie brave defendants . . . who
in the lower end of the roome had erected a very delicat and pleasant place, where
in private manner they and their traine remained, which was so very great that no
man imagined that the place could have concealed halfe so many . . ." (quoted
in Orgel and Strong, p. 164).

been achieved, the king appeared at the extreme point of that perspective, representing the pinnacle of the social pyramid and of Jones's art.

Inigo Jones's ambitions for the masque go far beyond the world of the graphic arts; and that shift in perspective from two to three dimensions ought to remind us that he was above all an architect. Even without the Orgel and Strong compilation, we could well have guessed that the architect of the Whitehall Banqueting House would certainly have filled it with architectural theater designs, and the drawings themselves make this point very clear. The representation of architecture highlights many of Jones's masque designs. He persistently introduces architectural elements into his Arcadian landscapes, or depicts an urban world defined by architectural vividness and variety. Clearly the wonderment that Jones hoped to inspire was based at least in part on the creation in little of grandiose piazzas filled with Italianate structures: and this creation exemplifies the imperialism of Jones's art.

But it is clear from virtually every design that Jones's use of architecture is not confined to the mere representation of buildings but shapes his whole visual imagination. His sense of the structuring of space—something we can just begin to perceive from pondering the drawings and visualizing their realization—has much in common with the requirements of monumental architectural units and vistas. Perhaps it is his talent for combining grandeur with a fine sense of proportion. For all that he worked with decorative elements, he virtually never seems to have seen anything in only two dimensions. It is no great exaggeration to say that his settings are architecture and his costumes sculpture. The pinnacle of his inspiration is in the use of multiple layers or levels: in separate pairs of wings, layered elements of a costume, relief carvings on a proscenium or a three-dimensional structure. Jones is determined to have the viewer experience from any distance a multiplicity of perceptible levels between himself and the horizon. And the complexity of three-dimensional perception is used to make up for the fact that the viewer of a stage-set, unlike that of an architectural work, is basically sedentary. The magnificent moving stage sets that Jones constructs increase these layers and levels.

Given a decidedly architectural vision of theater design, Jones embodies in his drawings a special glorification of architecture, in particular the monuments of contemporary English splendor that he was himself producing in the real world. In *Time Vindicated to Himself and to His Honours* (1623; #122) Jones begins with an exterior prospect of Whitehall and the surrounding buildings with his own creation taking the lion's share of the space. This representation of the building in which the masque is taking place induces a reflexive awareness in the spectator, reminding him of the experience he is having and of the fact of architectural monuments and, in this case, their ubiquitous creator. But Jones's effect seems to have gone yet further. This prospect of Whitehall is a downstage shutter, and the scene that takes place in front of it serves as a kind of elaborate fanfare to the main masque, at once cajoling the audience to take an interest in the proceedings and also criticizing the potentially seditious nature of the "Curious," who spy on the court merely for their own entertainment. These figures, joined by their poet laureate, the self-admiring satirist Chronomastix (a caricature of George Wither), may seem to be harmless in themselves but, by carping shortsightedly on the minor corruptions of the Time, endanger the fame of the great (and presumably uncorrupted) figures at the court.[10] Now in this masque, Jonson is utterly silent on stage designs and effects; indeed the only impression the text gives about the first scene is that it takes place indoors, an impression contradicted by Jones's design. Jones is in fact staging his own drama of architecture. To set this scene outside the monumental front of the Banqueting House is to demonstrate first that the "Curious" and their poet Chronomastix are forever on the outside looking in, second, that they do represent a threat to the court, and third, that it is the walls of the building themselves that stand between the detractors of the Time and King James. So the present experience, i.e., of beholding the masque in Whitehall, while an embattled one, is nonetheless safe, thanks to the art of Inigo Jones.[11]

10. The best analysis of the issues here is to be found in W. Todd Furniss, "Ben Jonson's Masques," in *Three Studies in the Renaissance* (New Haven, Conn., 1958).

11. It should be pointed out that there is a striking contrast between the criticism of self-admiration in the text and the designer's decision to represent his own buildings on the stage. One is tempted to speculate that this apparent contradiction may explain Jonson's neglect of any stage descriptions in this particular masque. His epigraph, drawn from Martial (XIII.ii.7-8), seems almost too perfect a Jon-

Jones extends the architectural drama further in the next scene, which includes the discovery of the masquers and the beginning of Time's vindication from its small-minded detractors. The mood changes radically: in place of the satiric world and the London setting we have a serene, mythological atmosphere in which Venus and Saturn, Love and Time, unite to praise the court. The drawing, too, appears to change in style. Instead of direct imitation of a familiar vista, Jones designs a symbolic perspective surrounded by clouds and allegorical images. But architecture is still at the heart of the matter. The main element in the design is a great arch with side colonnades. In one sense, this seems to be imaginary architecture, a great open structure almost floating in the clouds and decked with symbols like the hourglass, the signs of the zodiac, and allegorical representations of day and night. But Orgel and Strong make the convincing suggestion that this structure may be a representation of or at least an allusion to work designed by Inigo Jones as part of the Duke of Buckingham's New Hall. If this is true, then the opening of the shutter to reveal this design is a kind of apotheosis of architecture (and particularly Jones's): by protecting the glories of the court from potential detractors, the architect earns his place in the heavenly scheme, just at the point where the real and the ideal cross.

With this intersection of the real and the ideal, we may begin to see that Jones's emphasis upon architecture is more than mere self-advertisement (though it is that too). Architecture becomes for Jones a favorite metaphor bearing a variety of meanings. As early as *Prince Henry's Barriers* (1610; #36,37) Jones designed settings with an almost absurd conglomeration of vibrant architectural styles to fit a text by Jonson that turns on an architectural metaphor:

> Only the House of Chivalry (howe'er
> The inner parts and store be full, yet here
> In that which gentry should sustain) decayed
> Or rather ruined seems, her buildings laid
> Flat with the earth that were the pride of time,
> And did the barbarous Memphian heaps outclimb;

sonian comment on Jones: "Qui se mirantur, in illos / Virus habe: nos haec novimus esse nihil" [Keep your venom for those who admire themselves; I know that these things of mine are worth nothing].

> Those obelisks and columns broke and down
> That struck the stars . . .
>
> (ll. 32–39)

Architecture is an image of potential wholeness and of historical continuity; and so it is logical that the shutter depicting architectural ruins opens to reveal an equally eclectic but unruined vista of buildings once the knights are about to appear. And much later in his career, in *Britannia Triumphans* (1638; #334), Jones gives us a perspective of London houses with his own work on St. Paul's at the precise vanishing point. The description, probably written by the designer himself, makes his own line of thinking clear:

A curtain flying up discovered the first scene, wherein were English houses of the old and newer forms intermixed with trees, and afar off a prospect of the city of London and the river Thames; which, being a principal part, might be taken for all of Great Britain.

> (ll. 59–62)

This is an aesthetic of synecdoche: the architectural masterpiece stands for the city, and the city stands for the realm. Architecture becomes an image of the whole and the part, of Britain and of Britain's participation in world history.

In *Albion's Triumph* (1632) Jones realizes his complete vision of architecture as an expression of artistic and political imperialism, ranging from self-advertisement to glorification of England. It is for this masque that he designed his famous architectural proscenium:

in the midst of which was placed a great arm of the King's, with angels holding an imperial crown, from which hung a drapery of crimson velvet fringed with gold . . . ; in the frieze were festoons of several fruits in their natural colours, on which in gracious postures lay children sleeping; . . . and at the foot of the pilasters, on each side, stood two women, the one young, in a watchet robe looking upwards, and on her head a pair of compasses of gold, the points standing towards heaven, the other more ancient and of a venerable aspect, apparelled in tawny, looking downwards, in the one hand a long ruler, and in the other a great pair of iron compasses, one point whereof stood on the ground, and the other touched part of the ruler. Above their heads were fixed compartments of a new composition, and in that over the first was written THEORICA, and over the second PRACTICA, showing that by these two all works of architecture and ingining have their perfection. . .

> (ll. 24–40)

The definition of architecture is clearly all-embracing: art and nature, theory and practice, heaven and earth, real and ideal.[12] But what may be even more significant is the direct association of architecture with an imperial vision of the British monarchy. *Albion's Triumph* as a whole expresses monarchist imperialism by constant diverse allusions to imperial Rome. The settings that fill up the architecturally oriented proscenium are magnificent representations of Roman building design: the perspective Roman atrium discussed above (p. 272), *"The forum of the city of Albipolis, and Albanactus triumphing, attended like a Roman emperor,"* and an elaborate colosseumlike amphitheatre. These buildings are specific emblems of imperial power. Jones, having glorified himself and architecture, now demonstrates that the glory of an imperial realm is inextricable from its architecture. The monarch and the architect are engaged in similar and mutually interdependent arts. We should not be surprised, then, at the final twist in the architectural drama, the last of the settings: *"The scene is varied into a landscript in which was a prospect of the King's palace of Whitehall and part of the city of London. . . ."* The architect creates the empire, and the architect's masque celebrates and defines that creation.

Architecture represents one important side of the masque's imperialism; the complementary side is provided by technology. Where architecture celebrates monumental and stationary values, technology is nearly always put in the service of complex forms of motion. Jones's very first scenic sketch, the House of Fame from the *Masque of Queens* (1609; #15), already conveys something of the abstract drama of stage movement. The previous scene, which opens the piece, is an antimasque of witches that takes place in *"an ugly hell, which flaming beneath, smoked unto the top of the roof"* (ll. 24-25). The stage imagery is concerned with the contrast between the permanent and the transitory. The "ugly hell" seems substantial to begin with, but the appearance of the House of Fame (when

12. The standard, and very revealing, essay that best analyzes this proscenium in terms of the tension between word and image is D. J. Gordon, "Poet and Architect: the Intellectual Setting of the Quarrel between Ben Jonson and Inigo Jones," *Journal of the Warburg and Courtauld Institutes*, XII (1949), 166–178. Gail Kern Paster modifies Gordon's assertions and further illuminates the subject in "Ben Jonson and the Uses of Architecture," *RQ*, XXVII (1974), 306–320.

the shutter is drawn away) makes the previous scene seem altogether evanescent: *"not only the hags themselves but the hell into which they ran quite vanished, and the whole face of the scene altered, scarce suffering the memory of such a thing"* (ll. 350–353). That last phrase of Jonson's is a key to the meaning of what he and Jones are doing in this effect. Stage motion dramatizes the impermanence of the witches' disordered nature, and it is contrasted with the extreme monumentality of the architectural construction that the motion discovers.

Jones's drawing shows the House of Fame itself to be a multisided, two-story construction perhaps forty feet high. The lower story, relatively classical with statues as columns,[13] includes a central arch with double doors, while the upper story has a distinctly Gothic flavor with trefoil arches, in particular on the central face, leaving room for a great three-level tableau of the queen and her ladies. Nothing could be more monumental. Judging from Jonson's description, the statues were famous poets and heroes, precious stones and metals abounded, and the structure was topped off with figures representing Honour and Virtue.

Given the solidity of the House of Fame (indeed, of Fame itself, as the masque repeatedly tells us), the stage drama takes on a new quality when parts of the building are set in motion. The twelve ladies are discovered in tableau in the upper central arch, and they remain there for a speech by a figure of Perseus celebrating heroic virtue and the fame of the ladies' mythological counterparts. After this speech, the throne in which they are placed proves to be a revolving machine, the ladies are rotated one hundred and eighty degrees out of sight, and on the other side of the machine Fame herself appears. The juxtaposition, indeed implicit equation, of the twelve and the one suggests that Fame is the essential principle of which the ladies are emanations. In her speech Fame gives an iconographic gloss on eagles, griffins, and lions, the animals who draw her chariots. While she speaks and then while loud music sounds, the ladies (now out of sight) are given time to descend to the lower level and mount chariots drawn by these three different animals. Then the great doors on the lower story open, and the ladies emerge in their chariots. They move toward the audience, descend from their chariots,

---

13. See Jonson's detailed description of the House of Fame at ll. 647–671 of the text.

and take up the whole space in dances that contrast strikingly with the grotesque dances of the witches in the first scene.

The drama of stage motion has come full circle in a decidedly Platonic fashion, beginning with the insubstantial motions of disorder, proceeding to the monumental image of the good, and culminating in motion that defines the good and then sends it forth into the world. Even in this early example of Jones's technology, we can note certain abiding characteristics. First there is a strong element of mobile stage spectacular for its own sake. Suddenness, surprise, radical changes: these, quite apart from any meaning, were surely crucial to Jones's art. Second, there is a natural and highly exploitable tension between architectural effects and technological ones. Finally, stage motion is ostensibly placed in the service of glorifying the monarch; but the drama it actually produces tends much more toward the abstract, philosophical, Platonic.

Looking at such an early design as that from the *Masque of Queens*,[14] one has the impression that Jones is just discovering the possibilities of stage movement. The individual effect must have been powerful and exciting, but prodigies of technology were still too rare in Jones's theater to be consistently worked into the design and meaning of the whole event. Just how or when a change takes place is not easy to pinpoint, since Jones's work gradually changes in a number of ways through the 1620's and into the early 1630's. The technology itself improves in time, with a number of developments necessary to provide for the mid-air displays that eventually become the hallmark of Jones's spectacle. Cloud machines and air-borne cars were standard early on, but they needed to be joined by more stable effects with the full use (around 1620) of the two-story stage; and all of these gained their highest potential for elaborate effects when they were joined by the fly gallery around 1630.

Another crucial factor was the departure of Ben Jonson. It is no coincidence that Jonson's last masque, *Chloridia*, is the first in which all these technological possibilities were realized. Not only was Jonson inimical to a creation in which pure spectacle overwhelmed the spoken word; even more significant is the fact that his imagination tended to emphasize

---

14. We find a similar mixture of architecture on the first story and movable machinery on the second in the Release of the Daughters of the Morn from *Love Freed from Ignorance and Folly* (1611; #74).

the specific, the concrete, and the individual, while technological prodigies, as we saw even as early as *The Masque of Queens,* nearly always celebrate the abstract. Finally, we cannot fail to notice in the drawings that Jones, even apart from the question of Jonson's influence, becomes increasingly abstract in his interests. The tension within Jones's own work between abstract and concrete forces is visible, for instance, throughout *Coelum Britannicum* (1634), one of his masterpieces. The general drift of Carew's text is to suggest that the old classical vision of heaven has become corrupted and that heaven will be purified by adapting itself to the analogue of the British court. Jones makes this statement with a good deal of visual and technical particularity. He asserts the decadence of the past powerfully with a magnificent perspective drawing of monumental classical ruins, while the birth of the British kingdoms is placed in a gigantic three-tiered set of intricate and busy design, and the presentation of the king comes in a setting (if the Orgel and Strong attribution is correct: #281) with wings quite naturalistically depicting trees and a shutter scene that is a detailed representation of a villa and formal gardens. All these settings take us up to the last hundred lines of the text, and to this point text and settings logically culminate in the king.

Here there is a significant change, for the king does not directly close the masque:

for conclusion to this masque there appears coming forth from one of the sides, as moving by a gentle wind, a great cloud, which arriving at the middle of the heaven, stayeth; this was of several colours, and so great that it covered the whole scene. Out of the further part of the heaven begins to break forth two other clouds, differing in colour and shape; and being fully discovered, there appeared sitting in one of them Religion, Truth, and Wisdom. . . . In the other cloud sat Concord, Government, and Reputation. . . . These being come down in an equal distance to the middle part of the air, the great cloud began to break open, out of which struck beams of light; in the midst, suspended in the air, sat Eternity on a globe.

(ll. 1051–1072)

The mid-air display coincides perfectly with the sudden turn in the drama to abstract values. The appearance of the clouds, their opening and closing, and the emblematic figures inside them: all this comes from the world of cosmic, rather than peculiarly British, forces. Jones graces King Charles with the references to abstract universals, but he also sets these apart from the king.

What Jones is moving toward in these middle years of his career is not only a more prominent place in the stage drama for abstract ideas but also an imitation of God's greatest masque: the motion of the cosmos itself. The stationary, architectural side of the masque is limited to a rather concrete political assertion, but the complex mechanics of stage motion transcend these. As soon as his technology becomes sufficiently flexible, Jones seeks dominion over not only the commonwealth but also the skies. In *Chloridia* (1631) he uses cutout clouds flown on from several directions to indicate a change of weather; and then in this same mid-air arena he stages a tableau centering on Juno, and he climaxes the masque with the discovery of Fame on a hill rising out of a trap and then the pulling of Fame up into the heavens on a wire. The following year, in *Tempe Restored*, Jones takes the next step by designing a great masque of the spheres in the sky:

In the midst of the air the eight spheres in rich habits were seated on a cloud, which in a circular form was on each side continued unto the highest part of the heaven, and seemed to have let them down as in a chain.
To the music of the spheres there appeared two other clouds descending, and in them were discovered eight stars; these being come to the middle region of the sky, another greater cloud came down above them, which by little and little descending, discovered at her glistening stars to the number of six.

(ll. 186–194)

The motion of the forces of heaven is equated with the machines of the masque. At the same time, the experience is kept familiar rather than altogether otherworldly because the earthly setting under this pageant of the heavens (#217) is a strikingly naturalistic, peaceful, and attractive seascape. Jones is still attempting to be all-embracing in his art. It is British, natural, cosmic.

But it is in the very last masques that the cosmos and the masque are truly united. *Luminalia: the Queen's Festival of Light* (1638) abandons in its text virtually all particularity and becomes an entirely symbolic drama of darkness and light. For the depiction of night, Jones uses a style vastly more impressionistic than anything he had hitherto created. The wings consist of trees that seem mutually intertwined; less clear than their foliage are the shadows between them, which amount to a kind of darkness visible. The back shutter is even more impressionistic. The greenery has lost all its definition and consists rather of treelike shapes of darkness. The central action of the masque consists of the coming of light. Hesperus and Aurora make mid-air entrances, preparing the way for the Queen, who has taken the sun's place. Her own entrance is significantly without elaborate mechanism, for Jones is choosing to keep the celebration of royalty separate from the cosmic dance. The queen bestows her blessing upon the newly created, newly relit cosmos; but that cosmic renewal is the achievement of the masque itself.

The last of the masques, *Salmacida Spolia* (1640), serves as a fitting conclusion because it unites many of preoccupations that Jones was expressing in his late work. Technology is paramount in this very elaborate spectacular, which includes setting changes, chariots, and flying machines of all sorts. Jones is concerned here with the equation between cosmos and masque; that equation is expressed not simply by means of celestial mechanics but a combination of all the elements at his disposal. The settings themselves, while ostensibly representational, take on an even more symbolic tone. The storm scene, with which the masque begins, is minutely symbolic of a disordered world, an impression conveyed equally by the design or the description:

No glimpse of the sun was seen, as if darkness, confusion, and deformity had possessed the world and driven light to heaven; the trees bending, as forced by a gust of wind, their branches rent from their trunks, and some torn up by the roots.

(ll. 111–115)

The celestial masque takes over when Zephyrus appears in the heavens and in a sense causes the change of scene to a peaceful landscape: again cosmic motion and the set design work hand in hand.

The true coming of light takes place again through Jones's cosmic machine, first, in the discovery of the queen and her ladies, who are revealed in their lightness by the passing of a great cloud, and finally by a magnificent series of clouds full of people:

From the highest part of the heavens came forth a cloud far in the scene, in which were eight persons richly attired representing the spheres. This joining with two other clouds which appeared at that instant full of music, covered all the upper part of the scene; and at that instant, beyond all these, a heaven opened full of deities; with celestial prospect . . . filled all the whole scene with apparitions and harmony.

(ll. 458–465)

This last of all the stage directions to Jones's masques can well serve as their summation (and epitaph). It was a scene of great magnificence, to judge by the rather sketchy drawing, almost Michelangelesque in its grandeur and composition. It audaciously celebrates the Stuart monarchy by suggesting that Charles and Henrietta Maria preside over a new heaven full of new deities. It is a strikingly abstract vision, with vast numbers of people at a great distance; yet at the same time it celebrates triumphs of Palladian architecture, since the landscape under the scene of relieve depicts the suburbs of a great city with a central bridge and monumental classical buildings.[15] Finally, it is a daring celebration of the masque itself, which, as Jones sees it, alone of all the arts can recreate the heavens.

15. It is particularly interesting in this regard that John Webb, Jones's assistant refers to this setting as "the / sceane of Architecture" (Orgel and Strong, p. 756), even though architecture accounts for a small part of the whole.

Notes on Contributors

Louis E. Auld has taught at Smith College and Duke University. Specializing in the art and civilization of seventeenth-century France, he has recently completed *The Lyric Art of Pierre Perrin, Founder of French Opera.*

Leonard Barkan, who teaches at Northwestern University, is the author of *Nature's Work of Art: The Human Body as Image of the World.* His current interests are in theater and in the heritage of mythology in Renaissance drama and painting. Beginning with N. S. VIII, he will be the editor of *Renaissance Drama.*

John A. Bertolini, Assistant Professor of English at Middlebury College, is currently working on a book-length study of the dramaturgy of Italian and French Renaissance tragedy.

Nan C. Carpenter, Head of the Department of Comparative Literature, University of Georgia, has published widely on the stage music of the Middle Ages and Renaissance.

Ernest B. Gilman, Assistant Professor of English at the University of Virginia, is at work on a book on seventeenth-century English poetry and the visual arts.

R. W. INGRAM, Professor of English at the University of British Columbia, has published numerous essays on the stage music of Renaissance England. Most recently he has completed a book on John Marston and an edition of the dramatic records of medieval Coventry for the Records of Early English Drama series.

JOEL H. KAPLAN, guest editor of *Renaissance Drama,* N. S. VII, is Associate Professor of English at the University of British Columbia. He has published a number of articles on Elizabethan and Jacobean drama, and is now co-editor of the Clarendon Press edition of *The Works of Thomas Middleton.*

JILL L. LEVENSON, Associate Professor of English at Trinity College, University of Toronto, is editor of the journal *Modern Drama.* She has published essays on Shakespeare and the bibliography of English Renaissance drama, and is working on a book-length study of the Troy legend during the Middle Ages and Renaissance.

TIMOTHY J. MCGEE is Assistant Professor of Music at the University of Toronto and Director of the Toronto Consort, a group performing medieval and Renaissance music. His edition of *Fifteen Medieval Dances* will be published early in 1977.

MICHAEL NEILL teaches English at the University of Auckland, New Zealand. His study of the *Maid's Tragedy* appeared in *Renaissance Drama,* N. S. III (1970). He has also published articles on Dylan Thomas, Shakespeare, and the Stuart theater, and is currently working on a book dealing with Mannerism in the drama.

R. B. PARKER, Professor of English at Trinity College, University of Toronto, has published extensively on Renaissance and contemporary drama and has served as Head of the University of Toronto's Graduate Drama Centre. He has prepared editions of *A Chaste Maid in Cheapside* and *Volpone* for the Revels series of plays.